The 1986 Oil Price Crisis:
Economic Effects and Policy Responses

The 1986 Oil Price Crisis:
Economic Effects and Policy Responses

Proceedings of the
Eighth Oxford Energy Seminar
(September 1986)

EDITED BY

ROBERT MABRO

Published by Oxford University Press
for the Oxford Institute for Energy Studies
1988

Oxford University Press, Walton Street, Oxford OX2 6DP
Oxford New York Toronto
Delhi Bombay Calcutta Madras Karachi
Petaling Jaya Singapore Hong Kong Tokyo
Nairobi Dar es Salaam Cape Town
Melbourne Auckland
and associated companies in
Beirut Berlin Ibadan Nigeria

Oxford is a trade mark of Oxford University Press

OIES books are distributed in the United
States and Canada by PennWell Books, Tulsa, Oklahoma

British Library Cataloguing in Publication Data
Oxford Energy Seminar (8th : 1986)
The 1986 oil price crisis : economic
effects and policy responses : proceedings
of the Eighth Oxford Energy Seminar
(September 1986).
1. Economic history—1971- 2. Petroleum
—Prices—History
I. Title II. Mabro, Robert III. Oxford
Institute for Energy Studies
330.9 HC59

ISBN 0-19-730007-3

Typeset by Oxford Computer Typesetting
Printed in Great Britain
by Billing & Sons Ltd., Worcester

CONTRIBUTORS

Nordine Aït-Laoussine	President, Nalcosa, Geneva
Ralph E. Bailey	Chairman, Conoco Inc.
Burckhard Bergmann	Executive Board, Ruhrgas
Pierre Desprairies	Honorary President, Institut Français du Pétrole
John Flemming	Economic Adviser to the Governor, Bank of England
Edward R. Fried	Senior Fellow, The Brookings Institution
John C. Gault	Oil Consultant, Geneva
Abdlatif Y. Al Hamad	Director General, Arab Fund for Economic Development
Ed A. Hewett	Senior Fellow, The Brookings Institution
Mohammad Farouk Al Husseini	Oil Consultant, Ministry of Petroleum and Natural Resources, Saudi Arabia
Ibrahim B. Ibrahim	Director, Economics Department, OAPEC
Ryukichi Imai	Japanese Ambassador to the Conference on Disarmament, Geneva

Ali M. Jaidah

Formerly Secretary General, OPEC

James T. Jensen

President, Jensen Associates Inc.

Arve Johnsen

President, Statoil

Aman R. Khan

President, GDC Inc.

Robert Mabro

Director, Oxford Institute for Energy Studies

Said El Naggar

Formerly Professor, Cairo University

Masahisa Naito

Director General, Petroleum Department, Agency of Natural Resources and Energy, Ministry of International Trade and Industry, Japan

Silvan Robinson

President, Shell International Trading Company

Ian Seymour

Editor, *Middle East Economic Survey*

David Simon

Managing Director, British Petroleum

The *Oxford Energy Seminar* is an international conference designed for government officials, industrialists, managers and other professionals engaged in the field of energy. The Seminar is sponsored by St Catherine's College and co-sponsored by OPEC and OAPEC. It was established in 1979 and its sessions are held annually at St Catherine's over a two-week period in September.

The Seminar, which is fully residential, has educational objectives. Its aims are to enhance the professional qualifications of participants; to improve the understanding of factors and forces which influence the operations of energy markets and the behaviour of policy-makers and economic agents; and to provide a privileged opportunity for contacts and debate between participants from petroleum exporting and importing countries.

A most distinctive feature of the Seminar is the balance of speakers and participants between nationals of petroleum exporting and importing countries and between representatives of government and industry. Each annual session of the Seminar involves fifty to sixty participants and approximately forty speakers. The organization is delegated by the co-sponsors to a Board of Management consisting of the Secretary General of OPEC, the Secretary General of OAPEC, Mr Wilfrid Knapp and Mr Robert Mabro.

The *Oxford Institute for Energy Studies* was established in 1982 to pursue through research and advanced study of problems of international energy the same objectives as the Seminar. The Institute is an association of members, including Oxford University and three of its constitutent colleges, OAPEC, the EEC, the UK Department of Energy and other national or regional institutions from Sweden, Norway, France, Japan, Mexico and the Arab world.

The Institute is committed to the idea of co-operation between scholars representing different sides of the international energy debate. This international character is reflected in the composition of both the membership and the research staff of the Institute. The Institute is also committed to achieving high academic standards in the study of real-life problems in the energy world. The aim is to combine excellence in research and relevance to important policy issues.

The Institute has a board of governors representing all members. Dr Ali Attiga is the Chairman, Sir Rex Richards the Vice-Chairman and Robert Mabro the Managing Director.

The views and opinions expressed in this book are those of the respective authors. They do not necessarily reflect those of the governments, companies or organizations to which they belong. They should not be construed as representing the views of the Oxford Energy Seminar, the Oxford Institute for Energy Studies, the sponsors, members or management of these two institutions.

ACKNOWLEDGEMENTS

The papers in this collection were presented in September 1986 to the eighth annual session of the Oxford Energy Seminar. In the interest of rapid dissemination, the Seminar has long-standing arrangements with *Middle East Economic Survey*, *OPEC Review* and *Petroleum Intelligence Weekly* for immediate publication of a few contributions without prejudice to the rights of the Seminar for eventual publication of these papers in book form. I wish to thank the Editors of these journals for their valuable co-operation. I also wish to thank David Guthrie for sub-editing the papers, Susan Millar and Margaret Ko for their patient work on the word processor, and Gordon Davies for designing the jacket.

Robert Mabro

PREFACE

This book presents a selection of papers given at the Oxford Energy Seminar in September 1986. This was the year of the oil price collapse, and naturally the question which most concerned all Seminar participants was that of the impact of the price decline on countries, economies and energy industries. The speakers were asked to address this question, each one of them from his particular vantage point and with reference to his own area of interest in the oil industry, the oil-exporting countries, the international economy, the developing world, the non-oil energy industries or the major industrialized oil-consuming countries. They were also asked, whenever relevant, to evaluate the policy responses of the various parties to the oil price decline.

This collection of papers is of interest for three major reasons. First, it captures the initial reactions of important decision-makers in industry and governments, and of eminent experts, to the consequences of the oil price collapse. Oil prices sunk to their lowest levels in July 1986 and the Seminar was held in early September, barely six weeks later. These initial reactions reveal more about the perceptions and behaviour of the main actors on the energy scene than statements made at later dates when everybody had had time to define a position *vis-à-vis* the others and take a public stance.

Secondly, although the price of oil was raised in 1987 well above the very low levels attained during the collapse, there is still no denying that a significant discontinuity has taken place. Today's world of $18 oil is not the same as the world of $30 oil in which we lived earlier on in the 1980s. The change in the average level of oil prices must be construed as an important change in a critical economic parameter which may have significant consequences on both energy-dependent countries (producers as well as consumers) and energy industries. The full consequences will take a long time to unfold because many of the economic responses to an oil price shock are in the nature of policy decisions by governments and investment decisions by companies, and all these inevitably involve time-lags. In short, the subjects of the oil price decline (unless the price fall is suddenly reversed by unforeseen factors) and its impact on OPEC, the oil industry and the world economy in general are likely to remain topical for a number of years to come.

Thirdly, a distinctive feature of this book is that it presents diverse views, the views of parties with different, and often conflicting, interests in the energy world, on the same set of issues. It reflects the approach which guides the work of the Oxford Energy Seminar and the Oxford Institute for Energy Studies. The underlying principle is that issues of international energy policy are studied and understood more fruitfully in a setting which allows every side to express freely its point of view and to listen carefully to the other side's point of view than in places where a single viewpoint dominates the research or the debate.

The book includes papers arranged in seven parts which cover all the main areas of the energy debate. The coverage, though not fully comprehensive, is sufficiently wide to include most important issues. Ideally I would have liked to present a paper on coal and additional papers on developing countries and on non-OPEC exporting countries. But there are limits on how much can be presented in a Seminar even when its session lasts for two full weeks and on how much can be incorporated in a book. The Introduction is a short synthesis of views about the likely impact of low oil prices on the demand for and the supply of petroleum, and on the oil industry. The paper of which this Introduction is but an updated version was written in February 1986 before the actual price collapse. It accurately predicted the advent of $15–18 oil and some of the effects of the price decline. This paper was used to initiate the debates of the 1986 Seminar, and may now help the busy reader by providing a condensed view of the issues discussed in certain parts of this book.

CONTENTS

Part VII: The Financial Problems of Developing Countries

TABLES

FIGURES

ABBREVIATIONS

AGR	Advanced gas-cooled reactor
AMOE	Arab major oil exporter
ANOE	Arab net oil exporter
API	American Petroleum Institute
ARAMCO	Arabian American Oil Company (Saudi Arabia)
bcf	billion cubic feet
bcf/d	billion cubic feet per day
b/d	barrels per day
BIS	Bank for International Settlements (Basle)
BNOC	British National Oil Corporation
boe	barrels of oil equivalent
boe/d	barrels of oil equivalent per day
BP	British Petroleum
CEGB	Central Electricity Generation Board (UK)
c.i.f.	Cost, insurance and freight
CPE	Centrally planned economy
DAC	Development Assistance Committee (OECD)
DM	Deutsche Mark
EDF	Electricité de France
EEC	European Economic Community
ENI	Ente Nazionale Idrocarburi (Italy)
f.o.b.	Free on board
GDP	Gross domestic product
GNP	Gross national product
IAEA	International Atomic Energy Authority
IMF	International Monetary Fund
kl	kilolitres (1 kl = 6.2898 barrels)
km	kilometres
kW	kilowatts
kWh	kilowatt hours
LDC	Less developed country
LNG	Liquefied natural gas
LPG	Liquefied petroleum gas
mb/d	million barrels per day
mboe/d	million barrels of oil equivalent per day
mBtu	million British thermal units
mcf	million cubic feet

MITI	Ministry of International Trade and Industry (Japan)
MOE	Major OPEC exporter
mtoe	million tonnes of oil equivalent
MW(e)	megawatts (of electricity generated)
n.a.	not available
NEA	Nuclear Energy Agency (OECD)
NGLs	Natural gas liquids
NOE	Net oil exporter
NOI	Net oil importer
NYMEX	New York Mercantile Exchange
OAPEC	Organization of Arab Petroleum Exporting Countries
OECD	Organisation for Economic Co-operation and Development
OIDC	Oil-importing developing country
OPEC	Organization of the Petroleum Exporting Countries
PIW	*Petroleum Intelligence Weekly*
PWR	Pressurized water reactor
SDR	Special drawing right
tcf	trillion cubic feet
TWh	terawatt hours
UAE	United Arab Emirates
URENCO	Uranium Enrichment Corporation
WTI	West Texas Intermediate

1 INTRODUCTION

Robert Mabro

The Origins and Causes of the Fall in Oil Prices

The collapse of oil prices on spot and futures markets for crudes and products in 1986 was the result of important structural and economic developments that began to unfold in the late 1970s, and which have radically transformed the features of the world oil industry. It is useful to describe very briefly these main developments, familiar as they may be to observers of the energy scene.

First, world oil consumption began to decline in 1979 and the downward trend continued to assert itself over a number of years. This phenomenon was not well perceived at its start because everybody's attention was then concentrating on the supply interruptions and the price rises brought about by the Iranian Revolution. The price rises of 1979–80 did not initiate this demand fall but contributed to the continuing decline in subsequent years; they provided renewed inducements for energy conservation and for substitution of coal and gas for oil.

Secondly, there was a considerable expansion of non-OPEC oil supplies, beginning in the mid-1970s and continuing unabated to date. This growth was partly due to the re-emergence of Mexico as a major world producer and to the development of the large North Sea oil reserves, and partly due to new smaller-scale production in a large number of countries all round the world. The decline in world demand for oil and the growth of non-OPEC supplies were accommodated by a considerable reduction in OPEC's output. The aggregate production of OPEC's member countries fell by about 45 per cent between 1979 and 1985.

Thirdly, the demise of the old oil concession system in the OPEC region, timidly begun in the late 1960s but virtually completed by 1979–80, transformed the structure of the world petroleum market. The large volume of internationally traded oil that used to move through the internal channels of vertically integrated companies is now traded at arm's length in external markets. These markets involve a large number of participants on both the supply side (the national agencies of OPEC member countries) and the demand side (major and minor oil companies, independent refiners, oil traders and other trading houses).

The demise of the old concession system in the OPEC region coincided with the emergence of the North Sea, a new oil province explored and developed under a competitive, free-enterprise regime involving a large number of licensees. The North Sea made a significant contribution to the expansion of an open market in international oil. A very big proportion of North Sea oil output is traded at arm's length. This reflects partly the role of fiscal factors, and partly the significant involvement in the North Sea of firms with no downstream interests in North West Europe.

Fourthly, the deregulation of US oil completed by the Reagan Administration in the early 1980s strengthened the links between the vast domestic oil market in the USA and the world petroleum market. Spot and futures trading in WTI became closely influenced by trading in Brent and vice vesa. Through the mediation of Brent, an internationally traded crude, changes in the conditions of the US oil market are now being transmitted to the markets for African, Mediterranean and Gulf crudes.

In short, the current situation is characterized by a huge imbalance between *potential* supplies and *actual* demand for oil and by the externalization of oil trade in dynamic and competitive markets.

Supply/demand imbalances were, of course, important in the past, during the concession era; but they were then absorbed internally by oil companies and their host countries. The concession system and the integrated structure of the industry enabled companies to respond to changes in demand by varying almost automatically the extraction rates from their prolific Middle Eastern fields. In the subsequent period, which we may call the OPEC era, any excess of potential supplies over demand was also absorbed fairly passively by OPEC member countries as was perfectly evident in 1975–8 and in 1981–5. The behaviour of oil companies in the 1950s and 1960s and of OPEC in later years caused prices to remain fairly stable during the relevant episodes; it also limited the amplitude of price variations in open markets.

Today the situation is radically different. The major oil companies have long ceased to perform a price stabilization role because of a fundamental change in circumstances. OPEC, which took over from the companies in the 1970s, attempted to perform this role during 1974–8 and 1981–5. It was successful during 1974–8, but faced increasing difficulties in 1981–5. In 1986, following Saudi Arabia's lead, OPEC abandoned its attempt to fix the price of oil in international trade and by the middle of that fateful year the oil price had collapsed from a previous level of $25–28 per barrel down to $8–12 per barrel. A new attempt was made in 1987, following the OPEC meeting held in Geneva in December 1986, to stabilize prices around a reference level of $18 per barrel. Whether OPEC will succeed in maintaining its control of the market during the next few years is uncertain.

So long as an imbalance between potential oil supplies and demand *at any price* persists, there is a serious risk that oil prices will fall once again to a low level and that they will fluctuate erratically around a declining trend in both spot and futures markets.

There is no doubt that we are facing today a situation of unstable oil prices in weak and nervous markets. For the purposes of this paper, let us assume that oil companies, governments and all relevant economic agents will soon begin to perceive future energy developments in terms of low and volatile oil prices. We will then address a number of fundamental questions about the effects of these expected price movements on the demand for oil, the supply of non-OPEC oil and the structure of the petroleum industry.

The Fall in Oil Prices and the Demand for Oil

Low oil prices could induce the substitution of fuel oil for coal in power stations equipped with dual burner facilities, or a switch from coal-fuelled power stations to idle oil-fuelled power stations in countries with excess capacity in electricity generation. Today the spot price of coal in Rotterdam is approximately $50 per tonne. Allowing for calorific differences, transport and handling differentials, the equivalent fuel oil price is $100 per tonne. This suggests that crude oil could begin to displace coal in power stations and in steam-raising industrial plants when its price fluctuates in the $15–18 per barrel range. Some observers believe that at these prices the room for substitution of oil for coal is significant, even in the short term, and particularly in the OECD region where many power stations have fuel-switching facilities. They believe that these effects tend to be underestimated; and they argue that the substitution of fuel oil for coal would rapidly stabilize crude oil prices at around $17–18 per barrel without any outside intervention.

If this view turned out to be correct, the system would be self-stabilizing at prices little different from those attained on spot markets for crude oil in 1987. It should be noted, however, that the speed of adjustment, and thus the time required for self-stabilization to take place, depend more on price expectations than on the level of prices actually attained at any given time. The short-term adjustment relates to long-term perceptions of price movements. If the oil price levels of 1987 are perceived as a temporary anomaly, no attempt will be made to substitute coal or gas for oil, irrespective of the short-term advantages of such a process.

Can we really expect a large substitution effect from low oil prices in the short run? To answer this question it is necessary to review briefly the situation in the OECD countries. In France, EDF will switch to oil as soon as prices tilt the balance in favour of this fuel. There will be no political or institutional inhibition against such a move. Within a few months coal could be displaced giving rise to a new demand for 4 million tonnes of oil. In Italy, very little coal is used for electricity generation, and the coal/fuel oil substitution issue does not really arise. In West Germany, the coal industry is a political 'sacred cow'. Some substitution against coal may take place but a significant shift is likely to be resisted by policy intervention. In the UK the scope for fuel oil substitution is significant but the CEGB may be constrained by its contractual arrangements with British Coal. The financial and political impact on British Coal of a switch against coal could inhibit the adjustment. In the USA it is thought that crude oil prices would have to fall below $15 per barrel to make fuel oil competitive with coal.

The picture is therefore patchy and uncertain because fuel oil substitution may be retarded by political and institutional restraints in some of these countries. Furthermore, some experts point out that South African and Australian coal is extremely cheap and could compete with fuel oil at lower prices than those mentioned in this paper. Some also remark that the prices of substitutes – namely coal and gas – will themselves fall in response to a decline in oil prices.

The short-term impact of lower petroleum prices on the demand for oil may also come from an increase in motoring stimulated by lower oil prices and from some increase in petrochemical production in response to brighter expectations of economic growth. Some growth in gasoline consumption occurred in 1986 for a variety of non-price reasons (for example, a change in holiday patterns in the USA in the summer of that year). This simply continued a trend that began in 1985: oil prices need not fall to produce such short-term and rather incidental effects. Finally, growth in petrochemical production, though probable, is unlikely to be very significant in the short term. To sum up, we may witness a small overall stimulus to the demand for oil in the short term (a year or eighteen months) but we should not expect too much.

It is evident that lower oil prices are more likely to stimulate demand in the longer term, that is after three or four years, than in the immediate future. The interesting questions are: how? and by how much? To approach these issues we need to assume that oil prices remain fairly stable for a substantial period of time within the $15–18 per barrel range. We shall also assume *at this stage of the argument* that the benefits to the final consumer of lower prices are not cancelled out by tariffs or excise taxes. These assumptions are required for the clarity of the analysis; they do not necessarily reflect our views about likely developments.

A 40 per cent reduction in oil prices from 1985 levels

(allowing both for a fall in nominal dollar prices and for a drop in the exchange value of the dollar *vis-à-vis* the yen and European currencies) could increase the demand for oil by 1990 by as much as 3–4 mb/d through the substitution effect and by another 1.0 mb/d through the price impact on world GDP growth according to optimistic experts. If we assume that the price elasticity of demand is half as large on the way down as on the way up, then the substitution effect on oil demand will be no higher than 2–3 mb/d.

To these increases we must add the 2 mb/d rise in the demand for oil which was expected to obtain by 1990 had oil prices remained pegged at $27–28 per barrel. In short, lower oil prices could add between 3 and 5 mb/d to the expected level of demand for oil in 1990. There is a significant difference between the end-values of this range, but such are the state of the art and the effects of uncertainty.

The questions of import levies and excise taxes, which we set aside for a moment, must now be addressed. In the USA there is much talk about tariffs and taxes. There are lobbies in favour of an import levy or a gasoline tax and lobbies committed to free trade in energy which are staunchly against any intervention. The introduction of a tariff on oil now appears unlikely, largely because of administrative difficulties and problems arising from pressures to exempt a number of oil-exporting countries from an import duty. But the introduction of a tax on gasoline (perhaps after the Presidential election) remains possible because of the budget deficit; the US Government could be strongly tempted to impose such a tax in order to find an easy source of revenue. Despite a strong US policy commitment to free energy trade, revenue considerations may prove overriding. This is not to say that the introduction of an excise tax is a foregone conclusion; there is still a large but continually shrinking margin of uncertainty on this issue.

The EEC is unlikely to introduce an import duty on oil because its member countries would find it difficult to agree on a common external tariff for oil (or energy) imports. Such a measure would require the agreement of all member countries and their interests on this issue are sufficiently diverse to preclude an unanimous decision. However, governments can impose excise taxes on petroleum products (or vary their rates) independently of one another. This is the course European governments are likely to follow and their stated objectives will include the familiar lines on the long-term need to conserve 'scarce' energy resources and to reduce dependence on oil imports. Of course, the revenue motive will also be attractive, and the need to protect coal in West Germany or other energy elsewhere will play a role.

Japan is unlikely to change its fiscal or tariff regime in response to lower oil prices. It would gain a competitive advantage over Europe and the USA if these countries pushed oil prices up domestically through taxation and Japan did not.

To sum up, lower oil prices will elicit a small demand response in the short term, and will contribute more significantly to demand growth in the medium and long term, if economic forces are allowed to operate without political or fiscal intervention. As it is natural to expect some government intervention, at least in a few OECD countries, and particularly in the USA, we can conclude that the long-term demand effects will be dampened. With tariffs and taxes, the drop in oil prices may not add more than 2–3 mb/d to the level of expected oil demand in 1990.

Lower Oil Prices and Non-OPEC Supplies

Lower oil prices will shut down stripper wells in the USA but have little immediate effect elsewhere. In fact some companies may respond to lower prices by increasing their production from equity sources in order to improve their cash flows. (Some observers believe that the opposite could happen, with companies holding up production and waiting for prices to rise again but this is unlikely.) Costs of production from existing oilfields are low in most parts of the world outside the USA, even in the North Sea where they are below $5 per barrel for 90 per cent of UK and Norwegian output.

There is no doubt that some small firms will face the prospect of bankruptcy because of cash-flow problems arising from their indebtedness to banks and their huge tax bills. But bankruptcy need not affect production: in most cases it will only lead to a change in the ownership of assets.

An oil price of $15 per barrel reduces oil production from US stripper wells by 70–100,000 b/d. A price of $10 per barrel in mid-1986 caused an output reduction of 700–800,000 b/d. The loss of production at this low price was fairly rapid; it occurred within a three-to-four month time-period. This volume of shut-in production caused serious concern in the USA, and the US Government had recourse to diplomatic pressure to persuade Saudi Arabia to stop the oil price war and to attempt to stabilize prices at around $18 per barrel. A price of $17 or $18 per barrel virtually restores US oil production to the 1985 level and cancels these particular supply effects of low oil prices.

It is certain, however, that low oil prices (i.e. prices in the $15–18 per barrel range) will affect exploration and the development of *new* oilfields, thus reducing potential output after 1990 in most of the world, and perhaps before 1990 in the USA. In the USA the oil reserve base is small in relation to output, and production responds very rapidly to a decline in the rate of exploration and development.

The adverse impact on oil investment will be due to the following factors. First, low oil prices will reduce the inventory valuation in balance sheets, thus reducing the equity base of companies and (other things being equal) their access to credit. Companies will have little option but to curtail investment budgets – even those already approved for 1986 or 1987 which were inevitably based on old assumptions about oil prices. Secondly, large companies will be tempted to use some of their cash resources to purchase cheap assets relinquished by less fortunate competitors. They will increase their oil reserves by acquiring existing resources, and the likely trade-off is a reduction of investment expenditure for the discovery of new reserves. Thirdly, investors may feel that the costs of new investment in areas such as the North Sea or the Arctic can not be justified at current prices and that they should delay or even scrap any plans for the development of high-cost oil.

The importance of these considerations should not be underestimated, but it is wrong to believe that they are the only determinants of the investment decision. Companies may take the view that the long-term prospects for oil demand require them to develop such additional sources of supply, or that prices will rise in the 1990s and yield a good rate of return on high-cost investment undertaken in the interim. If these views are sufficiently widespread, and if they are shared by bankers, finance will be found and investment will continue. It is instructive to note in this context that companies have recently been paying very large sums for difficult acreage in the North Sea, an indication perhaps of buoyant expectations for the 1990s.

The growth of non-OPEC supplies has been systematically underestimated by forecasters in the past ten years. Most predictions, made under old assumptions about oil prices, put the increase in non-OPEC supplies at 1.0 mb/d by 1990. Some observers, allowing for the underestimation bias, think that this increase could be as high as 3.0–3.5 mb/d. Lower oil prices need not affect the growth of non-OPEC supplies until the end of this decade, particularly if the US Government introduces fiscal measures to protect stripper wells and advanced recovery. After 1990 potential supplies in the non-OPEC region will almost inevitably decline because of a fall in investment in the preceding period, but the size of the reduction may be overstated by the current conventional wisdom. Only very strong expectations of a rosier 1990s can sustain a high level investment activity in the upstream.

Our quantitative forecast is that non-OPEC supplies will increase by 1–2 mb/d irrespective of what happens to the oil price. Should the US Government decide against the introduction of a tariff or of fiscal incentives to production and investment, non-OPEC supplies in 1990 might remain at their 1985 level.

The Supply and Demand Balance

These various estimates of the impact of lower oil prices on demand and supply can be now brought together. We assume that non-Communist world demand for oil would have increased by 2 mb/d between 1985 and 1990 under previous price assumptions; that non-OPEC supplies would have increased by 2.0–3.0 mb/d; and that OPEC production in 1985 averaged 16.0 mb/d. Under these assumptions OPEC production would be 15–16 mb/d in 1990 compared with 16 mb/d in 1985.

Lower oil prices and *unchanged* fiscal regimes in the OECD countries would increase non-Communist world demand for oil in 1990 by an additional 3–5 mb/d and change the level of non-OPEC supplies by 0.0–1.0 mb/d. This implies that OPEC production would rise in 1990 to 20–23 mb/d, compared with 16 mb/d in 1985.

Lower oil prices counteracted by tariffs and higher taxes in OECD countries (other than Japan) would increase non-Communist world demand for oil by a maximum of 2 mb/d above this base line and leave the initial forecast of non-OPEC supply increases unchanged (at 2.0–3.0 mb/d). In such a case total OPEC production would reach 17–18 mb/d in 1990, compared with 16 mb/d in 1985.

These results suggest that the benefits of lower oil prices to OPEC countries are subject to much uncertainty. It should be immediately stressed that non-OPEC exporting countries, being output maximizers, suffer a straight revenue loss from any drop in oil prices. There is no mitigation from increased production. The situation is different for OPEC countries as they would eventually see their output rising in response to lower oil prices (here assumed to be in the range of $15–18 per barrel). Table 1.1 shows that in the most favourable case output will be 4–7 mb/d higher in 1990 than would have been expected in the absence of a price fall. If industrial countries

Table 1.1: Demand for OPEC Oil in 1990 under Various Assumptions. Million Barrels per Day.

	Old Price	Price Fall and No Tariffs	Price Fall and Tariffs
1985 Demand	16.0	16.0	16.0
Increase due to GDP Growth	2.0	2.0	2.0
Substitution Effect	–	2.0–4.0 ⎫	
Additional GDP Effect	–	1.0 ⎬	2.0
Displacement from non-OPEC Supplies	−2.0–3.0	−0.0–1.0	−2.0–3.0
Total Demand in 1990	15.0–16.0	20.0–23.0	17.0–18.0

resort to protection, demand for OPEC oil in 1990 will be 2–3 mb/d higher than otherwise expected.

Assuming that OPEC exported 12 mb/d of oil in 1985, and would have exported 12.5 mb/d in 1990 in the absence of price changes, the more favourable case involves a maximum increase in exports of some 56 per cent and a minimum of 32 per cent above expected levels in 1990. The increases would be smaller, though rising, in the intervening years. To achieve this result prices would have been slashed by 33–45 per cent. It is easy to infer that the break-even point would probably not be reached before 1989, and that OPEC would not be able to recoup the revenue loss incurred from lower oil prices until 1991 or 1992 at the earliest. Things would naturally be significantly worse if the demand for OPEC oil increased by the smaller amounts predicted by our less favourable case (price fall and tariffs or taxes).

The conclusions of this analysis are that a low oil price strategy is likely to prove costly for OPEC in the medium term, and that such a strategy is totally irrational for non-OPEC exporting countries, particularly for those belonging to the Third World. It also follows that a strategy aiming at bringing the price of oil into the $22–25 range would be the least attractive: these prices involve revenue losses in the medium term and hardly any beneficial impact for OPEC in terms of higher demand and lower non-OPEC supplies. The gamble on low oil prices can not benefit OPEC countries until the 1990s and the risk is that the time needed to recoup the initial losses may turn out to be too long. Contrary to common belief, *all* OPEC countries with excess capacity today will be able to increase their output in the 1990s above the low levels attained in 1985. All have sufficient reserves to keep them in the market in the next decade. The differences of view within OPEC on the appropriate price strategy have more to do with immediate revenue needs (time-preference) than with the size of the countries' oil reserves.

Lower Oil Prices and the Oil Industry

We have assumed so far that oil prices will settle during the next five years within a definite range. This assumption was necessary for the analysis of the possible impact of lower prices on demand and supply.

Actual price movements will be more complex than as assumed above. So long as potential supplies exceed the demand for oil, price stability depends uniquely on producers' regulation. Otherwise prices will fluctuate: they will first tend to fall to very low levels (as they did in 1986), then bounce back (as in 1987), and then perhaps start declining again. On top of these cycles we may expect to see considerable day-to-day price volatility in both spot and futures markets. There are no automatic stabilizers for oil prices in the short term, no more than there are for copper, peanuts or foreign currencies. As the marginal extraction costs of oil are very low and as substitutes are not immediately available for the whole set of oil uses, petroleum prices could fluctuate over a very wide range. Of course, there is always a long-term equilibrium price, but its influence is slight and remote: long-term forces do not provide much short-term stability to oil prices.

The introduction of tariffs or other trade protection measures will segment the world petroleum market, restricting the area in which oil flows freely; and this segmentation will probably contribute to greater price fluctuations. The petroleum industry will have to live in a world where oil behaves like an ordinary primary commodity. Oilmen believe that they can learn to adjust and many will probably survive it all. Markets will continue to expand and diversify their functions; some like NYMEX may have to adapt to the changed features of a protectionist world.

Low oil prices will ultimately increase demand and the industry will no doubt welcome this growth in the aggregate size of its market.

Low oil prices may inhibit investment as mentioned earlier, but the extent of this effect is difficult to ascertain. They will also lead to greater industrial concentration: some small firms may disappear and some mergers may take place.

The industry will be forced to become more efficient. There is much gold plating in upstream investment and, therefore, there are opportunities for cost reductions and improved technology. The incentive to ensure that the downstream operates as an effective profit centre, which is already there, will be enhanced.

The economics of conversion refining may be adversely affected by an increase in the demand for fuel oil resulting from the displacement of coal. New adjustments of the refinery stock will therefore be required.

The oil industry tends to put on a brave face when the energy world is subjected to shocks. This was noticeable in 1973 and in 1979–80, and the same attitudes, albeit in very different circumstances, emerged again in 1986–7. Companies with large cash balances and favourable gearing ratios believe that their *relative* competitive advantage over others will improve. Cold comfort indeed: these relative gains must be set against an absolute fall in profits and a reduction in the valuation of companies on the asset side of the balance sheet.

Conclusion

The price shocks of 1973 and 1979 transferred income from oil-importing to oil-exporting countries. The price collapse in 1986 brought about just the same income transfer in reverse. The issue is essentially about the international distribution of income. There are no rights and no wrongs: all depends on which side one happens to be on. The economic interests of a net oil exporter are at odds with those of a net oil importer and no amount of sophistry will change this basic fact. Non-OPEC exporting countries lose revenues when prices fall; OPEC members lose revenues for some years but may reap advantages some time in the 1990s. If they have a choice, non-OPEC exporters should try to arrest the price decline. OPEC countries have cause to stop and wonder whether rewards in the 1990s are worth the heavy income transfer of the 1980s.

The avid reader will want to know what will happen in the years to come. Will OPEC's move to stabilize oil prices, begun with some success in 1987, produce lasting effects? Will non-OPEC countries lend their support to some OPEC stabilization plan? We shall simply state two general principles. First, as in all distributional issues, market power is a most critical factor. Secondly, the collective exercise of market power by a group of countries requires both strong leadership and commitment to the common interest. To guess the outcome of future OPEC efforts on price stabilization it is important to know: (a) how much power oil exporters still wield; (b) whether Saudi Arabia is still in a position to exercise strong leadership; and (c) whether OPEC members are now sufficiently worried by the prospects of a price collapse to accept the sacrifices of co-operation. But these are matters of difficult judgements on which reasonable persons may reasonably be expected to differ.

PART I

THE OIL INDUSTRY, ENERGY MARKETS AND THE PRICE COLLAPSE

2 OIL AND ENERGY DEMAND: OUTLOOK AND ISSUES

James T. Jensen

The 1985 demand for oil in the non-Communist world was 45.6 mb/d. At that level, demand was 5 per cent lower than it was in 1973 at the time of the first oil shock. Even if current expectations for 1986 are correct, and we see roughly 1 mb/d of extra demand this year, non-Communist world oil demand will still be less than it was in 1973. This is a truly remarkable turn of events, given the widespread expectations in the mid-1970s of chronic oil shortages and upward pressures on prices.

The dramatic collapse of oil prices during 1986, after an extended period of high prices and sluggish demand, raises two obvious questions: first, where did all that oil demand go, and, secondly, is demand likely to recover with the return of lower oil prices?

I believe that the answer to the first question is that oil demand has been lost: not to a simple and reversible response to the price increases of the 1970s, but rather to a very fundamental transformation in the way in which society utilizes energy. It follows then that the answer to the second question is: demand recovery will be slow at best.

During the past fifteen years, demand has been on a roller-coaster ride. Up to the time of the first oil shock, it was increasing at about 7 per cent per annum. Had it continued at that rate, demand would have inevitably challenged supply even without the Middle East war which triggered the first shock.

The price shock set off a recession in 1974, causing oil demand to fall for two years. Demand then grew at about 3 per cent per annum during the recovery period. The second oil shock in 1979 triggered another recession, but this time around oil demand has not recovered. In fact, demand has been almost steadily downhill since 1979, averaging a decline of about 2.2 per cent per annum.

An examination of the structure of the decline suggests that it can be attributed, broadly speaking, to four distinct factors. The first is the reduction in expectations for world-wide economic growth. The countries of the non-Communist world experienced a sharp decline in economic activity as recessions followed each of the two oil shocks of the 1970s, but were never really able to recover their earlier economic growth rates after the shocks were over.

The non-Communist countries maintained a growth in GDP of 5 per cent per annum for the decade preceding the first oil shock; they have been able to support slightly more than half that rate since then. Since economic activity is considered to be a significant determinant of energy demand, it should not be surprising that energy economists have had to lower their energy forecasts.

But changes in economic expectations explain only a portion of the decline. The second major factor is conservation. Consumers in every sector have become skilled at doing with less energy without any significant deterioration in their standards of living or in the quality of industrial production. Therefore, there has been a downward trend in unit energy consumption in all consuming sectors.

The third element of demand reduction, sometimes confused with conservation, can be described as industrial restructuring. We do many things in different ways today than in the era of cheap energy in the 1960s. The resulting restructuring has reduced energy intensity. The Japanese were actively building tankers in 1973, but they do not build many tankers today. Automobiles in the USA were large 'gas guzzlers' then; they are not now. The steel industry, as a result, has shown a distinct downward trend in almost all of the OECD economies since 1973.

The fact that the US automobile fleet now gets 19 miles per gallon when in 1973 it averaged 13 is evidence of conservation at work. The fact that one element in the reduction is 'downsizing' or producing smaller, lighter cars that require less use of energy-intensive materials, such as steel, is evidence of industrial restructuring.

Finally, oil demand has been reduced by fuel substitution or fuel-switching. It is fairly clear that the share of the energy market held by oil has declined since the 1960s, as nuclear power, coal and natural gas have increased their shares of the market. These four factors – the reduction in economic growth, conservation, structural change and fuel-switching – have all contributed to the decline in oil demand.

The Forecasting Dilemma

When economists forecast oil demand, they generally have two broad approaches at their disposal. The first, a broadly-based macro approach, attempts to relate energy utilization both to economic activity – income elasticity – and to price – price elasticity. The second, a much more detailed sector-by-sector approach, attempts to isolate the cause-and-effect relationships that drive the individual components of demand.

The macro forecasts commonly utilize econometric techniques. They state their results in the form of numerical coefficients that link the economic variables with demand. Despite their mathematical precision, the coefficients do not give the forecaster a flesh-and-blood feel for what is going on. When one can interpret a rising trend in automobile miles per gallon in terms of new car fuel efficiency standards and the trade-off between new car sales and automobile scrappage rates, the resulting forecast of gasoline demand has some underlying logic to it. But who can sense the meaning of a declining coefficient of energy growth per unit of growth of GNP and feel comfortable with the assumption that the trend will necessarily persist?

One of the major problems inherent in econometric forecasting is that the coefficient relationships may not survive a significant structural transition such as an oil shock. Thus, it may take an extended period of time before enough data are available to measure the new relationships. Those who criticize the macroeconomic approach liken it to driving rapidly at night on a highway with the headlights pointing backwards to see where the driver has been. Coefficients provide relationships that really do not have fundamental meaning to the forecaster. They are relationships that have occurred in the past; the interesting question is: will they occur in the future and therefore be predictive?

One particularly troubling problem with econometrics might be called the 'hysteresis effect' after a phenomenon in electromagnetic physics. Physicists, in looking at electromagnetism, recognize the fact that when an electric current is sent through a coil around an iron rod, there is a measurable relationship between the magnetism created in the rod and the electric current in the wire. But if the electric current is reversed, the magnetic field does not retrace the same path that it first exhibited. There is less magnetism for a given electrical current when the field is reversed. Physicists term the effect 'hysteresis'.

An example of the hysteresis analogy in econometric forecasting came from a study done in the United States about 1970 when policy-makers were struggling with the issue of removing price controls on natural gas. The Federal Power Commission commissioned a large econometric study of the effect of well-head price changes on gas supply from a prestigious economist. He had one significant problem. Since natural gas had been subject to price controls, over a period of time there had been no change in the nominal price of natural gas. However, the economist recognized that the price had been going down in real terms because of the effect of inflation. He therefore used a GDP deflator to derive a time-series of real prices. His analysis showed that the supply of natural gas had declined gradually as the real price slowly declined under the influence of the price deflator. He concluded that with the elimination of price controls, an increase in the price of natural gas would immediately lead to an increase in gas supply and that there would be no shortages. That study was accepted at face value by the then head of the Council of Economic Advisors who said, 'We in the US do not have an energy problem. All we need is natural gas price decontrol – we'll get a lot of supply and the overall energy problem will be solved.'

In this case, the basic argument was that if the price of natural gas had been declining slowly at the same time as supply was declining slowly, the process was reversible. A sharp increase in price would lead to a sharp increase in supply. Unfortunately, it has not worked that way. Natural gas prices in the United States have gone up dramatically in recent years but supply (as measured by proved reserves) has continued to decline.

The alternative to econometric forecasting is to do a sectoral analysis, in order to take apart cause-and-effect relationships in great detail. Those who favour such an approach are apt to be criticized for a failure to see the forest for the trees. The sum of all of the individual demand elements may not add up to a full total since many elements that are insignificant at present – and thus largely ignored in sectoral analysis – may have a significant and growing influence on demand in the future. The sectoral approach is thus often criticized because of the difficulties inherent in making a whole out of a sum of parts.

An interesting example of the pitfalls of the disaggregated sectoral analysis occurred in a major OECD study of energy demand following the first oil shock. Each government was asked to project what its oil and energy demand would have been in a 'before' case of $3 oil; they were then asked to estimate their post-shock demands for oil after reflecting the changes in price and government energy policy. In its estimate, the United States decided that one of the policy options to limit oil imports would be to increase the utilization of natural gas by increasing natural gas imports. The study neglected to observe that, at the time, the only country that exported natural gas to the USA was Canada. Implicit in the US projection as a result was an increase in gas imports from Canada. In its submission, Canada concluded that one way to reduce oil imports was to increase the natural gas market share by reducing the export of natural gas to the United States. Both forecasts went in to the OECD, with the implicit assumption that the same surplus Canadian gas could be used to reduce the oil demand forecast for both countries.

Thus, one of the inherent problems with the disaggregated approach is that it may be difficult to co-ordinate the different pieces of the analysis, and therefore to reaggregate them into a meaningful forecast.

Since each of the forecasting approaches has its own problems, many forecasters utilize both approaches at the same time – using one as a check on the other. That is the approach I intend to use today.

Econometric relationships between GDP and energy are a common part of many public forecasts. Chevron has recently published an excellent energy analysis; Figure 2.1 illustrates the GDP/energy relationship in the same way as the Chevron forecast. For OECD Europe, the USA and Japan, the relationship between real GDP and total energy demand has steadily declined from the pre-shock levels (1971–3 = 100).

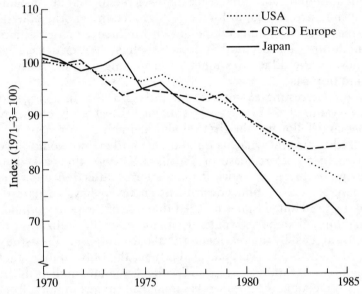

Figure 2.1: Ratios of Total Energy to GDP for Major OECD Regions. 1970–85.

Prior to the first oil shock, there was the widespread assumption that a God-given relationship existed between energy growth and economic growth, so that increases in the one automatically paced increases in the other. Had that relationship continued, OECD Europe, the USA and Japan would all show a straight, flat line in Figure 2.1 at the 1971–3 level of 100. As is evident from Figure 2.1, however, the relationship has been dropping sharply in all three major consuming regions. By 1985, OECD Europe has an index of 84, the USA an index of 77, and Japan an index of 70.

Since in OECD Europe, the overall relationship appears to

have levelled out at about 84, one might expect in looking at Figure 2.1 that an increase of GDP in OECD Europe of 1 per cent would result in a 0.84 per cent increase in the energy demand for the region. For both the USA and Japan, where the average relationship is still declining, the incremental increases that might be expected from a change in economic activity would be lower than their overall averages as shown in Figure 2.1.

The collapse in oil prices in 1986 should have a substantial impact both on economic activity in the industrialized world and on the relationship between economic activity and energy growth because of the effects of price elasticity. All things being equal, one might expect to see an increase in energy demand from the combined effects of higher consumption rates at lower prices (the price elasticity effect) and from a stimulus to economic growth which falling oil prices are expected to provide (the income elasticity effect). Unfortunately, the hysteresis phenomenon raises its head at this point. Obviously, economic growth has been under some pressure at higher price levels for the industrialized world and the effect of higher prices has been to reduce the rates of energy consumption. In the absence of hysteresis, one might expect the relationship between economic growth and energy to retrace its steps as prices go up. Hysteresis suggests that in fact that may not be true at all, but we do not yet have the data to determine how the energy economy will respond to the price change.

The Shifting Balance of Oil Utilization

The balance of oil utilization in 1984 is quite different from the balance that prevailed during the 1960s; and with a shift in the use of oil there is no assurance that oil demand now responds to changes in price or in economic activity today as it did in the earlier period.

Figure 2.2 illustrates the way in which the non-Communist world consumes oil. The figure is simply a proportional chart which subdivides 1984 non-Communist world oil demand by region and by sector. The United States accounts for slightly over one-third of total oil demand. With OECD Europe included, the two regions account for about 60 per cent.

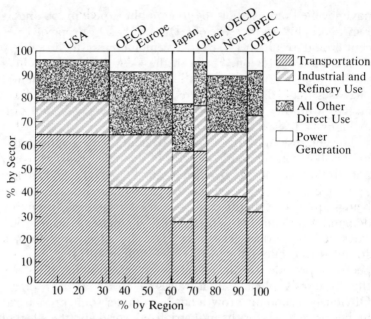

Figure 2.2: Non-Communist World Oil Demand by Region and by Sector. 1984.

Transportation uses – including road, rail, air and ships' bunkers – are responsible for nearly two-thirds of US oil demand but about half of total combined non-Communist world demand. Industrial demand (including refinery fuel) and 'all other direct use' (predominantly residential and commercial consumption) each account for slightly less than one-quarter of total non-Communist world consumption. Power generation rounds out total oil demand with slightly less than 9 per cent. In 1970, before the first oil shock, transportation was a smaller proportion of total demand (38 per cent) while industry was much larger in proportion.

The common presumption is that the demand for energy is closely related to changes in economic activity as measured by GDP. Given such an assumption, there is every reason to expect some rebound in oil and energy demand as a result of the anticipated stimulus to economic activity in the industrialized countries that lower oil prices are expected to bring about; but sectoral analysis suggests that not all oil demand sectors are likely to be equally affected by changes in economic activity.

One would expect to see a strong relationship between industrial activity and GDP; thus, if the OECD economies show a recovery from a recession, industrial energy and oil demand should increase. In the power generation sector, there should also be a similar relationship, since a significant portion of electric power goes to industrial activity. On the other hand, the transportation sector, while not totally insensitive to changes in economic activity, should be much less affected by the ups and downs of GDP. In Japan, for example, there is a heavy component of goods hauling which is sensitive to economic activity. On the other hand, in the United States, where so much of the transportation sector demand is driven by personal transportation requirements, there is serious doubt that gasoline demand moves significantly with short-term changes in GDP. The same reduced sensitivity to economic activity also tends to characterize the residential and commercial sectors.

To the extent that oil has been vacating its role as a fuel for industry and power generation in favour of greater concentration in transportation, the effect has undoubtedly been to desensitize oil demand to swings in economic activity. Although the possibility remains that oil may have retained some of its historic role as the 'energy supply of last resort' and may be disproportionately drawn back into the market with economic recovery, I do not believe that that is a strong possibility in today's market. Too much extra capacity for alternate fuel supply exists to come into the market and stifle this potential effect on oil demand. In any case, one cannot understand or predict a return to an 'upswing' role for oil without detailed and comprehensive sectoral analysis. Econometric relationships simply cannot capture the potential effect.

Oil Demand for Transportation

It is useful to examine the relationship between economic activity and demand on a sector-by-sector basis. Figure 2.3 plots the growth in oil demand for transportation within the

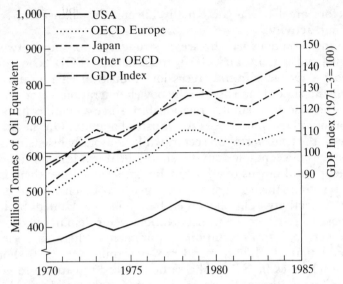

Figure 2.3: Transportation Demand for Energy and GDP Growth for the OECD. 1970–85.

OECD countries together with the growth of real GDP. Interestingly enough, there was a tendency for a rough tracking of GDP by transportation use until 1980 when a significant departure developed. This was particularly apparent in the United States. An econometrician would be quick to ascribe this change in the relationship between GDP and transportation demand to the influence of price, and might be tempted to measure the price elasticity of transportation demand. Unfortunately, it is not a simple relationship.

The influence of price elasticity during this period is complicated by the fact that the USA retained price controls on gasoline until 1981, so the consumer did not see the full impact of the price changes. The USA also had the effect of a very strong dollar during a more recent period when oil prices went down in the United States in dollars but went up in most of the West European currencies. The influence of price on demand was therefore subject to distinct cross-currents.

But, price elasticity aside, the most important element in the relationship between energy growth and oil demand is the fact that the USA finally sat down and started designing energy-efficient cars. It took a considerable period of time before efficient vehicles accounted for a high proportion of the total fleet – but now that the fleet is much more efficient, it is hard to see a rapid return to the higher gasoline consumption patterns that characterized the 1960s. If price increases originally set in motion the trend towards more fuel-efficient transportation, and thus a lowered relationship between GDP growth and transportation, lowered prices will not readily reverse the trend.

There is some suggestion in the USA that people are driving more this year with the lower oil prices. It does look as if demand growth in the USA may be up 2 per cent over the 1985 level. Some of this indeed may represent price elasticity at work, but there are other possible explanations as well.

This is the year that airline terrorism appears to have profoundly affected the American tourist. The airlines' and the hotels' loss in Europe may be gasoline's gain in the United States, since Americans seem to be reluctant to travel to Europe this year. To the extent that the US consumer is taking his vacation at home, it may be that that effect – as well as price elasticity – is contributing to the gasoline demand increase. In any case, it may take some time before we can measure how much of this increase is real and how much purely transitory.

Oil Demand in Industry

The changing relationship between industrial energy use and economic activity is quite dramatic. Figure 2.4 shows the steady decline in industrial energy consumption per dollar of real GDP for the three principal OECD regions. Whereas the index of total energy per unit of GDP in Japan had fallen to 70 by 1985, the index of industrial use to GDP had fallen to 50. The drops in the USA and in OECD Europe are nearly as dramatic.

While the more rapid growth of industrial electricity consumption with its higher purchased energy efficiency levels distorts the figures somewhat, most of the decline is attributable to conservation, restructuring and fuel-switching. The measurement of what is conservation and what is restructur-

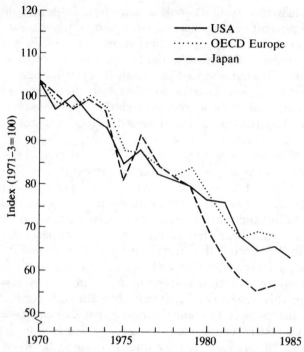

Figure 2.4: Ratios of Industrial Energy to GDP for Major OECD Regions. 1970–85.

ing depends in part on how one defines restructuring. In a sense, restructuring occurs where there is a definite change in the industrial mix that affects the way in which energy is used. It is important to recognize that restructuring is a time-related process, not an exercise in current comparative growth rates. The current rate of growth of energy-intensive industries may well exceed the growth of GDP or even that of industrial production; but if the growth of energy-intensive industry is substantially less than it was in an earlier period as a result of restructuring, it has had a depressing effect on energy demand.

Japan has been quick to focus its planning attention on industries that are heavy users of oil and energy, and has tried to cut losses in places where MITI felt there were losses to be cut. The Japanese appear to be making a conscious effort to get out of heavily energy-dependent activities in favour of industrial activities that contribute a higher value added without energy utilization. One can ask whether Japan's resulting energy loss is not really an energy gain in Taiwan, South Korea, Hong Kong or Singapore; to some extent energy-intensive activities have been moving out of Japan to the other economies of South East Asia.

We undertook a large study on the structure of world-wide industrial demand a year-and-a-half ago. We were trying to understand where oil demand for industry had gone. I entered the analysis with the tacit assumptions that Japan was a growth economy and that petrochemicals were a growth industry, and was surprised to discover that the use of energy in the petrochemical sector in Japan had been in absolute decline for several years. It became apparent that much of the petrochemical industry was being exported to nearby developing economies. But when we tried to determine the extent of fuel and feedstock growth in the other Asian countries, it was obvious that those countries' gains were smaller than the total Japanese loss, suggesting that the replacement capacity was more efficient than that which was being rationalized by the Japanese restructuring process.

The results of our study illustrated some of the things that happened to OECD industrial oil demand over the period 1975–84. We developed physical measures of growth for the oil-intensive industries, such as steel production, output of six tonnage petrochemicals, refinery runs, etc., and found that total OECD industrial growth had been 91 per cent over the period. We defined conservation as the extent to which total energy demand for the industrial sectors failed to grow as rapidly as the physical indices of production, and found this to account for some 90 per cent of the 'potential' growth. We also measured fuel-switching and the extent to which competing energy sources increased their percentage shares of the industrial market at the expense of oil. We found that oil had lost 13 per cent of its OECD industrial market share to electricity, 8 per cent to gas, and 46 per cent to coal. There was an overall reduction of industrial oil demand in the OECD region of some 63 per cent.

It proved extremely difficult, not only to develop reliable measures of physical production throughout the OECD, but even to find reliable energy consumption statistics by industry sector. The appearance of accuracy in the OECD energy demand statistics is deceptive for many countries, although this becomes apparent only when one begins to disaggregate the data by industrial sector and by country. Because of the difficulties inherent in developing the basic statistics, no effort was made to carry the exercise back before 1975 and thus no real measure of true restructuring (growth of the physical index of production for the study period relative to its growth in a comparable pre-shock period) was possible. Suffice it to say, the physical index grew only slightly less rapidly than OECD GDP or overall industrial production.

This observation itself was somewhat surprising, since I expected the energy-intensive industries to exhibit a *much slower* growth than either GDP or overall industrial production. One partial explanation was the important role of tonnage petrochemical production which maintained a substantial growth rate, even though it was clearly growing more slowly than it had grown in pre-shock periods.

Overall OECD industrial oil demand dropped by nearly 60 mtoe or about 1.2 mboe/d between 1975 and 1984. Had it actually increased at the rate at which physical output of the key energy-intensive industries grew and maintained its market share, it would have increased instead by nearly 90 mtoe. Thus, conservation, i.e. the reduction in demand needed to bring the pre-conservation, pre-share-loss consumption back to actual levels, was roughly equivalent to the potential growth.

The largest market share loss was to coal, with increased gas and electricity use important but less significant elements in fuel-switching.

Table 2.1 shows the breakdown of industrial use changes by industrial sector. The difficulty of providing a consistent update of national statistics by industry means that the cut-off date was left at 1983. For each of the industry sectors – petrochemicals, all other chemical demand, iron and steel, non-metallic minerals, pulp and paper and all other – we estimated what would have happened to oil demand over the period had it grown at rates of increased physical production. We next estimated the reduction attributed to conservation

Table 2.1: Changes in OECD Industrial Demand for Oil by Sector. 1975–83. Million Tonnes of Oil Equivalent.

Sector	Growth	Fuel-switching	Conservation	Net Change
Petrochemicals	76	2	−61	18
Chemicals	8	−14	−17	−21
Iron and Steel	−3	−25	−14	−42
Non-metallic Minerals	4	−27	−18	−42
Pulp and Paper	22	−21	−26	−27
All Other Industry	41	−17	−23	−2

and to loss of market share to alternative energy sources to explain this overall net change in oil demand.

The largest oil losses occurred in iron and steel and in non-metallic minerals. Iron and steel production declined slightly over the period, while the growth of cement and other non-metallic minerals was very limited. The primary losses in both cases were attributable to alternative fuels. For steel making, this is partially attributable to changes in the underlying technologies that make energy substitution more feasible. For cement in the minerals category, it is simply the fact that coal is a preferred energy source to oil or gas for kiln operation.

Petrochemicals showed remarkably strong growth in physical output with conservation being primarily responsible for limiting oil growth to modest levels. Fuel-switching was not an element in petrochemical oil demand changes.

Let me make a comment here about petrochemical demand. The data shown in Table 2.1 are total liquids figures including the gas liquids feedstocks such as ethane and propane. The figures are not limited to liquid products refined from crude oil. One interesting trend that Table 2.1 does not show is that the movement of the petrochemical industry away from naphtha-based utilization in places like Japan and Western Europe, say to the Gulf where it is ethane based, affects oil utilization. A naphtha-based industry provides crude oil-based by-product fuel which can be utilized for downstream activities. Petrochemical ethylene from the Middle East on the other hand utilizes ethane. The lower level of by-product fuel generated from the cracking process permits the substitution of natural gas for oil as fuel downstream.

The growth rate in the petrochemical industry has fallen fairly substantially from what it was before 1973, in much the same way that overall economic growth rates have fallen from their pre-1973 levels. This raises an interesting question: if high economic growth rates were to return, would the petrochemical industry revive or would it not? We were forced to say that it is almost an unanswerable question – we really do not know.

Oil Demand for Residential and Commercial Use

One would not expect residential and commercial energy consumption to be as sensitive to changes in economic activity as industrial use. While the economy might have some limited influence on commercial activity, most utilization in this sector is more closely related to space heating and other household convenience needs, which are not related to national economic performance. It should not be surprising then to note that the overall growth of energy demand in this sector is far below the growth rate of GDP.

Figure 2.5 illustrates the market share shifts among energy sources in the residential, commercial and 'other' sectors for the USA, OECD Europe and Japan. Energy consumption levels, which are lower in 1984 than they were in 1970, are shown as a negative increment on the left bar. Positive increments of energy consumption for 1984 relative to 1970 are shown on the right in each case. The amount by which the right-hand bar rises above the zero line is the net increase in consumption between the two years.

For the USA, total energy consumption in this sector rose by less than 10 mtoe, or only about 2 per cent, over the fourteen-year period, despite the fact that GDP grew by 50 per cent over that time. The principal change was an increase in electricity utilization, largely at the expense of oil. Coal and gas both gained slightly.

OECD Europe showed a much larger overall net increase of

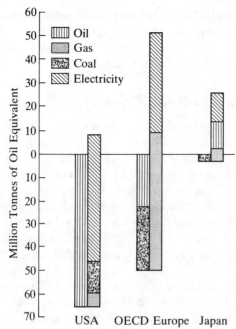

Figure 2.5: Energy Consumption in the Residential, Commercial and 'Other' Sectors Combined for Major OECD Regions: Changes from 1970 to 1984.

about 50 mtoe, although it still represented only a 16 per cent rise compared with a 43 per cent growth in GDP. Both gas and electricity gained at the expense of oil and coal.

Japan alone among the regions actually increased its oil consumption in the sector, splitting its overall energy growth among electricity, oil and gas. Residential and commercial energy consumption grew by 63 per cent over the period, while GDP growth was 93 per cent.

Although Figure 2.5 makes no attempt to measure conservation levels directly, the fact that sectoral demand is so much lower than economic growth suggests that there is a very strong conservation component. In the United States, which we have studied in substantial detail, conservation is large and continuing to increase. Furthermore, the moves in housing and equipment design and in construction are largely embedded in consumer and industry practices. No one is going to go back and build an energy-inefficient house now that good and relatively inexpensive equipment designs are standard because oil is now cheaper than it was. Oil demand recovery in this sector is not likely to be much larger as a result of accelerated economic growth or price elasticity.

Oil Demand for Power Generation

In many ways, electric power generation is the most interesting sector of all, because in a sense, at least in the United States, it is the balancing wheel by which inter-fuel competition determines oil market shares and competitive price levels. For much of the world, there is substantial surplus power generating capacity because the industry, faced with long lead times, built the capacity for demand growth rates that never materialized. Utilities that have surplus capacity and often have multiple fuel capability can fine-tune their oil use based on price.

Figure 2.6 illustrates the changes in US power generation relative to 1976 levels for the various energy sources. For every year except 1978 and 1979, the net increase in generation required by the market (relative to the 1976 base year) is *less* than the increments of increased coal- and nuclear-fired generation. The net result is that generation based on oil has steadily lost ground.

It is fairly clear that utility executives expected overall growth in electricity demand to be much stronger when they set their new projected plants in motion; but even with nuclear plant cancellations and construction delays, they have consistently found themselves with more capacity than they need. The high marginal cost of generating electricity from oil and gas has forced the oil and gas capacity to take the brunt of the cut-backs; and for the most part, in the USA, gas demand has held up, forcing the swing role on to oil.

One can make the case that the decline of oil generation will be arrested or even turned around as the capacity surpluses begin to dry up. But it will not happen quickly; nor will the incursion of new coal and nuclear capacity into the generation required from oil and gas combined be particularly influenced by price. The principal pricing effect will be the competition between gas and oil to take the brunt of the downswing.

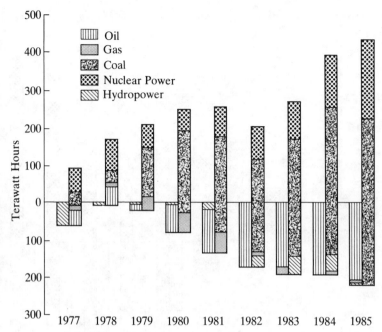

Figure 2.6: Changes in Demand for Various Fuels of US Power Generation
Sector from 1976 Base Level. 1977–85.

The pattern in Western Europe (data for the EEC–9 group
are shown in Figure 2.7) is similar to that in the USA. The
stronger role for nuclear power relative to coal is evident; the
increments of nuclear generation have exceeded total incremental generation required, again pushing oil into a downswing role. Gas has also been a loser.

In Japan (see Figure 2.8), there has been a greater rate of
growth in electricity demand, but the pattern of backing out
oil-fired generation is still similar to that which is found in the
USA and Western Europe. Nuclear power and natural gas-
fired generation based on LNG imports are the growth elements of the mix. There is also a small positive increment
based on imported coal.

Some Early Observations about 1986 Oil Demand

By now, everybody knows that oil demand is up this year. We

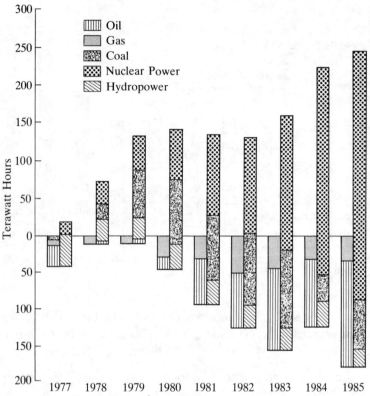

Figure 2.7: Changes in Demand for Various Fuels of EEC–9 Power
Generation Sector from 1976 Base Level. 1977–85.

talk about an increase in gasoline demand. We talk about
residual fuel oil demand being up. The questions are: Where
did the demand come from? Is it real? Will it stay? The
answers to these questions are really very hard to come by.
Physicists deal with something called the 'Heisenberg Uncertainty Principle'. It is possible to determine where an atomic
particle is located; but in the act of measuring where it is, you
lose the ability to find out how fast the particle is travelling.
Conversely, one can devise an experiment to establish how
fast the particle is travelling but one destroys the information
about where it is in the process. The Heisenberg Uncertainty
Principle thus states that one cannot at the same time know
both where a particle is and how fast it is going.

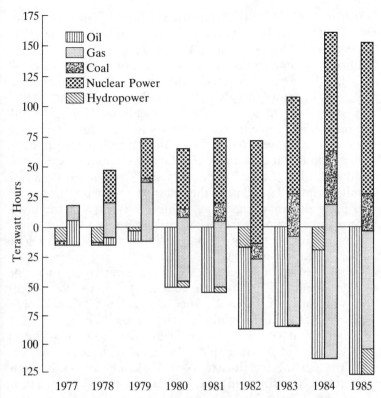

Figure 2.8: Changes in Demand for Various Fuels of Japanese Power
Generation Sector from 1976 Base Level. 1977–85.

There is an unfortunate statistical parallel. You can have
timely statistics and you can have accurate statistics, but you
cannot have, I am afraid, both timely and accurate statistics.
We have less than six months' experience with the market
consequences of the oil price collapse. While such a period
may be ancient history to a trader, it unfortunately still represents *terra incognita* for a statistical analyst, since so many of the
numbers one would like to see are so slow to come in.

We watch the natural gas market in the United States very
carefully. Our computer models suggested that natural gas
demand would be sharply reduced by the oil price collapse
because of losses to oil in fuel-switching. At the moment, US
natural gas demand is runnning about 7 per cent below what

it was in 1985. If it keeps that up, the final US gas consumption for 1986 will be more than 1 tcf below what it was in 1985. That is equivalent to about 500,000 b/d of oil.

Our computer models attribute much of the gas loss to oil switching. (Weather patterns also exerted some influence on the drop, but interestingly enough, it does not appear that oil has gained anywhere near what gas has lost.) Thus, we think we may have got our answers on gas right for the wrong reasons, I suppose proving the truth of the old adage that, 'it is better to be lucky than smart.' Of course, to the extent that residual oil has picked up some demand from natural gas as a result of the price collapse, the question of whether or not oil can hang on to that gain at stable price levels, let alone a return to higher oil prices, is a critical one.

One set of relatively current US statistics that can give some indication of what has been happening to switching between gas and oil is for electricity generation by fuel type and by region. They indicate that for the lower forty-eight states of the USA, taken together, gas has lost 250,000 boe/d while oil has gained slightly less than 100,000 b/d.

However, if you look at the regions in the United States where shifts have taken place, you discover very different patterns. In the North-east (New York, Pennsylvania, New Jersey and New England), gas lost and oil gained, an example of switching; but coal also lost as the increment of new nuclear exceeded the overall increase in generation.

Our analysis suggested that the North-east was one of the most likely regions to experience switching from gas to oil, largely because of the accessibility of this market to waterborne resid from the Caribbean. We did not foresee that oil competition would be so intense in the region that oil would also back out some coal-fired generation, but it obviously has.

Our models also suggested that California was vulnerable to fuel-switching from competition with Singaporean and Indonesian fuel oil. There has been intense price competition between gas and oil in this market and gas has lost significantly, superficially seeming to confirm our expectations; but the interesting fact that the generation data demonstrate is that oil has not gained significantly despite the price competition. The data indicate that gas's losses came from an increase in nuclear power generation and from a very good year for hydroelectric power. Oil's principal effect on this market was price related, not volume related. Oil tried to capture the market, but did not do so. All it did was drive down the price of gas.

The seven major gas-producing states of the US South-west also experienced a substantial decline in gas-fired power generation. Part of this was due to a sharp increase in nuclear generation, but part was also attributable to the reduction in generation overall as comparatively warm weather reduced the electric space-heating load and the economy of this oil-producing region suffered from the price collapse. In Florida, both oil and gas gained as nuclear was cut back and there was little overall growth in generation from within the state. The rest of the USA simply showed an overall decline in generation in which all fuels suffered.

The cross-currents in part explain why gas's losses have not necessarily resulted in offsetting gains for oil as might have been expected. Perhaps the 100,000 b/d of increased oil demand represents the actual exposure level of switches out of gas into oil. The remainder of the gas losses are attributable to a complex set of other demand and fuel substitution factors.

Conclusion

Econometric analysis suggests that oil demand should be stimulated by the fall in oil prices – both because of the income elasticity effect through the spur to GDP growth and through the price elasticity effect, largely through demand stimulation and fuel-switching. It is really too early to see any measurable response of GDP to the price effects of the late winter. Nevertheless, the analysis of where oil is now used – so heavily in transportation, for example – suggests that demand should not be particularly sensitive to an acceleration of GDP. It certainly should not respond as quickly as it did in the 1960s, when a much higher percentage of oil was used in the form of residual fuel oil in industry (or in power generation destined in large part for industrial markets).

The latest data for the USA suggest that oil demand to mid-year may have increased by about 2.5 per cent or 400,000 b/d. This is divided evenly between gasoline and residual fuel oil. The gasoline demand increase may be in response to the oil price decline, since recent normal growth in gasoline has been running closer to 50,000 b/d per annum rather than the 200,000 b/d we may be seeing this year. But before concluding that price is indeed the cause, it is wise to remember the shift in the US summer vacation pattern and wonder whether price is totally responsible.

The increase in demand for residual fuel oil does appear to be price related and to represent markets captured from natural gas (and possibly a bit from coal) as a result of the price drop. A legitimate doubt exists whether the increase in oil's market share can survive any significant oil price recovery. Thus, OPEC's effort to gain market share, which has set off the severe price competition, seems unlikely to achieve significant and sustainable gains in overall oil demand from the price collapse.

3 ON PRICES AND PRICE FORMATION

Silvan Robinson

As an international trading manager, I need to cope on a daily basis with the conflicting worlds of downstream markets and upstream suppliers. I see the pressures from both sides – from the marketing and refining side looking for ever cheaper and better supplies; and from the upstream, with legitimate interest in preserving some sort of price structure. I get squeezed in the middle and have to try to survive, so I try to understand both sides of the argument.

What has been happening to us over the last year? The basic fact has been that, all through 1985, the supply of formally priced crude from the upstream into the downstream was constantly being eroded, as less and less crude reached the final market other than as some form of spot crude. The pressures of an open downstream market steadily eroded the formal OPEC structure. Many OPEC countries offered discounts (in one form or another) below the official price structure in order to maintain markets and, of great importance in the non-OPEC world, the BNOC structure collapsed.

The real problem for the oil world has been first, that OPEC established too high a price – the $28–30 level was too high for OPEC's own good. It encouraged so many substitutes and it encouraged conservation. Secondly, OPEC left far too much to Saudi Arabia. Saudi Arabia was left as the sole swing producer and everybody else lived off this fat. Understandably, the Saudis gave up on it.

So we are now for the first time in any of our working memories in an environment where there is no formal structure for pricing. I would like to talk about some of the facts of price and some of the dynamics of price formation. Inevitably, the main pricing issue under debate today concerns the nature of netback deals. To some people they have acquired a bad reputation.

From a downstream point of view (and that may be different from the upstream) the main thing about netbacks is that they have been a mechanism for bringing long-haul crude into competition with short-haul crude. One can not understate the difficulties of moving something that you buy spot in the Gulf to a market which is six or seven weeks away, and then hoping to make money. The risk in a volatile market is simply too great. If you buy a spot cargo on a day when product values in Europe look as though they will cover your costs, the chances are that by arrival time the market will have collapsed. You may lose dollars a barrel on the transaction. Nobody is prepared to do that. Netbacks reduced this risk by pricing close to arrival date. They turned long-haul crude into a form of short-haul crude. It wasn't the only way that Saudi Arabia could have regained market share. In this Seminar last year, when Sheikh Yamani addressed it, he said 'We'll try this solution out but of course if it doesn't work, there are other ways. For example, we could price at Brent equivalent minus $1.'

Let me just take up one or two points about the nature of netback deals and give a view on some of the issues that they raise. I think there are four sorts of question. First, because there is a fixed refiners' margin, is there a downward propensity for crude oil prices created by netback deals? Secondly, have these fixed margins made refining profits risk free? Thirdly, have they created prosperity in the downstream to the disadvantage of the upstream? Fourthly, are netbacks permanent or is there something else that will take their place?

On the downward propensity of netback deals, you only have to look at what has been happening in the last month or so to see that they have not created automatic downward pressures. We have seen the market rise back from the $10 level to $15–16 for Brent in the last month or so and netback deals have still been in place. So empirically the fact is that they do not always create downward pressures.

I think it is correct that during the period of the rapid price fall it was spot crude that led the netback deals. It is just as well to look at facts and not just rely on logic. When they started, netback deals were priced at a level that was very competitive with Brent and this was of course the idea, so that they gained market share. But when the price fell, starting roughly at the end of 1985, spot Brent fell much faster and further than netback deals, again for very logical reasons. The netback deals had captured a certain market share. Brent is by and large sold spot and in order to maintain a market position it had to be sold at prices lower than the netback arrangements. Later on the Saudis discounted by another dollar or so. Relationships constantly varied. The market is now rising again. The trend of price movements is quite independent of the instrument that was used to push Middle East crude into the European market.

The second question is whether these arrangements actually create a risk-free environment for the refiner. The answer is that they reduce risk. They create some security for the refiner but you then have to look at the details. There is not just one sort of deal. Not all netback deal terms are public knowledge but the fact is that they span an enormous spectrum of arrangements. The time-period in which prices are determined is different for different arrangements and that contains an element of risk. The fees and the yields are different for different arrangements. Some are comparatively complex with relatively high fees – though nothing that would do more than cover a proportion of the full costs of refining. In other cases, the yields are simple and the fees are quite low. The dynamics of these two sorts of arrangements are quite different. If gasoline prices, for example, rise very fast, a refiner with a simple yield arrangement will probably do better, because he will be able to add more value from the products actually made in a complex refinery than would be the case with the simple yield in the netback calculation. If differentials narrow, a refiner with a more complex arrangement and higher fees will probably do better. So it is a constant question of judgement and commercial optimization and commercial opportunity. Some netback deals have a fixed freight element. If crude is hauled from the Middle East under a netback arrangement assuming a fixed freight rate, the refiner's margin may vary because real freight rates can vary enormously. Indeed, spot freight reached very high levels in 1986, so that some refiners lost a lot of money relative to the fixed freight elements in their deals. Again, the products will probably be priced well before they actually have to be sold, so refiners will lose money in a falling market. They may want to add value to *Platt's* (on which netback calculations are based) but in an over-supplied market they will probably have to sell at *Platt's* minus.

So there is nothing certain or secure about a netback deal. It is quite different from the sort of full realization netback deal that was practised in some Venezuelan cases or for example between Shell and Gulf in the old Kuwait agreement.

Netbacks are, to my mind, commercial transactions. Their terms are constantly under renegotiation because a refiner will always be unwilling to lose opportunity value compared with his alternatives. If he can buy from the Soviet Union or from the Brent market or under various other arrangements at cheaper prices than the netback deal seems to produce, then he will not go on buying on the old terms; and vice versa, as the market turns, the supplier will be trying to tighten the screws. The negotiator of netback deals does not sit back after he has negotiated the initial deal. Every few months there will be a renegotiation of the terms to correspond to the changed commercial environment.

This is quite different from integration. It is simply another method of pricing. One has to remember also that very few refineries will actually run 100 per cent on netback crude. A prudent refiner will take a proportion of crude this way because it looks as though it creates at least the opportunity of a stable relationship with a large producer; but will certainly keep a proportion of throughput, sometimes 50 per cent, sometimes less, sometimes more, for buying more opportunistically. I suspect it is the decision on the variable quantity of crude run that actually sets the refiners' margins; it isn't the base load. Another risk factor is that not all netback deals are determined by product prices in the area to which the crude is actually going. Some Middle East producers, for example, sell to Japan and the East not on Singaporean prices or Eastern prices but on European prices, and there have been times when this produces results $2–3 per barrel out of line with the alternatives, so tremendous frictions are created. Nigeria has a three-region pricing basis for establishing the price of its crudes – North West Europe, the Mediterranean and the US Gulf. I have to buy on a proportion of each but my customers won't buy on a proportion of each. If they are in the USA, they will say they want US prices. If they are in North West Europe, they will say they want something like North West European prices but a bit cheaper please. If I move to the Mediterranean I have to be sure that I am not selling too much that way because otherwise I will be losing on the average. People can play these markets off against each other. It is by no means a straightforward game. At different times different markets will be better outlets, but it is very difficult for a refiner to sell in a way that actually fits the pattern of his supply.

The third question is the refiners' margin. It is true that there have been better results downstream recently. None of us is the slightest bit ashamed of that – we certainly needed them. The downstream has been a poor business for many years, over-supplied with refining capacity yielding a return that no good business man should accept. Over the last three or four years, simple margins have been pretty well zero from beginning to end. Some money has been made out of complex refining, and complex refining was getting better during 1985, before netback deals or the price collapse. It wasn't just the netback deals that improved complex refining. Of course when crude prices collapsed people did feel 'My God, we are losing our money upstream. We must try and make more efforts to make money downstream.' This has undoubtedly run through the minds of many oilmen. But I would suggest that it is underlyingly due to a few other things, the main one being that we are running a different economic cycle in the downstream. It isn't just a fiction that there are two businesses, the upstream and the downstream. We have been through a period of great over-capacity, built because people were on the wrong trend, and there has been a massive effort of rationalization in the downstream. Refineries have been taken out of commission, restructured and so on. At the same time, white product demand has been growing. Black oils have been falling away. (There has been some fillip to black oil demand in 1986 but I don't think that it is permanent.) We have also been rescued by the environmentalists. The tighter lead regulations in the USA and now the tighter lead regulations in the Netherlands, Belgium and Europe generally are creating a shortage of high-octane material. The refining sector is now much more in balance than it was. As night follows day, if supply and demand come closer into balance, so margins improve. When the upstream gets supply and demand more into balance, crude margins will improve just as they have in the refining sector. But they are two different sectors and they are working on two different economic cycles.

I think it is also true that in the volatile market, refiners are more careful about how they run their capacity, and this is where there is perhaps some conflict between the netback situation and the natural inclination of refiners. Nobody likes to be caught today with surplus stock of any sort, so refiners tend to limit their production of co-products rather than maximize on the 'leading' product and not worry if some co-products are built up. This tends to strengthen the market. I believe that a strengthening of the downstream markets also strengthens crude prices, so it is a good thing for the crude market to see strengthened product values. This can be seen quite clearly from the behaviour of the US market. 50 per cent of the US market is gasoline, and there is a very clear relationship between US gasoline prices and US crude prices: when gasoline goes up, crude goes up and vice versa. The price of gasoline in turn is closely correlated with the level of gasoline stocks: high stocks, low prices; low stocks, high prices. And stocks in turn are a function of refinery runs. Refiners never manage to get it right; so prices yo-yo. WTI affects the price of Brent and the Brent market will affect the Middle East. It isn't just the OPEC balances that matter. It is also the behaviour of the refining sector. If you want to know what is going to happen this winter, I suggest you watch what happens to US refinery runs – quite as important as what happens in OPEC.

This leads to the fourth question – are netbacks a permanent solution? When you get around to asking what OPEC can do and how stability is to be created, everybody has to think very carefully about what sort of price structure is feasible. Let me list a number of the options. We have had government-established prices, fixed prices, etc. and prices with fixed differentials. That was an unwieldy system, and I hope it is never re-established in the old form. There are a lot of spot-based sales. Quite a number of countries are working on a 'price assessment' basis where they establish with their buyers and with a representative group of involved people what they think the price is. All the participants put their numbers in sealed envelopes and the result is a sort of averaging – not a bad system. As an alternative to either a fixed price system or a completely free system, one could envisage a system of bands. Each country would be free to move within a band but this system would only work within a rather strict quota structure. An even freer system would be to leave prices to move freely but for the producers to agree that if any one of them got beyond a certain point on volume then it would have to do something about its price. So far as I know, those are about the only systems of pricing that can work. The alternatives need a lot of thinking about because the subject is of great importance.

4 COPING WITH LOW OIL PRICES

David Simon

I will start with a simple introductory thought. If oil prices are too low today, they will give totally inappropriate signals for future demand and supply patterns. The potential consequences of this are profound and serious, not only for the oil industry but also for consumers and producers. Anybody who has lived through the effects of the oil price hikes of the 1970s and the price collapse of 1986 must surely believe that there ought to be a better way of running the system.

The objective of this talk is to show how recent changes in oil markets have influenced a company like BP in its approach to oil exploration and production, and also in its approach to financing.

The effect of the oil price collapse on BP is very clear. It has reduced our cash flow dramatically and changed our perception about the attractiveness of investments in future oil production. In 1985, when oil was priced at around $28 per barrel, we talked about the possibility of a price reduction; but we all thought it could be managed in a sensible way. It seemed realistic to assume that the price would settle at $18–20 for a two-to-three year period. This became the 'mindset' on the oil price scenario. But towards the middle of 1986, a very big change in our perceptions had taken place. People began to say that the price, then around $12 per barrel, could fall even lower – possibly to below $10, as indeed it did. Then, when the price subsequently edged back up to $15, people began to say that this was actually quite a good level. So much for 'mindsets' at work.[1]

---

[1] In early 1987, the oil price increased to $18 per barrel.

The Impact on Cash Flow and Profitability

The true impact of the oil price collapse on our current profits is somewhat hidden. I am not sure that the commercial world fully understands yet the wider implications for the industry. If we compare BP's results for the first half of 1985 and the first half of 1986 (see Table 4.1), the historic cost profit of £859 million drops to £236 million. If, on the other hand, we look at it in replacement cost terms, the profit of £859 million increases to over £1.2 billion.

Table 4.1: The British Petroleum Company plc. Group Results. January–June 1985–6. Million Pounds.

Profit after Taxation before Extraordinary Items	*1985*	*1986*
Historic Cost	236	859
Replacement Cost	1,215	859

Under the replacement cost method, stocks are valued on the basis of last in, first out. In effect, stockholding gains and losses are excluded. You just look at how your company is trading at the value that it is buying oil today in order to put it into the market the next day. A simple observer might say: 'Your company has done wonderfully well in keeping its trading profit in good shape, mainly because the fall in refined product prices lagged behind the fall in crude oil prices in the market-place.'

Time-lags in price movements should not cause any surprises. A business man will try to hang on to his profits as the cost of his raw materials falls, because if costs go up again he will be caught out. Nevertheless, the large companies are now in a state of pause and are assessing the current situation. They have all had to write down the value of their stocks even though they have done well on the trading account. I am not sure that by looking at the accounts, people really appreciate yet the impact that lower oil prices will have on companies' future investment plans.

Of course, in many countries the effect of the price fall has been softened by taxation. This is certainly true for oil companies operating in Europe, where a very high proportion of the value of oil is paid in tax. The drop in the value of the actual oil production has been far greater for the exchequers and finance ministries than it has been for the companies. This raises an important question in the world's financial markets: are governments going to give some incentive to the companies to reinvest? Because if oil prices stay low, our cash flows, which we use to help fund future developments, will be hit. Companies are now experiencing lower cash flows, and they cannot be expected to maintain their previous levels of capital expenditure – particularly on exploration. So, will governments give something back, or will private companies be expected to take all? This is still an open question.

How to withstand this problem is what the managements of all oil companies are looking at now. The first criterion for assessing a company's ability to finance projects is to establish how much debt it has in the balance sheet. Obviously, the greater the debt, the less the company's ability to go out and borrow more money at competitive prices. And if the cost of financing is high, any project investment it makes will be less competitive than it is for a rival company.

Companies' Debt/Equity Ratios

One thing that has emerged since the oil price collapse is that the integrated major companies have performed better than the specialist production and exploration companies. The majors are better able to withstand the shocks of oil price volatility because of their broader portfolio of activities. One of the reasons why oil stocks were blue chips (considered good stocks) was because a large debt element did not feature in the balance sheets of most of the majors. In the halcyon days before the price fall, or before price volatility, a debt/equity ratio of around 30 per cent was considered somewhat high; and for several companies the ratio was below that level (see Figure 4.1). Exxon, a financial giant, has generally been at the bottom end, and Shell and Amoco have held a steady position throughout the period.

But three of the so-called Seven Sisters – Mobil, Texaco and

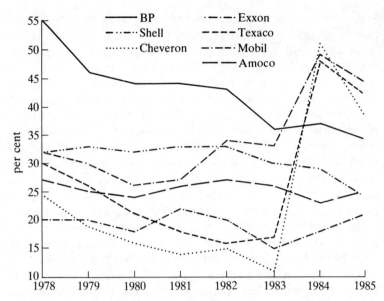

Figure 4.1: Ratios of Debt to Debt + Equity (Adjusted to Common Accounting Basis). 1978–85.

Chevron – show a considerable change of stance. Just before the price fall, they all borrowed heavily to purchase oil assets. Broadly speaking, they were trying to replace their reserves through acquisitions rather than by traditional exploration. The security for these loans was the relatively high price for oil in the ground. Because of their large borrowings, the debt/equity ratios of these companies climbed to over 50 per cent – and this took place just before the price collapsed! Now, of course, they have a lot of debt to pay back; and they are struggling to do this as members of an industry whose principal product has halved in value.

Before the collapse in the oil price in 1986, our planners had always considered that a price of $15 per barrel was a possibility, although that was our bottom marker. But because we were alarmed at even the possibility of this low price, we built up our liquid resources. At the end of 1985 we were carrying over £2 billion in our balance sheet. Why this large amount? Because of the shock that can happen when the price drops. Broadly, for every $1 drop in the value of oil, we lose about

$100 million of cash flow. If you think the price might fall $10 overnight, then it is only prudent that you have a cushion.

BP once was borrowing fairly heavily; but as can be seen from Figure 4.1 our debt has been brought down steadily over recent years. In British accounting practice, cash does not feature in the debt/equity ratio. If you include cash, the slope of the graphs will move down even further. At one time, Shell were holding $7 billion in cash and Exxon were holding $4 billion.

After four months of 1986, the oil industry's cost of borrowing deteriorated by about 1 per cent. Thus, had we borrowed, say, £500 million, it would have cost us £5 million a year more to service that debt than it would have done a year earlier. Now, bankers have an unsentimental way of looking at a business. They will listen to the argument that a $15 oil environment is not likely to be sustained for long. But they will still want to know how a company would position itself if low oil prices were to continue. Here, it is important to recognize that during the first half of 1986 we were no longer talking about the normal pattern of risk and reward that had characterized the oil industry previously. We were having to face the financial community in the light of the new reality.

The Range of Oil Price Forecasts

At any point in time, a very wide range of prices is possible. However, there is a narrower range within which prices will tend to vary and to which they are likely to return after periods of exceptionally low or high levels. This band of $15–30 per barrel is set by the costs of alternative fuels and by the effect of price on demand.

It is quite possible to believe that a sustained period of low prices will eventually lead to high prices, as the twin effects of price on demand and supply work through. But it may be risky to assume that prices will rise continuously, or that there will be little likelihood of lower prices in the long term. The market may have cycled from low to high and back to low again by the time today's long-term project has moved from the drawing-board to production.

From today's perspective, long-term projects whose

viability depends on their producing oil at costs above today's levels are risky. All of us use discounted cash-flow methods, and we know that the value of money at the front end of the project is absolutely crucial. So there is a tendency to try to get maximum value out of a project in the earlier part of its life. The view that you should invest on a continuing basis and that volatility might be ironed out is one now being discussed in financing circles.

Knowing that we were getting into this debate and seeing the terms of finance hardening against us, what actions can a company like ours take? There are the obvious knee-jerk (but nevertheless sensible) reactions – such as striving to improve efficiency in order to keep costs down. This will apply not only to employee numbers and productivity but also to the company's financial structure. And here it is not just a question of high liquidity or how much debt there is in the balance sheet: it is the degree of flexibility a company can achieve in a volatile world.

We are now reviewing our upstream exploration and development plans to take account of the changed circumstances. But first, let me say a word about the downstream sector. This part of our business had its tough period between 1980 and 1985. Its asset base was fundamentally restructured to take account of the value of its assets when demand was declining as a result of the high oil price. All companies rationalized their downstream assets and began operating them in a more flexible way. The downstream business was seen as a collection of assets that had to remunerate themselves. Their job was to add value to a base price of oil and so make money. I believe the cycle has swung round and we must now do exactly the same thing for our upstream assets.

People ask us what we are going to do with our exploration and production budgets. Today, as I speak, everything is on pause because the mindset has not yet totally come to grips with the $15 per barrel price. The future level of investment will depend on a mix of factors: how far cash flows are encouraged by taxation policies, whether drilling becomes less expensive, whether offshore production – given the signals of demand – becomes cheaper, and at what level oil prices might stabilize, to mention but a few. Only when the interaction of all the relevant factors has been evaluated can we realistically assess the future level of investment in the upstream sector.

The Extent of Cut-backs

Two recently published surveys show the extent of the cut-backs in capital expenditure and exploration budgets in the USA. A survey by J. S. Herold estimates that capital expenditure in the upstream part of the industry in 1986 will be down by some 24 per cent compared with the 1985 level (see Table 4.2). However, I doubt whether any of these cuts have been carefully thought through at this stage. BP has trimmed its 1986 exploration expenditure (as opposed to production expenditure) by 20 per cent compared with 1985; but I have to say that this reduction is still something of a shot in the dark.

Table 4.2: Changes in US Oil Industry Capital Expenditure Plans. 1985–6. Million Dollars.

Group	Number of Companies	Capital Expenditures		Change (%)
		1985	1986	
Integrated	19	43,833	33,740	−23
Producing	27	1,535	969	−37
Gas Pipeline	9	3,609	2,353	−35
Contract Drilling	3	178	91	−49
Service and Supply	13	756	690	−9
Total	71	49,911	37,843	−24

Note: 1986 figures are preliminary estimates.

Source: J. S. Herold Inc., *Business Week*, 25 August 1986

Another recent report published in the *New York Times* shows that total capital expenditure on exploration in the USA could eventually be down by 50 per cent (see Figure 4.2). That is a juddering halt to a big machine, and it is vitally important that people understand fully the effect of such a reduction.

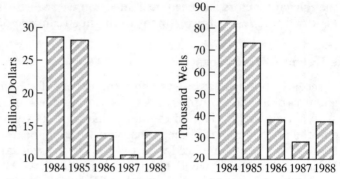

Source: Data Resources Incorp., *New York Times*, August 4, 1986

Figure 4.2: Forecasts of US Exploration Expenditure and Thousands of Wells Drilled. 1984–8.

How have Markets Responded?

So what does the industry do now? How do markets cope with the low price environment? And how is the industry to be financed?

Financial and other markets have responded to the oil price collapse in different ways. An early casualty was the Brent spot market. After a rough period, confidence in this important price-setting and trading market is now largely restored. New contracts are once again providing greater safeguards for sellers in falling markets. I have always argued that the role of the Brent market was effectively to respond to the supply and demand pressure in the US market.

The next thing that ought to be said is that financial markets, as big structures, have also responded to the changed environment. Their treatment of companies has varied according to how they perceive companies' relative strengths. Three examples illustrate this point. First, if you look at the combined market capitalization of Shell and BP over a period in which the value of oil has halved, it is quite extraordinary that investors seem prepared to value these two companies more highly than they did when the oil price was almost double what it is today (see Figure 4.3).

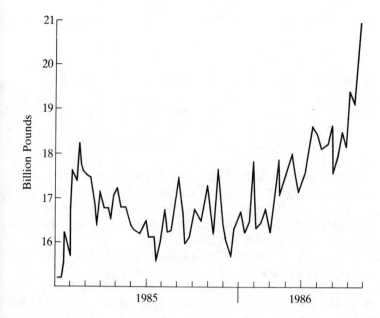

Figure 4.3: Combined Market Capitalization of BP and Shell. January 1985–August 1986.

Secondly, with the capitalization over the same period of several independent UK exploration and production companies, there is exactly the opposite reaction in terms of their market values. The different trends shown in these figures provide the evidence for my assertion that the people who are really in trouble are the independents and not the integrated oil companies. I am not saying that this should or should not be the case, but simply pointing out how the financial market views different types of company.

The final point is that the cost of debt has risen for almost everybody in the market. Certainly an independent exploration and production company would find the cost of finance high if it tried to borrow, say, £500 million to develop the North Sea's Miller field. In terms of relative competitiveness, it would probably cost an independent 2–3 per cent more to obtain its money than it would a top-grade major company, and this increase represents a large slice of the profit margin.

What Else can we Expect from the Market-place?

In the present climate, raising equity and debt finance for new developments is going to be more expensive for any producer or explorer who does not have a portfolio balance. In discussing today's oil market it is commonly asserted that prices are 'low' and that they are likely to rise in the future; but this belief finds little expression in the current market. Whilst it is true that oil markets have followed financial and other markets in recent years in using futures and options to trade forward and to hedge, this has been for relatively short periods. There is, as yet, no long-term futures market. If everybody really believes that future oil prices are going to be stronger than those at present, why hasn't a financial way of taking that punt been devised?

We ought to establish some form of hedging technique because the reality is that future oil prices are still uncertain. The consequences for consumers of drawing the wrong conclusions have inhibited the development of any long-term futures market at prices that would encourage the continuing investment in higher-cost projects.

The best innovation I have seen has come from The Standard Oil Company – BP's principal US subsidiary. By issuing bonds that are linked to the price of oil, Standard has reduced the cost of its debt by linking the rate of return on the debt to the price of oil forecast in the 1990s. By being prepared to give up potential value in the future – at a time when it will be receiving at least $25 per barrel for its oil – Standard is reducing its costs now in an environment of sub-$20 oil. And the financial institutions will benefit too, because if oil is priced at, say, $30 in the future and they have been given title to that oil at $25, then they will recoup $5 on every barrel.

Spreading the risk on the future price of a commodity is not new. The timber world began practising it over fifty years ago – when more wood was used in house-building – but we seem to have forgotten this. The financial market is still sceptical about where the oil industry will position itself in the next year or two, and it is partially unsure about the future value of oil – though not sceptical enough to say that integrated companies (in whom they see a hedge) aren't good value! So they are buying into these companies at the same time as they are selling production-only companies and writing down their value. I find these actions difficult to reconcile.

What Governments Can Do

Governments can help the industry in two ways: first, by alleviating the tax terms on companies' current production so that cash flows are improved; and secondly, by granting tax incentives for new developments. In the latter area, a number of incentives have already been introduced because most governments know they are in a competitive game.

But governments appear highly sceptical about increasing oil companies' cash flows. It would be difficult for them, politically, to make improvements, given the recent experience of the speedy fall in the price of crude oil and the time-lag in the fall of refined products prices. The proof of the pudding will be in the cash flows of the oil industry in 1987. I hope we will not see the industry in an extreme state of recession before people can take sensible decisions.

Recent changes by the Norwegian authorities in encouraging continued commercial development are a step in the right direction. A major review of the UK tax system is warranted.[2]

Conclusions

The downturn in prices has undoubtedly affected the willingness of private oil producers to commit resources to high-cost production. I think it has blunted the flow of normal banking capital and equity routes into the oil industry at competitive prices. Indeed, the evidence in the short period between August 1985 and August 1986 is that there has been a relative deterioration of credit ratings for many companies. Terms have worsened unless a company's debt in the balance sheet has been reducing, or unless it has a large cash pile to absorb the risks that bankers won't take themselves.

---

[2] The improved terms introduced in the UK Budget of March 1987 will bring some benefits.

Markets are giving us limited options to reduce that deteriorating cost – a factor that will certainly slow down new, high-cost developments. They are not yet being very subtle about how we can hedge price volatility. There is no doubt that one consequence of low oil prices today will be a severe reduction in exploration and development spending in the next two years – unless cash flows improve in the next six-to-nine months.

In structural terms, the integrated companies will probably get stronger, whereas companies concerned solely with exploration and production – unless they are government-owned and don't have to take account of the normal laws of economics – will face problems. That trend is something that we should worry about because it may mean falsification of market relationships if it is not handled carefully.

My final view is that I do not believe the oil price is going to go down. In fact, I am one of the optimists who think it will go up. Certainly at present it appears to have stabilized, although some volatility in the future must be expected. But I believe that the laws of supply and demand, and the good sense of all the participants, will see that this particular story has a relatively happy ending.

5 THE IMPACT OF LOW OIL PRICES ON US ENERGY MARKETS

Ralph E. Bailey

It was at this Seminar that Sheikh Yamani quietly introduced the topic of 'netbacks' in September 1985. According to the *Guardian*, 'the select gathering of international oil experts was quick to grasp the point: the world's leading oil exporter was preparing to declare a price war'.

In the United States – as in other countries – we realized that Saudi Arabia was tired of losing market share in its efforts to prop up prices for the rest of the world's producers. And we realized it was preparing to take some countervailing action. But we did not immediately appreciate the full extent of what this would mean to the economics of the oil industry, in the United States and elsewhere. By April 1986, when the price of crude oil had fallen below $10 per barrel on the spot market, from a high of $32 in November, *then* we fully recognized the significance of the Minister's comments.

What we would like to know now, is where oil prices will go in the future. This is a question pondered daily by those at Conoco who are responsible for making supply and demand forecasts for our strategic planning. Having a rough idea of future price levels is, of course, an essential element in projecting rates of return on petroleum investments that are under consideration.

Given the uncertainty about the future path of crude oil prices, we have developed several price scenarios for planning purposes and, along with them, a number of contingency plans.

Our most likely case is that prices will average in the mid and upper teens for the next several years, and then rise rapidly in the early and mid-1990s as the market tightens.

Today, I would like briefly to review the Conoco forecast based on this most likely case. I shall focus on the US aspects of the Conoco world-wide energy study, with particular emphasis on oil and coal.

In the Conoco forecast, looking to 1995, we project US econonic growth at a little below 3 per cent per annum. Growth in energy consumption is projected at 1 per cent per annum. In this forecast, US oil demand grows at an average of 1.5 per cent annually to almost 18 mb/d in 1995. This represents a return to consumption levels that preceded the price run-ups of the early 1980s.

US natural gas demand falls by 0.5 per cent per annum on average until 1995. In the short term, gas use will be constrained in the important utility market by competition from low-priced residual fuel oil. In the 1990s, the constraining factor is expected to be availability of supply. The current gas surplus is expected to evaporate within a few years because of the decline in gas development associated with weak prices.

US coal use has the same percentage increase as oil – 1.5 per cent. This is less growth than would have occurred if oil prices had stayed in the $25–30 range, because the incentive for utilities to use more coal instead of oil and gas has been reduced. In fact, at oil prices below $15, substantial amounts of coal might be displaced. The potential for displacement in the United States would be about 80 million tons of coal per year – the same volume of coal that displaced oil in the period 1978–85, when utilities were responding to high oil prices. This is equivalent to about 900,000 b/d of residual fuel oil. The theoretical displacement factor would be about 10 per cent of 1985 coal use.

The response by some utilities to price changes can be swift. For example, during March and April 1986, when the price of crude oil fell below $10 per barrel, there was a 50 per cent increase in oil-fuelled electricity generation. Of course, the load can shift just as quickly back to coal. The reason for this flexibility is excess and varied generating capacity – coal, oil and gas – not just within a particular utility system, but nation-wide. For example, when coal prices are attractive, a utility in the north-east may elect to buy coal-generated power from West Virginia – 400 miles or so to the south-west – as well as using its own coal-fired capacity. But very low oil and gas prices would put the load on petroleum. However, under

Conoco's most likely price case of mid-to-upper teens, the competition from petroleum would only slow the increase in coal use, rather than causing a downward trend. It is also worth noting that the United States has huge coal reserves, that there is political interest in using more of those reserves to help the economies of the coal-producing regions, and that the coal industry itself has proved remarkably resilient. Cost reductions have been achieved, largely through productivity gains. Our coal company has increased productivity in its underground mines by 100 per cent since 1978, and these gains are continuing. These factors would tend to mitigate the effects of low oil prices on coal use in the United States over the long term.

Nuclear generation is forecast to grow at an average of 4.4 per cent per annum. We project rapid growth until 1990 as a number of new plants under construction finally enter commercial service. After that, nuclear generation is expected to level off and then decline during the 1990s, as old plants are retired and no new facilities come on stream. No new nuclear capacity has been ordered in the United States since 1978, and most plants ordered since 1974 have been cancelled. Nuclear power in the United States has been cursed with cost-overruns, delays in obtaining permits, well-organized opposition and intense, adverse publicity triggered by the accident at Three Mile Island. The recent accident at Chernobyl in the USSR has served to support the anti-nuclear cause.

Finally, in our forecast, hydropower growth is negligible, because of the limited availability of new sites in the United States. There is no separate category for synthetic fuels because their share is insignificant. With oil at recent price levels, synthetic fuels are simply not economic.

Given the trends I have outlined, the US energy use mix in 1995 would be led by oil at 42 per cent of the market, followed by coal with 24 per cent, natural gas with 21 per cent and nuclear and hydropower accounting for the remainder. This is essentially unchanged from 1985, except that natural gas loses about three percentage points and nuclear gains about three points, over the ten-year period.

US production of crude oil and NGLs is forecast to decline

by an average of 2.5 per cent per annum, from 11.3 mb/d in 1985 to a little over 9 mb/d by 1995. This would leave a gap of 8.7 mb/d to be filled by imports. This is more than double the volume imported last year, and is based on our forecast of prices in the mid-to-upper teens.

Of course, the United States would be dependent on oil imports, even under the most optimistic price scenario. The fact is, although the United States is the largest oil producer in the non-Communist world, that it is a mature oil province, and most of the big fields have already been discovered. So the level of prices does not determine *whether* a gap exists between domestic oil supply and demand but simply how large or small the gap will be. For example, last year, when oil prices were around $25 per barrel, we forecast import dependence of about 40 per cent by the year 2000. But the USA could approach 50 per cent dependence on imports by 1995 or sooner, with oil prices in the mid-to-upper teens.

As you know, low prices affect oil production in three phases. First, there is a near-term impact, in which wells with lifting costs above realized prices are shut in. These would be primarily the so-called stripper wells, which produce 10 b/d or less. Actually, the 453,000 stripper wells that were operating in the United States in 1985 averaged only 3 b/d. The National Stripper Well Association estimates that 100,000 of these wells are probably uneconomic at prices of $15 per barrel or less. The API has studied the potential effect of various price levels on US oil production. In a comparison between $15 and $20 per barrel, they estimate 500,000 b/d would be lost at the lower level, in one-to-two years.

Secondly, there is an intermediate impact, in which development plans are cut back or postponed. On a broad scale, there is a negative impact on such development work as infill drilling. And there is an impact on major projects. Conoco's decision not to go ahead at this time with the second phase of a development project on the North Slope of Alaska is one example of this. There are obviously many others involving other companies. Decisions such as these will affect supply up to five years in the future. The API estimates a loss of 1.3 mb/d by 1991, at $15 versus $20 per barrel.

Thirdly, there is a long-term effect, resulting from cuts in exploration budgets. Cut-backs in this vital area are showing up in low numbers of seismic crews engaged in geophysical surveys, and in drastically reduced drilling activity. Current exploration cut-backs will adversely affect US production up to ten years from now – at about the same time as we had expected a tighter market even without the 1986 price collapse. As I indicated, Conoco is forecasting a production decline of over 2 mb/d by 1995. I think the biggest long-term impact will be felt in offshore projects, with their long lead times and high costs. This is unfortunate, because offshore exploration offers the best prospects for significant new discoveries in the United States.

I should mention that low oil prices have an adverse impact on investments in enhanced recovery in all three time frames – near, intermediate, and long term. Most enhanced oil recovery systems already in place and operating will remain economic at $15 per barrel, but some projects that are in the pipeline will be stopped, and new plans will be shelved for the time being. The effect of low oil prices on enhanced recovery will be to hamper efforts to offset the natural decline in our mature fields.

Low oil prices will increase the rate of decline in US production. But there are broader and perhaps more serious effects, in the impact on the oil industry world-wide. For example, there is the effect on the industry's ability to develop new technology and perhaps – in the field of enhanced recovery – to sustain current standards of applied technology. In the past, we have moved from decade to decade on the crest of successive waves of new technology. New technology has enabled us to develop petroleum provinces previously beyond our capabilities. But budget cuts will undoubtedly affect investments in technology. This would have adverse consequences, not only for new frontier areas, but also for established producing regions, including the prolific fields of the Middle East. Advanced petroleum technology will be required to increase ultimate recovery in these fields as well.

A related area of concern is human resources. The final numbers are not yet in for autumn enrolment at the petroleum schools, but I understand from Conoco's recruiters that the recession in our industry has turned many young people away. And the thousands of experienced geologists, geophysicists and engineers who have been squeezed out of the industry may be lost to us for ever, because they may have found other careers or settled permanently into retirement.

I think all producers, OPEC and non-OPEC, have a commonality of interest in maintaining a strong technological base. This depends on the ability of the industry to continue to invest in technology, and on our ability to attract the talented young people who will be our managers, scientists and technicians in the future.

I believe we also have a common interest in maintaining market access, under the principles of free trade. In that regard, it is worth noting that sentiment has been rising in the United States for some sort of oil import tariff. Ostensibly, such a tariff would be to protect the US oil industry from low-cost imports – but I think at least part of the attraction for legislators is in its revenue-enhancing potential. In addition to the money from the tariff itself, there would undoubtedly be some tax on the higher prices that US producers would realize behind the tariff wall. My own view is that a tariff would do more harm than good, because it would raise US energy costs above world prices. This would further undermine the ability of US manufacturers to compete with foreign manufacturers at home and abroad, and it would be inflationary. But, with a Presidential election looming, and the electoral leverage of the oil-producing states (particularly Texas), I would not rule out the possibility of protectionist legislation including, possibly, an import tariff. This would apply, in all probability, to refined products as well as crude oil; otherwise, a tariff would simply skew imports towards products, damaging the refining industry.

It is also worth noting that, although the US Government is ideologically committed to free trade and free markets, it is nevertheless closely monitoring the oil situation. In fact, the US Energy Secretary has asked the National Petroleum Council for a thorough study, which is now under way. The Council consists of representatives of the energy industry, financial institutions and academia, and its role is to advise the Federal Government. As Chairman of the Council, I can tell you that we are focusing on a number of factors that may affect the US petroleum outlook. These include political, geological, economic, technological and environmental considerations. The object is to evaluate how the United States might avoid a recurrence of the energy shocks that occurred in the 1970s, or at least lessen the adverse impact of such shocks. This study is scheduled for completion in early 1987, although some preliminary results may be reported in autumn 1986.

Finally, I believe all producers – OPEC and non-OPEC – have a common interest in a more stable oil market. The price volatility of the past few months has wreaked havoc with the cash flows of nations and companies alike. And the boom-and-bust cycles of the past few years have been highly disruptive to the economies and social fabric of both oil-exporting and oil-importing countries.

In the United States, the conventional wisdom is that the benefits of low oil prices to the economy as a whole far outweigh the negative impact on the oil industry. But, so far, the conventional wisdom has been wrong. Instead of responding vigorously to lower energy costs, the economy has acted in a sluggish manner. In some regions, particularly the southwest, the negative impact of a depressed petroleum industry is seen in reduced capital expenditures, higher unemployment, higher social costs and declining government revenues. Nation-wide, capital spending by the oil industry accounts directly for about 10 per cent of all capital investment. But there is a far greater ripple effect, and it is very likely that oil company budget cuts averaging more than 25 per cent this year are a significant factor in the economy's lack of vigour.

In general, I believe the US energy policy of relying on the free market is appropriate. I am sceptical that there is an ultimate benefit to be derived from direct government intervention. However, I am concerned about the overall air of complacency in the general public with regard to future domestic energy supplies. This is reflected in attitudes in Congress. For example, Congress repeatedly invokes moratoriums on offshore leasing, preventing exploration of some of the most promising acreage. It seems unable to bring itself to eliminate the remnants of price controls on natural gas, or to end the windfall profit tax. I believe this inertia is a fair reflection of public attitudes.

In the private sector, some painful lessons have been learned. I think it will be a long time before we see a repeat of the excesses of the early 1980s, when anyone who could buy, beg or borrow a drilling rig came into the oil business, and banks were falling over themselves to lend money for energy projects, even of dubious merit. Many operators have gone out of business, and I doubt that they will be back in large numbers – ever.

I hope now that some stability will return to the energy markets, and that we will see an end to excessive price swings. Oil-exporting and oil-importing nations, consumers, and the oil industry itself would all be better served by an environment of moderate, predictable prices, with appropriate incentives for oil companies to invest in the technology necessary to maintain adequate, reliable supplies of energy to the world.

Such an environment would assure that petroleum would remain the pre-eminent chosen energy source far into the twenty-first century.

PART II

OPEC SUPPLY AND PRICING POLICIES

6 PRODUCERS' POLICIES: PAST AND FUTURE

Ali M. Jaidah

At the time of the first Oxford Energy Seminar, in 1979, we were generally told by the news media and the petroleum industry that the world was facing an oil crisis. This was perceived as a problem of supply security which naturally manifested itself in sharp increases in the price of oil. The circumstances of this crisis were the Iranian Revolution and the sequence of market responses that followed the first interruption of Iranian production.

We are meeting now, several years later, for the eighth Oxford Energy Seminar and we are also facing a crisis which I shall call an oil demand crisis. Those who are primarily affected are not the consuming countries but the producers by which I mean all countries endowed with hydrocarbon resources and companies with upstream investments and assets. The culprit this time is not tight and insecure supplies. On the contrary, supplies are available to anybody who cares to purchase crude oil, and despite the damaging effects of the Iraq–Iran war and the US embargo on Libya, supplies remain potentially abundant and can always be secured from alternative sources. This time the problem arises from low or stagnant demand for oil. Through a sequence of events this decline in demand has led to a sharp drop in the price of oil and to fundamental changes in the process of oil price determination.

Since this new crisis affects producers rather than consumers and because producers are much less vocal than the powerful political lobbies of the industrialized countries, the current petroleum situation is not generally described as a crisis.

Let us simply accept the fact that any significant change in the oil situation can represent a crisis for some group and bestow advantages on other groups but that no situation can be correctly described as a world crisis. This is why I have been careful in referring to the 1979 events as an oil supply crisis, stressing supply security as a cause, and to the 1986 event as an oil demand crisis.

My purpose today is to try to examine how we moved from one extreme situation to the other. Essentially, the story is about a change in the balance of power. Ten years ago in a lecture given at Harvard, I introduced the concept of 'controlling power' as a way of interpreting the main developments in the history of oil. This concept remains eminently relevant for an understanding of these recent developments. In 1979 OPEC appeared to have this controlling power over price developments and supplies and in 1986 OPEC appeared to have lost that power. This, however, raises a number of questions. The most obvious one relates to the causes of this apparent shift in power and the more subtle ones raise doubts about the exact nature and the reality of this controlling power. For example, is it true that OPEC in 1979, as was widely believed then, not only by the world at large but by OPEC members themselves, was in the driving seat leading and steering major oil developments? And is it true that the market in 1986, as most people today seem to believe, has completely taken over the process of price determination? In 1979 most people thought that OPEC's power was there to stay, that supplies would always remain tight and that oil scarcity would always cast its shadow over the immediate horizon. In 1986 many people seem to think that the victory of the market over an OPEC system of price administration is final and permanent, that supplies will always remain abundant and that the recovery of oil demand, if it ever takes place, is so far beyond the horizon as to be an irrelevant prospect.

In trying to explain how the oil world moved from the extreme situation of 1979, when prices seemed to rise so rapidly and to such high levels that nobody could identify a ceiling for this movement, to the situation of 1986, when on some days prices were falling so fast and so low that people began to wonder whether there was any firm floor capable of arresting this movement, I will look at the interaction of OPEC's policies with economic and political forces that operate on the market. In this context it is important to emphasize that I subscribe neither to theories that explain all developments exclusively in terms of OPEC's behaviour and OPEC's policies, nor to theories that focus entirely on the market and consider that OPEC's actions are irrelevant. A proper understanding of what happens to oil must take into account both the role of OPEC and the role of the market, and the complex interaction of these two forces.

Let me briefly go back to 1979. There is no doubt that the price increases were then initiated by competition between oil buyers, companies and governments of consuming countries which were, for perfectly understandable reasons, in a panic about possible supply disruptions. OPEC countries, like all other producers, naturally benefited from the price rises, which generated high revenues, but they were in no position to regulate or arrest the movement for the simple reason that buyers were competing for all available supplies. OPEC appeared to be the 'controlling power' because it was reaping the immediate benefits that the exercise of that power normally yields, but this was an optical illusion. The benefits accrued to the producing countries through the actions of others who were responding to a situation created by an independent political event, namely the Iranian Revolution.

It is important in this context to recall the very simple proposition that producers can only attempt to control price movements when the market is slack. This is because the regulation of price requires an adjustment of supply to the level of desired demand and this adjustment can only be made if producers have some margin of manoeuvre over supplies. When buyers demand more oil than producers can extract or shift, supplies can not be adjusted upwards and the price rise movement takes on a life of its own.

Paradoxically, OPEC began to have a role to play in 1980–81 when demand for its oil started to slacken. By then prices had reached a high level and it was open to OPEC to decide on an appropriate pricing strategy that would best serve the long-term interests of producers. In my view, this is when things began to go wrong for OPEC. The origins of the 1986 crisis go back five years earlier to these very important years 1980–81. At that time, precisely because demand was slackening, OPEC potentially had the power to determine by itself the future course of prices. It had no need to accept any longer the autonomous determination of prices which had resulted from the competition of buyers for limited supplies. Nor had it any need to accept passively the new competition of non-OPEC sellers trying to maximize their output under the price protection of OPEC.

Unfortunately, OPEC in 1980–81 did not take advantage of the opportunity. Most member countries considered that the fortuitous price increases of 1979–80 should be permanently preserved. Their implicit belief was that a price gain, however obtained, must be treated as a sacred bench-mark and that any future change decreed by OPEC must go above this bench-mark. In other words, OPEC and its individual members believed that the oil price should be either kept at whatever level had just been attained or raised above that level but that on no account could prices be decreased. It did not matter whether the level attained was due to temporary and totally incidental factors. It did not matter whether the prices attained were the product of forces outside OPEC's control. Very few people within OPEC raised the question of whether the price level reached accidentally in 1979 was the price that served OPEC's long-term economic interests best. One can understand the psychological and political considerations that were making it very difficult for most OPEC members to question the price level that was then attained. We can say now with hindsight that it was a mistake not to try to steer prices back towards a path that would have been planned to provide OPEC with greater long-term benefits, but we must understand that such a move would have then been perceived as a defeat and that very few people would have been able to persuade the relevant authorities that a price decrease causing an immediate and significant loss in revenue was beneficial and worth implementing for the sake of hazy long-term gains.

I do not want to go in detail over all the developments that took place between 1981 and 1985 and which are familiar to you. It would be sufficient to highlight a few important points. OPEC's policy during that period was to defend as best it could the unified official reference price agreed in 1981 after long and painful debate between those who wanted to retain all the gains obtained in 1979–80 and stick to a $36 per barrel marker price and those who preferred the lower marker of $32 per barrel.

To defend the $34 marker price did not prove very easy. On the one hand, non-OPEC prices were lower than official OPEC prices, and on the other hand the structure of price differentials for OPEC crudes was not correctly rationalized. But it is remarkable that despite very adverse market conditions OPEC was able to avoid a drastic retreat on the price front until the end of 1985. There was only one major official price adjustment in March 1983 when the marker was revised to $29 per barrel and a very minor adjustment in October 1984 when it was reduced to $28 per barrel. These adjustments were made only to match the prices then prevailing in the North Sea. The forces with which OPEC had to contend during that period are well known to you. Demand for energy was not rising very much because of conservation and the economic recession. Oil was losing part of its share of the energy market because of substitution by gas, coal and nuclear power, and demand for OPEC oil took a considerable plunge from a peak of 31 mb/d to a low of 16.0–16.5 mb/d as a result of all these factors and an additional one of major importance – the significant growth in non-OPEC oil production. OPEC held the price line essentially by agreeing to absorb these very significant decreases in demand. It also had recourse to a production policy consisting of an output ceiling and a quota distribution in order to buttress the price defence policy. The first attempt at introducing the production programme was made in March 1982 but did not prove very successful. The second attempt made in March 1983 in London provided the world market with eighteen months of relative price stability. But then, again under the impact of the North Sea, prices began to give way and a new crisis led to the OPEC meeting of October 1984. OPEC once again attempted to shore up the price defences by introducing a tighter production programme with a 16 mb/d ceiling and a new quota allocation. But by that time things had gone too far and most observers familiar with OPEC could see that the price defence strategy could not be maintained for much longer on those terms.

Having recognized that OPEC misjudged the situation in

1980–81 when it failed to appreciate the importance of implementing the price strategy based on long-term economic factors and economic interests, and taking into account the immediate threat posed by the lower prices set by non-OPEC producers, I must now emphasize that the non-OPEC exporting countries also misjudged the situation during that period. The non-OPEC exporting countries were increasingly becoming a major force. The situation that prevailed until the end of the 1970s and the situation that began to emerge in the early 1980s were drastically different in one important aspect: in the former OPEC had a virtual monopoly of world oil exports, whereas in the latter the non-OPEC exporters commanded an ever increasing share of the world oil market. The non-OPEC countries believed that OPEC would always have the ability to defend the price of oil on its own and to maintain it at a level that would enable them to increase their investment and their production at the expense of OPEC. The non-OPEC countries were unduly complacent about the ability of OPEC to continue to play the same role despite a continual erosion of the volume of its exports. Simple common sense should have made them realize that one cannot rely on an institution to perform these functions when that institution is weakening from day to day. Surely there must be a point when continual weakening will paralyse this institution. Things are even worse when the institution on which one relies is being weakened by one's own actions. Together with many OPEC spokesmen and analysts aware of the reality of OPEC, I have warned in previous Seminars and on other occasions that OPEC cannot be taken for granted for ever. Although I accept that before October 1984 non-OPEC exporters could claim that their belief in the ability of OPEC to continue to defend the price was justifiable, it became abundantly clear in October 1984 that the writing was on the wall. I remain amazed at the complacency and blindness that prevented the non-OPEC exporting countries from attempting to protect their true interests, a protection that can only be achieved through some sort of co-operation on the part of all producers on the issue of the oil price. I am even more amazed that this perception today is not as sharp as it ought to be. An oil price collapse is not catastrophic for OPEC only: it harms all producing interests even if in different degrees and by different amounts.

By 1985 the situation had become untenable for OPEC. The residual demand for OPEC oil had become so low as a result of the total squeeze caused by low world demand and increases in non-OPEC supplies that competition for market share both between OPEC and non-OPEC and also within OPEC had become inevitable. On the one hand it was virtually impossible to obtain an effective agreement within OPEC on an allocation of a meagre 16 mb/d output among thirteen countries, all of whom were hard pressed by revenue needs. If a cake that has to be shared is so small that everybody will only get a minute portion that cannot satisfy his hunger, it will be impossible to agree in advance on how to share the cake. The natural instinct is for everybody to fight in the hope of obtaining through his independent actions a larger portion. This is in essence what competition is all about. Furthermore, what I may call the 'law of residuals' comes into play. When small producers try to increase their small shares by little amounts they can legitimately think that their own small increase has no effect on the global picture. However the sum total of all these small increases make a significant dent in the share of the residual supplier. This is exactly what happened both between non-OPEC and OPEC and within OPEC between the majority of member countries and Saudi Arabia. Wittingly or unwittingly, the non-OPEC exporters have pushed OPEC into a tight corner and, wittingly or unwittingly, a large number of OPEC members have displaced some of the burden on to the traditional OPEC residual supplier which is Saudi Arabia. This sequence of moves was bound to produce a crack in the system. In my judgement this is exactly what happened in late November 1985.

When the story is put in this long perspective it appears very clearly that it is simplistic and misleading to blame a single factor or a single actor for the oil crisis of 1986. Everybody has played a part. Everybody has contributed to this outcome through actions of his own and through reactions to the actions of others. We have also seen that the 'controlling power' has never been an exclusive attribute of either OPEC or the market and that there is a constant interaction between producers and the market and we have also seen that the non-OPEC exporters have taken a back seat and enjoyed the benefits of the game without making a positive contribution. They contributed to the 1986 crisis through their passivity.

In examining what can be done to resolve the current crisis we must keep all these points in mind. There is no effective solution which can depend exclusively on the actions of OPEC alone. Co-operation between OPEC and non-OPEC exporters is going to be essential to any attempt to stabilize the movement of oil prices and one should also realize that price stability can be achieved neither by abandoning the system of price determination entirely to the market nor by ignoring the role of economic forces altogether. We must move towards a more complex concept of the 'controlling power' that involves a sharing of roles between OPEC and producers must establish new and appropriate types of relationships with the market. Let me develop these points. The producer's interest is to ensure that the oil price is set at a level that reduces some of the current short- and medium-term imbalance between supply and demand and ensures that long-term supplies remain forthcoming. The aim is to avoid the emergence of an energy supply or demand crisis in the long term. It is important to reduce the current imbalance because its scale is so considerable as to make it a very powerful cause of instability. But it is also important to avoid such a rapid increase in demand and such a significant inhibition of supplies that would recreate within a few years or even within a decade a new tight oil market situation with all its adverse consequences for the producers and for the world economy. This is not an easy problem to solve but it is to my mind the most important problem. This point has certain implications. It indicates that the priority for producers is to determine a price policy. The urgent task that faces OPEC is to define as best as it can a price policy that takes these factors into account. As a first step OPEC should revert immediately to its traditional role which is to set again and to hold firmly a reference or marker price for oil. This can be set as a floor price, below which OPEC members will refuse to sell. Price administration by OPEC would be limited to the reference price. The thorny issue of price differentials could be easily solved by an arrangement that settles the differential on the basis of relative netbacks one month after the oil is lifted. In this situation production programmes and quotas play an important role but not as the sole policy instrument. Their purpose is to buttress the price policy. The second step is to foster co-operation between OPEC and non-OPEC on the determination of an optimum price strategy, taking into account this floor price and the need to restrain output and the production maximization made at the expense of OPEC. Co-operation is needed, not only because the price issue is difficult and its solution requires inputs from all those concerned but also because the implementation of a good price policy can not be successful if OPEC applies it on its own. It is not necessary to envisage a formal agreement between the whole of OPEC and every non-OPEC oil exporter. Sharing of views on the pricing issue could begin informally between the major players within OPEC and non-OPEC. It could be posed initially as an intellectual question provided that all the parties concerned accept that it is in their interests to investigate the issue dispassionately for their own good. Formal understanding could come later.

The relationship between the producers and the market is another important issue. It is essential to remember that producers remain the major agents on the oil market. After all, they have the ultimate word on supplies. If the basics of the market are supply and demand, let us not forget that producers reap half of the equation. If we remembered the simple fact we could see very clearly but all those who believe that the market is a force on its own, independent of producers' policies and objectives, are misrepresenting the truth. The difficulty is to work out the appropriate forms of interaction between producers' policies and market forces. This depends on a correct understanding of the functions of the market. Markets give two types of signals. They give very short-term signals through volatile price fluctuations and they reveal the long-term tendencies of fundamental economic forces. The first set of signals are the most visible, and modern technology through the video screen and swift communication increases the visibility and influence but the signals are confused and confusing. They largely reflect spontaneous reactions to information and disinformation. Their economic value is doubtful or limited. But they can be used for the determination of price differentials. The long-term tendencies of economic forces are much more difficult to discern. They require interpretation and analysis and producers can only ignore them at their peril. In determining their price and production policies they must take into account as best as they can the long-term effects of prices on demand and on investment decisions that determine future supplies. We would be mistaken if we allowed ourselves to be unduly influenced by short-term volatility. In fact the aim should be to stabilize this short-term movement but not to the point that would blot out the long-term signals.

I am aware that this is a difficult task, that it is a very tall order indeed. But the problems facing the world of oil are too serious and the consequences are too damaging for their solution to be sought in half measures and half-baked strategies and policies. To devise good policies, however sophisticated, is not beyond the skills of those engaged in the oil world but what may be lacking is the political will. My only hope is that a growing awareness of the damage that the present oil price situation can cause if it persists will mobilize this political will. Once that is achieved, the policy question may not be more than a difficult technicality.

7 THE 1986 OIL PRICE WAR: AN ECONOMIC FIASCO

Nordine Aït-Laoussine and John C. Gault

During the first eight months of 1986, OPEC pursued a strategy to increase market share which implied, as an unavoidable consequence, a substantial drop in crude oil prices. What has OPEC gained by pursuing this strategy, and should it be continued? This paper estimates the positive and negative effects of the price war on OPEC as a whole, with particular reference to the gains and losses in collective (total OPEC) export revenues.

It is clear that OPEC has succeeded in increasing its output since the beginning of 1986 (comparing actual January–August average production of 18.6 mb/d with pre-war projected average production of 15.9 mb/d for the same period), at the cost of a substantial price drop (of the order of $20 per barrel during the same period). The immediate net result has been a $50 billion loss in actual revenue compared with potential revenue. But what of future gains and losses?

In the short run, some of the gains in volume experienced so far in 1986 will prove temporary. Indeed, we calculate that 2.1 mb/d of the apparent 2.7 mb/d increase in OPEC's market share during these eight months should be attributed to transient factors which may not be repeated in the immediate future. As a consequence, our projection of net demand for OPEC oil in 1987 is only slightly above that for 1986. This means that if OPEC seriously intends to stabilize the price in the $17–19 per barrel range targeted by most of its member countries and recently endorsed by the Gulf Cooperation Council, the temporary quota agreement reached for September–October 1986 should be extended at least until the spring of 1987.

In the medium term, if oil prices do not collapse further but instead rise gradually from $17 per barrel in 1987 to $20 per

barrel in 1990, then limited expansion of world-wide oil demand and some contraction of non-OPEC supply (compared
with pre-war projections) may be foreseen. The resulting increase in OPEC's market share, however, will not be sufficient
to offset the decline in prices from pre-war levels. OPEC's
total revenues in the 1986–90 period will fall some $170 billion
below pre-war estimates which, discounted at 12 per cent, is
equivalent to $130 billion in present value terms.

Even in the long run, OPEC's gains from the war will be
insufficient to outweigh the short- and medium-term losses.
Although continued low (relative to pre-war) oil prices in the
1986–90 period may prompt an acceleration of demand
growth in the early 1990s as well as some further slippage in
non-OPEC supply, the maximum revenue gain to OPEC may
be severely limited by restrictions on OPEC production.
These restrictions, which result both from physical and production policy limits, will hold OPEC total output to no more
than 26.0 mb/d in the mid-1990s.

If we discount (at the same 12 per cent rate) the difference
between pre-war and post-war projected OPEC export revenues over the entire 1986–95 period, and if we assume prices
jump to $30 per barrel in 1992 as OPEC's 26.0 mb/d produc-
tion ceiling is approached, the 'present value' of the price war
to OPEC remains negative. In other words, for OPEC to
achieve a positive net present value, i.e. a net gain from the
price war, either future production ceilings must be relaxed or
prices must reach significantly higher levels than in the immediate pre-war period. From the perspective of most member countries, the price war would therefore have served only
to bring forward by a few years the time when they will again
be producing at or near capacity limits.

Rather than establishing the 'market share' objective
(which implied a price war and the subsequent revenue loss),
OPEC should have defined its objective in terms of a revenue
target. It would have been possible, for example, to obtain the
same export revenues as in our post-war scenario by cutting
production to 10.0 mb/d in 1986, 13.0 mb/d in 1987 and 14.0
mb/d in 1988, thus defending the pre-war $28 per barrel price
level. OPEC's market share would in any case have grown in
the 1990s. This alternative policy would have the additional

advantage that oil not produced today would be available for production in the long run when prices are higher; oil produced and sold at today's (relatively low) price is, in contrast, gone for ever.

Questions Raised by the Price War

The oil industry has experienced in 1986 its most dramatic upheaval in recent history. This upheaval was prompted by the decision taken by OPEC in late 1985 to abandon its traditional role of residual supplier in favour of pursuing a larger market share.

Although the final communiqué issued at the end of the December 1985 Geneva Conference was not specific as to the means by which the organization intended to achieve its new objective, it soon became evident that this novel strategy meant that OPEC would no longer be concerned with the defence of the oil price and that member countries would indulge in competitive pricing to improve their output at the expense of other producers. Most member countries realized that, in view of their large unused production capacity, this competitive pricing would bring about a substantial drop in crude oil prices which would, in their view, stimulate demand, reduce non-OPEC supplies, and result in an increased market share for OPEC.

This is how the price war was set in motion. The rest of the story is known: a price crash of the order of $20 per barrel in six months (see Figure 7.1). It can be said therefore at this point that OPEC has done extremely well in bringing about a rapid price decline which was one of the objectives endorsed, willingly or unwillingly, by its members in December 1985 in Geneva. But what other objectives has it achieved?

The purpose of this paper is not to discuss the reasons why the oil-exporting countries managed to place themselves in their current predicament nor to assign responsibility for this state of affairs. Its purpose, instead, is to address a question which must be haunting the minds of the policy-makers who endorsed the December 1985 OPEC decision.

The answer to this question requires an economic assessment of the gains already realized or to be expected by OPEC

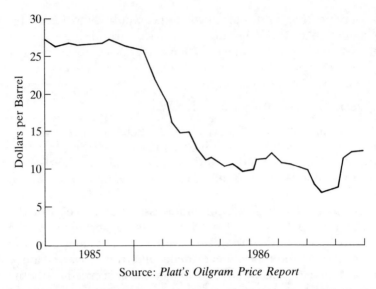

Source: *Platt's Oilgram Price Report*

Figure 7.1: Average Spot Assessment for Dubai Crude. October 1985–
August 1986.

as well as the costs associated with these gains. In this respect,
we propose to examine in turn: the pre-war perception of the
future, the post-war outlook, and the overall balance, in terms
of the resulting gains and losses for OPEC as a whole.

In our concluding remarks, we will offer some suggestions
on how we believe the exporting countries can bring the
current crisis to an end, restore market stability, and protect
their long-term interests.

The Pre-war Perception of the Future

(*a*) *The Demand Outlook.* In 1985, forecasters generally expected
that 1986 non-Communist world oil demand would broadly
remain at the 1985 level and that oil consumption would rise
very slowly over the next fifteen years at rates of about 1 per
cent per annum up to the late 1980s and at slightly higher
rates during the 1990s.

A number of general assumptions underlay this perception
of oil demand growth for the remainder of the century:

(a) Constant nominal oil prices were assumed (and even, in some forecasts, constant real prices).

(b) Average world economic growth rates of some 2.5–3.5 per cent per annum were projected, with the OECD expected to average around 3 per cent per annum (Japan above and Western Europe below) and the Third World forecast to average some 4.5 per cent per annum (OPEC above and most of the rest below).

(c) Total world primary energy consumption was expected to rise at average rates of 1.5–2.0 per cent per annum, with a continued decline in average energy intensities although the rate of decline was expected to slow down.

(d) Within the structure of primary energy, the share of coal was forecast to rise (from 20 to 23 per cent). The contribution of natural gas was also expected to increase, but only marginally (from 18 per cent to around 19 per cent), with most of the increase taking place in the Third World. Nuclear power was expected to double its contribution from 4 to 8 per cent, while hydro and other marginal fuel sources were forecast to remain broadly static at around 10 per cent. The petroleum share was generally forecast to decline from just below 50 per cent to around 40 per cent by the year 2000. Non-Communist world demand was expected to reach some 48.0–48.5 mb/d in 1990, rising to 52.0–53.0 mb/d in 1995 and to around 55.0 mb/d in the year 2000. Most of the increase in oil demand was expected to come from Third World countries.

(*b*) *The Non-OPEC Supply Outlook.* On the supply side, most forecasters expected that non-OPEC petroleum availabilities would peak out in the late 1980s and would gradually decline throughout in 1990s.

The consensus was broadly based on the following perceptions:

(a) Conventional crude oil production was expected to be some 23.0 mb/d in 1990 and to decline, mostly in the OECD area, to 22.0 mb/d in 1995 and 20.0 mb/d by the turn of the century.

(b) NGLs output was projected to increase by about 1.0 mb/d

and to reach 3.5 mb/d by the turn of the century (excluding OPEC NGLs).

(c) CPEs net exports were forecast to remain at current levels until the late 1980s or early 1990s (China up and USSR down) with some forecasters projecting a total phase-out of these exports by the turn of the century.

(d) Limited developments of syncrude were anticipated, reaching about 300,000 b/d in 1990 and about 1.0 mb/d by the year 2000.

(*c*) *The Prospects for OPEC's Output.* As a result of these forecasts, the general consensus was that substantial excess producing capacity would persist until the mid-1990s and that oil supplies would become relatively tight before the turn of the century. Under the then prevailing assumption that OPEC would continue to administer prices, the outlook was for a continued constraint on OPEC crude oil production for the rest of the 1980s. This implied no increase in OPEC output in 1986 as compared with 1985 (16.0 mb/d) and a modest gradual improvement in the following years with most forecasters expecting a level of the order of 18.0–19.0 mb/d by 1990.

Thereafter, OPEC crude oil production was forecast to continue to rise during the 1990s to reach some 23.0–24.0 mb/d by 1995 and to push against capacity soon thereafter.

To sum up, the pre-war perception of the future was that OPEC was getting out of the tunnel, so to speak, with the prospect of a gradually rising market share from the low point of 16.0 mb/d in 1985–6 to full capacity before the turn of the century.

The Post-war Outlook

(*a*) *The Experience of January–August 1986.* OPEC's crude oil production has recently approached 21.0 mb/d and has averaged about 18.6 mb/d for the first eight months of 1986. This increase in output, as compared with a pre-war forecast of 15.9 mb/d for the same January–August period, has perhaps given to some member countries the impression that much progress has been made, within a short time, towards improving OPEC's market share. But a closer look into the various components of this apparent increase reveals that this progress is illusory since most of the gain achieved in 1986 is temporary in nature.

A comparison of the pre-war and post-war views of the supply/demand balance for the January–August 1986 period (see Table 7.1) shows that the apparent gain of 2.7 mb/d results from the combined effects of a 500,000 b/d increase in oil demand, a 1.1 mb/d decrease in non-OPEC supplies and 1.1 mb/d of inventory build-up.

Table 7.1: OPEC Production and Market Share.
January–August 1986. Million Barrels per Day.

	Pre-war Forecast	Post-war Actual	Gains in OPEC Market Share		
			Apparent	Permanent	Temporary
Total Demand[a]	45.5	46.0	0.5	0.3	0.2
Non-OPEC Supply[b]	29.6	28.5	1.1	0.3	0.8
Residual OPEC Supply[c]	15.9	17.5			
Actual OPEC Production[d]	n.a.	18.6			
Inventory Movement	0	1.1	1.1	0	1.1
Total			2.7	0.6	2.1

Notes: (a) Excluding CPEs.
(b) Including processing gains and OPEC NGLs.
(c) Before adjustment for stock changes.
(d) Assuming August at 20.5 mb/d.

Looking first at the demand component of the increase, the observed improved consumption levels in the OECD region can be attributed, in part, to a sudden surge in economic growth in the United States in early 1986, spurred by lower oil prices. Real GNP growth in the first quarter of 1986 soared to 3.8 per cent, compared with only 2.7 per cent on average for 1985. However, this was accompanied by a sharp deceleration in economic growth in West Germany and Japan in the first quarter, and second quarter US growth (at an annual rate of a

mere 1.1 per cent) fell well below earlier expectations. Virtually all projections of OECD economic growth for 1986 made in
1985 were first revised *upwards* in the spring to reflect the
hoped-for consequences of the oil price decline, but were later
revised *downwards* on the basis of the sluggish performance
during the first half of the year.

Moreover, given the concurrent decline in the value of the
US dollar, one might expect that the increases in oil demand
observed so far would be greater outside than inside the
United States, but such is not the case. A significant share –
perhaps as much as half – of the unanticipated increase in
non-Communist world demand has taken place in the USA,
and much of this has been concentrated in motor fuels. This is
explained by a more intense utilization of each automobile
(miles driven per car per month) rather than by a shift to
larger cars, which would require years to have a noticeable
impact upon the average fuel consumption of the fleet.

More intense car utilization, however, is a transitory phenomenon, resulting as much from Americans' preference to
avoid travel outside the USA during the 1986 summer driving
season (owing to the low value of the dollar and fears of
terrorist attacks) as from the depressed price of gasoline.
Previous alterations in driving habits, following the 1973 and
1979–80 oil price increases, proved equally temporary. Over
the long run, Americans (whose intensity of car use is already
among the highest in the world) seem reluctant to alter the
number of miles driven per year or (which amounts to the
same thing) the number of hours spent behind the wheels of
their private cars.

Thus, while the increase in world oil demand so far in 1986
compared with pre-war projections is real, some of it, which
we estimate at 200,000 b/d, may not be repeated so that the
net permanent gain attributable to the price decline is of the
order of 300,000 b/d. The pace of world-wide oil demand
growth experienced in January–August 1986 cannot simply be
projected indefinitely into the future (see Table 7.1).

Similarly, the pace of reduction in non-OPEC supply
already observed in 1986 may decelerate in the short term.
Most of the 1.1 mb/d reduction, compared with pre-war expectations, is not the result of economically induced cuts nor

of political decisions to turn customers away. It is rather due to unusually low levels of CPEs exports in the winter of 1985–6, strikes in Norway and Australia in spring 1986 and various losses of output elsewhere, particularly in Mexico and Egypt, due to inappropriate pricing policies which have now been corrected. These cuts are therefore of a temporary nature and may not be repeated unless a production pact is concluded between OPEC and non-OPEC producers. At this time, only the loss of 300,000 b/d due to the shutting-in of high-cost tertiary production and stripper wells in North America and some uneconomic Australian production can be considered as a permanent gain for OPEC under the present pricing environment.

Finally, the massive inventory build-up observed so far in 1986 (1.1 mb/d) is, by definition, a one-time phenomenon due to perceptions by consumers and purchasers that oil prices had reached bargain levels. It cannot be repeated since worldwide stocks have now returned to comfortable levels as compared with those of early 1986. Indeed, these stocks can only contribute to a weakening of apparent demand during the 1986–7 winter season.

To sum up, the 2.7 mb/d apparent increase in OPEC's market share achieved so far in 1986, as compared with pre-war estimates, can be roughly broken down into 2.1 mb/d of temporary gains that cannot be extrapolated into the future and a mere 600,000 b/d of permanent gains that can really be attributed to the $20 per barrel price drop that occurred during this period.

Such a small real improvement in OPEC's market share is clearly not worth the cost associated with it. But the proponents of the price war take the understandable view that it is premature to draw the 'profit and loss balance' at this stage of the game and that, over the medium-to-long term, the gains expected in terms of a substantially improved market share will ultimately offset the per barrel revenues forgone under the new price regime.

(*b*) *The Medium-term Picture*. Since the dramatic drop in oil prices which started in early 1986, forecasters have revised their medium- and long-term views of oil demand and supply trends. In the wake of the price war, in an environment of lower oil prices, world-wide demand will expand somewhat more rapidly than was previously expected, and non-OPEC supply will grow more slowly. Thus, the net world-wide demand for OPEC oil is now anticipated to increase faster than in projections made prior to the price war. These conclusions appear to be valid even if one assumes that crude oil prices will rise towards the level of $17–19 advocated for the medium term by the majority of OPEC countries and recently endorsed by the Gulf Cooperation Council.

In the medium term, roughly until the end of the 1980s, the foreseen boost in world-wide oil demand is due primarily to an assumed acceleration of economic growth. Lower oil prices are expected to contribute to the achievement of higher levels of income and economic activity in oil-importing countries (in spite of the disappointing economic performance during the first half of 1986 mentioned in the preceding section). The OECD Secretariat has recently estimated that each $3 per barrel fall in the price of crude oil should, in the short-to-medium term, add about 0.5 per cent to the annual rate of growth of industrial activity in the OECD region, and about 0.25 per cent to the annual rate of real GNP growth. Our own detailed studies of oil consumption in the OECD countries have revealed that oil demand begins to expand when OECD economic growth exceeds about 3 per cent per annum (see Figure 7.2).

If we assume that oil prices remain in the range of $17–19 per barrel and that OECD economic growth accelerates to 3.8 per cent per annum in the period 1987–90 (the upper bound of recent post-price war private economic forecasts) then oil use should expand at about 1.0 per cent per annum over the same period. This would add roughly 2 mb/d to OECD oil consumption in 1990 compared with pre-war predictions. A similar acceleration in economic growth in oil-importing countries outside the OECD would add an additional 850,000 b/d to non-Communist world demand by 1990 (compared with pre-war views), but this would be partially offset by slower growth of oil consumption in the OPEC countries themselves (see Table 7.2).

A smaller and more temporary boost to oil demand will

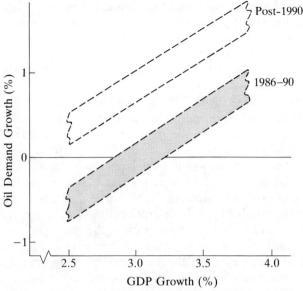

Figure 7.2: Approximate Relationship of Growth of Potential Oil Demand and Growth of GDP for the OECD. 1986–90 and Post-1990.

Table 7.2: Post-war and Pre-war Predictions of Non-Communist World Demand. 1986–90. Million Barrels per Day.

	1986	1987	1988	1989	1990
Post-war	46.4	47.1	48.1	49.2	50.2
Pre-war	45.8	46.3	46.8	47.4	47.9
Gain	0.6	0.8	1.3	1.8	2.3

come from modifications of consumer behaviour and from substitution of oil for other fuels. The most direct impact of lower prices upon consumer behaviour observed so far has been an increase in motor gasoline consumption, particularly in the United States. We have already explained why we believe this phenomenon to be temporary.

Other immediate behavioural responses to lower oil prices appear equally temporary in character. Turning up the thermostat in the winter heating season of 1986–7 will probably have a trivial effect on demand (under normal winter heating conditions), since most consumers in Europe and North America have already returned to the levels of comfort achieved before the first oil price increase. Improved home insulation and superior design of residential and commercial buildings will not be reversed.

As for major substitutions of oil for other fuels in industry and electric power generation, we believe these will be of minimal importance in the medium term. Many OECD industries have switched so completely away from oil that a reverse substitution would involve major capital commitments and/or a return to earlier technologies. Even an acceleration of economic growth is not anticipated to bring any sudden switch back to the use of mothballed, older, oil-fired equipment. Electric power generation, the one significant area where a substitution of residual oil for gas or coal is imaginable, will probably not make the switch, provided that gas and coal prices move in sympathy with the price of oil. Such sympathetic movements of gas and coal prices appear likely in the $17–19 per barrel oil price range over the medium term (many gas contracts are linked by escalation formulae to crude oil or petroleum products prices, and both gas and coal contracts generally include price renegotiation clauses).

On the supply side, non-OPEC crude oil production will be affected in the medium term by the lower oil prices prevailing in the wake of the price war (see Table 7.3). Much of the anticipated reduction in oil production will take place in North America, home of the world's costliest oil. As much as 800,000 b/d of US production may be lost by 1990 if oil prices are expected to stay in the range of $17–19 per barrel (com-

Table 7.3: Post-war and Pre-war Predictions of Non-OPEC Supply.[a] 1986–90. Million Barrels per Day.

	1986	1987	1988	1989	1990
Post-war	28.7	29.3	28.9	28.7	28.4
Pre-war	29.8	30.0	29.8	29.7	29.7
Gain	−1.1	−0.7	−0.9	−1.0	−1.3

Note: (a) Includes OPEC NGLs and processing gains.

pared with estimated production if prices were expected to remain around $28 per barrel); this estimate is based on the results of a survey of major oil companies undertaken in March 1986 by the API. In Canada, further expansion of syncrude, tar sands and frontier oil development may be halted, though most pre-war forecasts counted on increases of as little as 100,000 b/d from these sources between 1986 and 1990. Other countries showing reductions of projected 1990 oil production as a result of the price war include Australia (45,000 b/d) and the UK (65,000 b/d); the latter estimates are based upon research by Wood Mackenzie. The sum of all of the above reductions in 1990 OECD production is of the order of 1.0 mb/d.

The effect of lower oil prices upon medium-term production capacity in non-OECD, non-OPEC countries is, however, expected to be so small as to be almost unmeasurable. Development projects already well under way will increase oil production in these countries by 1.5 mb/d by 1990 (compared with 1985) at oil prices as low as $17 per barrel. Even lower prices in the medium term will probably not affect these developments, as their planning is based upon expected higher prices in the 1990s. Reductions in exploration efforts in LDCs, although significant, are not expected to affect the volume of available crude oil until 1989 at the earliest, given the long exploration lead times prevailing outside the OECD and OPEC regions. On the other hand, voluntary contributions of production cuts may be obtainable from some non-OPEC producers such as Mexico, Egypt and Malaysia, credit for which should be attributed to the price war. We have allowed for such cuts amounting to 500,000 b/d for the remainder of 1986, declining to 100,000 b/d in 1990. In 1990, even so, the net loss in expected production due to the price war (i.e. compared with pre-war projections) is only 280,000 b/d (including 100,000 b/d of voluntary cuts).

The net effect of all of the above modifications in anticipated demand and supply in the wake of the price war is to increase the expected demand for OPEC crude oil to 17.7 mb/d in 1986 and 21.8 mb/d by 1990 (assuming prices remain in the range of $17–19 per barrel in the medium term (see Table 7.4).

Table 7.4: Post-war and Pre-war Predictions of OPEC Market Share.[a] 1986–90. Million Barrels per Day.

	1986	1987	1988	1989	1990
Post-war	17.7	17.8	19.2	20.5	21.8
Pre-war	16.0	16.3	17.0	17.7	18.2
Gain	1.7	1.5	2.2	2.8	3.6

Note: (a) After adjustment for stock changes.

Before we examine the overall 'profit and loss account', it is important to make two observations at this stage:

(a) In view of the excessive OPEC production that occurred in the summer of 1986, the 17.7 mb/d residual demand calculated for 1986 will be exceeded even if OPEC restrains its output for the remainder of 1986 to the level of some 17.2 mb/d agreed as part of the cease-fire concluded at Geneva in August 1986. This means that if OPEC seriously intends to stabilize the oil price in the targeted range, the temporary quota agreement reached for September–October must be continued at least until the end of 1986.

(b) Little gain should be expected in 1987 (as compared with 1986) in terms of OPEC market share (17.8 mb/d versus 17.7 mb/d), owing to the temporary nature of some of the gains achieved so far as explained above.

(*c*) *The Medium-term Overall Balance.* An overall profit and loss balance has been drawn up for the entire period 1986–90 (see Table 7.5) for both the pre-war and post-war scenarios. This balance attempts to compare OPEC crude oil export revenues resulting from, on the one hand, OPEC's market share profile under our own pre-war forecast valued at an average price assumed to remain at $28 per barrel and, on the other hand, the new market share profile under the post-war outlook valued at an assumed average price of $13 per barrel in 1986, rising to $17 in 1987 and increasing by $1 each year to reach $20 per barrel in 1990 (CPEs exports, OPEC NGLs and

Table 7.5: The 1986–90 Overall Balance.

| | Pre-war Forecast | | | | | Post-war Outlook | | | | |
	1986	1987	1988	1989	1990	1986	1987	1988	1989	1990
Net Demand on OPEC Crude (mb/d)	16.0	16.3	17.0	17.7	18.2	17.7	17.8	19.2	20.5	21.8
OPEC Local Consumption (mb/d)	3.3	3.4	3.6	3.8	4.0	3.0	3.1	3.2	3.3	3.4
OPEC Exports (mb/d)	12.7	12.9	13.4	13.9	14.2	14.7	14.7	16.0	17.2	18.4
Average Price ($/Barrel)	28.0	28.0	28.0	28.0	28.0	13.0	17.0	18.0	19.0	20.0
Revenues ($ Billions)	130	132	137	142	145	70	91	105	119	134

$ Billions

Cumulative Export Revenues:	Pre-war	690
	Post-war	520
Cost of the Price War over the Period:	Undiscounted	170
	Discounted (at 12 per cent)	130

processing gains have been kept at the same level under the two scenarios).

The net balance is that OPEC *as a whole* will, as a result of the price war, suffer a significant cumulative loss in oil revenues amounting to $170 billion over the five years 1986–90, which, discounted at 12 per cent, is equivalent to $130 billion in present value terms. This latter figure represents a significant amount of money, approximately equal to OPEC's total oil revenues in 1985 (estimated at $125 billion). It is much in excess of the total foreign bank debts of all OPEC countries at the end of 1985 ($110 billion, as reported by the Bank for International Settlements) and amounts to roughly twice the total reported international monetary reserves of OPEC countries at the end of 1985 ($62.1 billion according to the IMF; Iran and Iraq do not report their monetary reserves).

(*d*) *The Long-term Outlook*. On balance, therefore, the price war appears to be a losing game for OPEC in the medium term. However, a somewhat more favourable picture emerges in the 1990s. Even so, one may ask whether it is worth the price cut.

As stated earlier, the pre-war view of the 1990s foresaw accelerated growth of oil consumption in the non-Communist world. This was due not to an anticipated acceleration of economic growth but to the maturation of many of the fuel substitution and energy conservation trends that commenced in the 1970s and early 1980s. Some industries, as already mentioned, have in 1986 completed planned conversions away from oil as a fuel, and further substitution in these industries is hardly likely. Others will arrive at a similar situation in the next few years. For this reason, the curve relating expected oil demand growth to economic expansion will shift gradually upward (see Figure 7.2). Thus, for the 1990s, even if economic growth did not accelerate, forecasters anticipated more rapid growth of oil demand.

One dramatic example of this 'playing out' of the conservation trend may be seen in the plans for new nuclear power facilities. Very few new nuclear plants are on order or scheduled for completion during the early 1990s, compared with a large number of completions planned for the 1985–90 period. Given the long lead times required to design, win approval for, and construct nuclear power stations (ranging from six to twelve years in most OECD countries), it would be difficult to add substantial new capacity before 1995 beyond that which is already planned. Conventional thermal generating plants, including existing oil-fired capacity, would have to take up any supply insufficiency in the early 1990s.

While the acceleration in oil demand growth was widely anticipated in pre-price war projections, the effect is accentuated by the more rapid rates of economic expansion associated with lower oil prices in the post-war world. Our own projections show OECD oil demand now rising to 38.1 mb/d by 1995 (compared with 34.5 mb/d in the pre-war forecasts). Non-OECD demand projections are also increased, but not by as much as OECD demand since economic and oil consumption growth in the OPEC countries has been interrupted by the price war (see Table 7.6). Total oil consumption in the non-Communist world may now reach 56.8 mb/d in 1995 compared with 52.5 mb/d in pre-war projections, for an overall increase of about 4.3 mb/d attributable to the price war.

Table 7.6: Post-war and Pre-war Predictions of Non-Communist World Demand. 1991–95. Million Barrels per Day.

	1991	1992	1993	1994	1995
Post-war	51.5	52.7	54.0	55.4	56.8
Pre-war	48.7	49.6	50.5	51.5	52.5
Gain	2.8	3.1	3.5	3.9	4.3

Non-OPEC oil supplies will also be affected significantly by the lower oil prices now assumed to prevail in the 1990s. Based on the same studies referred to earlier, downward revisions of OECD oil production projections for 1995 amount now to nearly 3.0 mb/d compared with pre-war views (see Table 7.7). This includes losses in the USA of roughly 1.7 mb/d and in Canada of nearly 500,000 b/d. Other OECD downward revisions include the UK (450,000 b/d), Norway (150,000 b/d) and Australia (100,000 b/d).

Outside the OECD region, losses will still not be so great.

Table 7.7: Post-war and Pre-war Predictions of Non-OPEC Supply.[a] 1991–95. Million Barrels per Day.

	1991	1992	1993	1994	1995
Post-war	27.9	27.4	26.9	26.4	25.9
Pre-war	29.6	29.5	29.4	29.3	29.1
Gain	−1.7	−2.1	−2.5	−2.9	−3.2

Note: (a) Includes OPEC NGLs and processing gains.

To be sure, a slower pace of exploration during the remainder of the 1980s will begin to have an effect on production capacity by the early 1990s. However, the reductions in seismic and exploratory drilling activity will not necessarily be proportional to the oil companies' announced budget cuts. Declines in exploration and drilling costs are already apparent, so that the same amount of exploration can be maintained with a lower overall expenditure. On the basis of a recently completed Petroconsultants' estimate (see Figure 7.3), we expect exploration outside of the OECD region to proceed during the second half of the 1980s at about two-thirds the physical intensity (measured as number of wells drilled or seismic kilometres recorded) observed in recent years.

Cut-backs in exploration activity, moreover, will be made selectively by oil companies. As difficult choices are made,

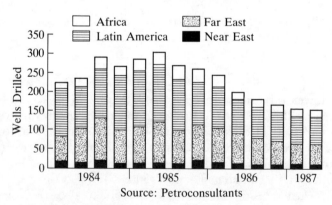

Figure 7.3: Numbers of Exploratory Wells Drilled per Quarter in the Third World. 1984–7.

exploration departments will defend most tenaciously their best prospects. For this reason, reserve additions in the early 1990s will probably not fall off nearly as sharply as the expected decline in physical exploration activity in the next few years.

Another reason why a dramatic downward adjustment in non-OECD production capacity in the 1990s may not result from lower oil prices is that exploration decisions are made on the basis of expected future prices, not current or even medium-term price levels. A new exploration project in Africa or Latin America, commenced today, would be unlikely to yield a commercial discovery for several years, and unlikely to be developed and brought into production until well into the 1990s, at which time prices are expected to have returned to pre-price war levels.

Expected declines in exploration and development activity must, in addition, be moderated by the very great likelihood that, if low oil prices prevail for some time, governments will revise fiscal systems to encourage a resumption of activity. This is already taking place in Morocco, Pakistan and Tunisia, and on an *ad hoc* basis in many other countries. For all of these reasons, we have revised our projected 1995 production in non-OECD, non-OPEC regions downward by only some 400,000 b/d compared with the pre-war outlook. No further voluntary production cuts by non-OPEC producers are projected after 1990, as these cuts are assumed to be no longer required by that time. Finally, the other components of non-OPEC supplies, such as CPEs exports, OPEC NGLs and processing gains, have not been revised and have been kept at the same level as under the pre-war outlook.

The net effect of the upward adjustments in non-Communist world oil demand and downward adjustments in non-OPEC oil supply under the new price regime is further to increase OPEC's market share to about 25.3 mb/d in 1992 and to almost 31.0 mb/d in 1995, compared with pre-war projections of 20.1 mb/d and 23.4 mb/d respectively (see Table 7.8).

The question is whether OPEC members could meet the additional demand. It is widely believed that OPEC's total production capacity is currently of the order of 26.0 mb/d and

Table 7.8: Post-war and Pre-war Predictions of OPEC Market Share. 1991–95. Million Barrels per Day.

	1991	1992	1993	1994	1995
Post-war	23.2	25.3	27.1	29.0	30.9
Pre-war	19.1	20.1	21.1	22.2	23.4
Gain	4.1	5.2	6.0	6.8	7.5

that this capacity will be lower in the 1990s, perhaps 25.0 mb/d, even if one assumes a capacity increase during the intervening period as Iraq and Iran attempt to return to full production potential (see Table 7.8). OPEC member countries may, therefore, be physically prevented from taking advantage of the long-run positive effect of the price war. From the perspective of these countries, the price war would have served only to bring forward by a few years the time when they will again be producing at or very near capacity limits. At such a time – and even in anticipation of such a time – we would expect oil prices to rise so as once again to encourage energy conservation and fuel substitution, and to stimulate non-OPEC oil production.

The long-term 'benefit' of the price war to OPEC depends, therefore, not only upon the pace of oil demand growth and the decline of non-OPEC oil supply levels, but also upon OPEC's production capacity and the timing and magnitude of price increases as OPEC production approaches capacity limits. We have calculated the 'benefit' (for the period 1986–95) under a variety of price and OPEC capacity scenarios and have found the net present value of OPEC's revenue stream (discounted at the same 12 per cent rate) to continue to be negative in nearly all plausible cases. For a 26.0 mb/d capacity, losses ranged from $20 billion to $105 billion (in present value terms), depending upon the price assumptions for the early 1990s. We found that, in order for the price war to achieve a *positive* net present value to OPEC as a whole, the crude oil price would have to return to about $32 per barrel in 1992, assuming that OPEC's capacity is limited at that time to 26.0 mb/d.

Conclusions

The conclusion that emerges from the above analysis is that the oil price war waged by OPEC in late 1985, either willingly or unwillingly or even unwittingly, has already resulted in huge economic and financial losses for all oil-exporting countries, whether developing or industrialized, members or non-members of OPEC. But while the damage caused to most of the Third World countries has reached a critical limit, for the other producing countries it has perhaps created some concerns and worries but, by and large, it is still manageable. For the OECD oil-producing countries, prices have to remain low for quite a while before the alarm bells awaken the relevant politicians and decision-makers; meanwhile, some OECD countries may very well institute import taxes to sustain their domestic oil or energy output.

Although the war was originally planned to constrain non-OPEC exporters, the battle front has shifted over time as the economic and financial losses have been unevenly distributed among OPEC member countries. Those who have not been able to mitigate the impact of the price drop on their revenues by increasing their production have been more severely affected. The confrontation is today no longer between OPEC and non-OPEC countries but between economically strong and economically weak producers, between rich and poor exporters. If the war goes on, the dividing line will tend to be drawn, as in the past, between the industrialized OECD countries and the developing countries of the Third World. In this respect, the 1986 oil price war will turn out to be not only an economic fiasco but also the biggest strategic political mistake ever made by a group of developing countries capable of pursuing the permanent struggle of the Third World for a better and more equitable share of the world's income.

It is indeed an economic fiasco because the expected increase in oil exports falls far short of the per barrel revenues forgone. We have seen that in the short term the real net 'booty' is minuscule in comparison with the 'casualties'; in the medium term, the cumulative losses resulting from the price drop far outweigh the revenue gains derived from the expected improvement in OPEC's market share; in the long term, OPEC, as a whole, will not be able to reap the fruit of earlier sacrifices because of physical limitations. The war is also a strategic political mistake because it divides OPEC, demobilizes its own ranks, and weakens its natural allies outside the organization (the Third World oil-exporting countries).

Yet it is within the Third World ranks, with the tacit agreement of the CPEs (who are known to be very pragmatic when their vital interests are threatened), that the resolution of the current unnecessary and damaging price crisis must be found. This resolution, which would involve a larger OPEC group composed of all significant Third World exporters, must rest on the following minimum conditions:

(a) The parties to the deal must globally and equally accept the role of residual supplier. This means that their individual quotas must proportionally go up and down to match the anticipated residual demand for the group; such demand should be assessed each year, preferably on a quarterly basis, to take account of seasonal fluctuations.

(b) The group must collectively agree upon and defend a pricing strategy capable of stimulating oil demand and increasing oil's share in the world energy balance in the medium and long term so as gradually to increase the call on the group's aggregate supplies. Such a strategy must involve a minimum base price (or marker crude) and differentials calculated monthly on the basis of a standard netback formula and reflecting the specific quality and location of each crude.

(c) The initial base price will need to be higher than the current level so as to entice the parties to the deal with the prospect of increased revenues. The agreed base price should then be gradually increased over time. An increasing base price would indeed provide an incentive to curb production when required, while ensuring stable or increased revenues (the reverse of the situation faced by OPEC in recent years when member countries had to incur losses on account of both volume and prices).

(d) The adherence by each party to the deal to price and production discipline should be ensured through an

adequate policing system enabling free monitoring by outside observers, unhindered by considerations of sovereign
rights.

Finally, some have argued and continue to maintain the
view that OPEC had no alternative and that the war was
inevitable because member countries could not indefinitely
sacrifice market share. We believe that the organization
should never have expressed its objective in terms of market
share only but rather in terms of overall revenues. As we have
seen, the losses already incurred, and those to follow in the
future, exceed any imaginable production sacrifice that
OPEC, as a whole, would have had to make to defend the
price prevailing on the eve of the war. Indeed, to achieve the
same level of export revenues under the same assumptions of
the post-war outlook, OPEC would have had to cut its overall
output to 10.0 mb/d in 1986, 13.0 mb/d in 1987, and 14.0
mb/d in 1988 to defend the $28 per barrel bench-mark.

Successful commodity agreements have always required
some sacrifice on production or exports. Most of OPEC's past
successes would not have been possible without output restraint to defend a given price level. It is most unfortunate to
have reversed a strategy that secured considerable material
benefits for member countries and so well served their political status on the international scene.

8   SOME ASPECTS OF THE SAUDI ARABIAN OIL SUPPLY POLICY

Mohammad Farouk Al Husseini

In the years immediately preceding the establishment of OPEC, particularly in 1958 and 1959, Saudi Arabia became convinced that it might not be able to achieve, single-handed, the oil policy objectives it had hitherto pursued with regard to the supply and pricing of its crude oil. The realization of those objectives was constrained by the subtle legalities of oil agreements, which had been so skilfully drafted by the concessionaires that no opening in them existed to permit of revision or change to take account of the emergent aspirations of a sovereign state. Consequently, in Baghdad in September 1960, Saudi Arabia joined with four other oil-producing countries, themselves labouring under similar conditions, to form the Organization of the Petroleum Exporting Countries (OPEC). In the Articles of Association of the new organization, the five founding members pledged, *inter alia*, that crude oil prices should be restored to their pre-August 1960 levels; that ways and means should be devised of ensuring the stabilization of prices in international oil markets, with a view to eliminating harmful and unnecessary fluctuations; that due regard should be given at all times to the interests of the producing nations and to the necessity of securing a steady income to the producing countries, an efficient, economic and regular supply of petroleum to consuming nations, and a fair return on their capital to those investing in the petroleum industry.

Those principles, which were embodied in Articles 1 and 2 of OPEC's Statute, guided the supply policy of Saudi Arabia for the following twenty-six years. In practical terms they meant that the supply of oil from producing countries, whether these countries were looked upon collectively or individually, should serve first and foremost the interests of member countries; in other words, it should provide those countries with optimal revenues. Resources should also be managed in such a way as to achieve the aforementioned objectives of price stabilization and to secure efficient, economic and regular supplies to consuming nations. Inherent in the applicability of those principles was the fact that the five founding countries, taken together, at that time controlled about 70 per cent of world crude oil reserves and about 85 per cent of world oil exports (excluding those from CPEs). The magnitude of those shares reflected the potential extent of the power that OPEC could exercise over world supplies and prices. That power was, in fact, exercised by OPEC member countries, both individually and collectively, in varying degrees over the next twenty-six years.

Although the organization's achievements in the early 1960s were so modest in concrete terms, they were nevertheless important, since they paved the way and provided momentum for greater achievements in the early 1970s. In the area of prices, for example, OPEC achieved some measure of success. Prices were stabilized in money terms at the levels that had prevailed in August 1960 and the organization was able to prevent their declining further for a period of ten years. In the supply sector, however, it should be noted that production levels in OPEC countries substantially increased over the period 1960–70. The production of the five founding members increased from 7.9 mb/d in 1960 to about 15.8 mb/d in 1970, an increase of 100 per cent. During the same period, however, Saudi Arabia's oil production was even more impressive, rising from 1.3 mb/d to about 3.8 mb/d, an increase of 190 per cent. For the purposes of illustration, if one considers OPEC's membership as comprising ten countries – the founding five, plus five new members – then its total production in 1970 would have reached 22.1 mb/d as compared with 8.7 mb/d in 1960, reflecting a rise of 154 per cent. By 1970 OPEC's share of world exports had reached 91.8 per cent, which had the effect of consolidating the organization's potential power in the area of pricing. Once again Saudi production had increased at rates that were more than proportionate to the increase in total OPEC production, such increases being possible, of course, on account of the Kingdom's huge reserves. Looked at from the standpoint of reserves, therefore, it may be noted that in 1970 Saudi oil production constituted about 0.98 per cent of its reserves. The total production of the ten member countries, including Saudi Arabia, in that year, constituted 2.1 per cent of total reserves, or double the ratio of that for Saudi Arabia taken alone. Taking the reserves/production ratio as the criterion the applicable to total OPEC reserves and production, Saudi production, even taking into account its already rapid growth, was still capable of expanding to twice the level produced in 1970. Since, however, in the 1960s, oil prices entered a period of stagnation, Saudi Arabia concluded that, in order to increase oil revenues in line with OPEC's objectives, the only course open to it was to develop the Kingdom's super-giant fields, unmatched anywhere else in the world, and thus to create production capacities of such a size as would permit, over time, more realistic ratios of actual production to reserves, ratios in line with those prevailing elsewhere, particularly in other OPEC countries. With the growth of world demand in the period 1960–70 having grown from 18.6 mb/d to 39.6 mb/d, an increase of 113 per cent, Saudi production policy could be said to have met in full the relevant objectives enshrined in OPEC's Statute, namely, utilizing the Kingdom's supplies in accordance with its interests and securing a steady flow of supplies to consuming countries. Saudi Arabian oil revenues thus increased from about $400 million in 1960 to about $1.214 billion in 1970, a net rise in excess of 200 per cent.

Despite these achievements, however, decision-making in the crucial areas of production and pricing continued to be exercised by the oil companies. Any concessions made to the Saudi Government, in these and other sectors, had to be accomplished by negotiation with the oil companies. This situation spurred the Saudi Government to renewed efforts to seek a more effective way of achieving its ultimate goal of absolute control over its indigenous hydrocarbon resources. These efforts began in 1968 with a call for participation in the ownership of the producing companies' assets. The negotiations to this end lasted a whole five years. By January 1973, however, the breakthrough had been achieved, and an agreement was concluded, under which the Saudi Government became entitled to purchase a share in the assets of ARAMCO, initially at the rate of 25 per cent, with that share increasing gradually until, in 1982, it should amount to 51 per cent. As matters turned out, however, progress in this direction was much more rapid than had been anticipated: by June 1974, Saudi Arabian participation had reached 60 per cent, and less than two years later, in January 1976, the Government assumed 100 per cent control over ARAMCO's assets.

During the three years immediately preceding this event, however, Saudi production had been increasing steadily, reaching, in 1972, more than 6 mb/d. In that same year, total OPEC production increased to 27.1 mb/d. This spectacular rise in Saudi production was a reflection of world demand for the Kingdom's oil. World demand, which had been rising by about 7.7 per cent per annum in the decade 1960–70, continued to grow at about 6.8 per cent per annum during the period 1971–3. Saudi production, however, which had been rising at a rate of 11 per cent per annum in the years 1960–69, made further impressive strides in 1973, increasing in that year by a massive 136 per cent over the 1969 level, implying a growth rate of 24 per cent per annum during the four-year period 1969–73.

Naturally, the new situation brought with it its own problems. Saudi Arabia had assumed the responsibility of spending huge sums of money on exploration and development, an area hitherto the exclusive preserve of the concessionaire companies. One area in which the producing companies had ignored the demands of the Saudi Government was that of gas. Gas was produced at a rate of 3.5–4.0 bcf/d during the 1970s, most of which was flared. Accordingly, in 1975, Saudi Arabia embarked upon a huge programme of investment in the gathering and fractionation of natural gas at a cost that exceeded $12 billion. By 1981 Saudi Arabia produced about 462,000 b/d of NGLs for export and 1.1 bcf/d of methane and ethane for local consumption. A huge petrochemicals industry sprang up from utilizing gas as a source of raw materials and energy, together with vitally needed water and electricity supply projects. By 1985, methane and ethane production had reached 1.7 bcf/d: on the other hand, owing to market weakness, the production of NGLs dropped to about 330,000 b/d.

The full acquisition of the oil companies' assets was pursued and achieved in keeping with the principle of the sovereignty of the state over its natural resources – an inalienable right. As a result all decision-making in the oil industry within Saudi Arabia had reverted to the Government. However, Government decision-making regarding production and pricing, although axiomatically now reconfirmed under full acquisition of oil assets, had been exercised fully by the Government a few years earlier.

The first time that the Government exercised a measure of control over production and pricing was in early 1971. During the first round of negotiations which took place in that year between the Gulf countries of OPEC and the oil companies regarding the upward adjustment of oil prices and income tax rates, the oil companies' primary offer in this respect was rejected by the OPEC governments. As a result Saudi Arabia warned that, unless countries' demands were met, it was prepared to take the necessary unilateral measures for securing those demands. Although these measures were not explicitly spelled out, they had inherently meant that the Saudi Government was prepared to price its crude as it deemed necessary under the circumstances, and would only permit exports at prices that secured its interests. However, agreement between the Gulf countries and the oil companies concerned was soon reached, prices were increased by 38 cents per barrel and income taxes were raised to 55 per cent. Saudi production in 1971 was running at a level of 4.8 mb/d which contributed about 19 per cent of total OPEC production, a rather sizeable amount that could neither be dispensed with nor substituted from sources elsewhere, not only in the short term but in the long term as well.

Another event which had demonstrated Saudi control of its production had taken place in October 1973 when Saudi Arabia reduced its production by 38 per cent as a result of implementing Arab countries' decision to boycott countries that helped Israel during the Arab–Israeli war. In 1974, however, the Government permitted production to rise again as the boycott measures had come to an end. Production in 1973 reached 7.6 mb/d. In 1974 demand for Saudi crude continued to rise and Saudi crude production was likely to reach exceedingly high levels as a result. But as crude oil prices had increased, first as a result of the Tehran Agreement and later as a result of OPEC's unilateral decisions taken in October and December 1973, oil revenue was likely to quin-tuple from $4.3 billion in 1973 to about $22.6 billion in 1974, thus mitigating the need for further production rises at pre-vailing prices. At the level of reserves management also, it was found that the life expectancy of Saudi reserves had fallen dramatically from 66.3 years in 1972 to 51 in 1973. If the same rates of increase had been permitted to continue, the life expectancy of Saudi reserves would probably have reached 45 years in 1980, a dangerously low figure by Middle East stan-dards. Thus, the expected decline in the reserves/production ratio, combined with a huge boost in revenues, caused the Government first to moderate previous production targets and later, in 1974, to impose a production ceiling of 8.5 mb/d. This ceiling became applicable immediately and was never ex-ceeded, except in 1979 and the following two years, when the Kingdom had to step in to make up for the supply shortfalls elsewhere, following the outbreak of the Iranian Revolution. Saudi Arabia was the only country in the world where produc-tion capacity was large enough to permit incremental supplies over and above actual production levels (ceiling) by a com-fortable margin equivalent to about 2 mb/d on a sustainable basis. Consequently, Saudi Arabia was called upon by the international community to increase its production in order to alleviate the adverse effects that might have been engendered by a world energy crisis. Production was accordingly in-creased to 9.5 mb/d in 1979, 9.9 mb/d in 1980 and 9.8 mb/d in 1981. Despite these increases the ceiling of 8.5 mb/d remained in effect the only official level of maximum production allow-able by the Government. Excess production over the ceiling was considered temporary and transitory, since it was implicit in the Government's decision that the needs of Saudi Arabia were safeguarded at a production level of 8.5 mb/d. It should be remembered, however, that oil produced in excess of the ceiling during 1979, 1980 and 1981 constantly fetched higher prices. The posted price per barrel of Arabian Light increased to $19.355 in June 1979, $25.806 in December 1979 and $34.409 in November 1980. In October 1981 it peaked at

$36.559 per barrel. As a result, oil revenues increased to $57.5 billion in 1979, $102.2 billion in 1980 and to an all-time high of $113.2 billion in 1981.

Although Saudi oil production and revenues peaked in 1981, signs of market weakness were already in the offing. Total OPEC production, which peaked in 1979, started to fall in 1980. By 1981 total OPEC production amounted to 22.6 mb/d, which represented a decline of 27 per cent or 8.33 mb/d from its level in 1979. The share of OPEC's oil exports in total world oil exports (excluding those from CPEs), which had invariably exceeded 90 per cent during the period 1960–78, started to fall in a pronounced manner in 1980. By 1981, OPEC's share in world exports had declined to 80.3 per cent. In 1984 it fell to 65.5 per cent. World demand for oil (excluding that of the CPEs), which peaked in 1979 at 51.2 mb/d, started to decline in 1980 and continued its uninterrupted downward movement until 1985. The recovery it made in 1984 was short-lived and almost wiped out in 1985. Many factors have contributed to this sharp decline in world demand and supplies. The most important, however, seems to be the major price increases applied by OPEC during the period 1979–81. Not only did these increases bring about a decline in world demand and supply in aggregate, but they were instrumental in inducing the development of new oil and energy supplies in non-OPEC areas, in quantities sufficient to substitute for a sizeable proportion of OPEC crude oil supplies, thus exacerbating their fall to unacceptable levels.

Non-OPEC countries, which used to apply a price for their exports consistent with the OPEC price, started to deviate from that system in the fourth quarter of 1981. They resorted to price cutting in order to gain a higher market share at the expense of OPEC. As the market price fell inexorably, eventually reaching a level $5 below OPEC's official price, the organization decided that something had to be done to rectify the situation. In March 1982, the Conference decided to defend a crude price of $34 per barrel by maintaining a production ceiling of 18 mb/d for member countries. Under this agreement, Saudi Arabia was supposed to bring its production down to 7.5 mb/d from the level of 8.1 mb/d that prevailed during the first quarter of 1982. In the wake of that

Conference, Sheikh Ahmed Zaki Yamani, the Saudi oil minister, announced that Saudi production would be reduced by a
further 500,000 b/d, bringing it down to 7 mb/d. These reductions on the part of Saudi Arabia pre-empted the market from
1.4 mb/d because actual production in April fell to 6.7 mb/d,
in addition to another 1 mb/d contributed by other member
countries. These measures had the effect of arresting the slide:
prices firmed up and rose to official levels again. However,
inroads from non-OPEC producers into OPEC's share continued unabated in a flagrant move to seize the opportunity
provided by OPEC's decision. Instability began to permeate
the market again with the emergence of low prices during
January and February 1983. Price deterioration in the crude
oil market again signalled for OPEC the danger of an imminent price collapse. This prompted member countries to meet
again in 1983 to seek measures to arrest the decline. They
subsequently met in London during March of that year. At
that meeting they decided to lower their production ceiling to
17.5 mb/d. They also decided to lower the official price of the
marker crude by $5 per barrel, bringing it from $34 to $29 per
barrel. The price reduction reflected OPEC's move towards a
more competitive, albeit restrained, position in the market in
line with sales elsewhere. The share of the twelve member
countries other than Saudi Arabia, which amounted to 10.5
mb/d as agreed under the 1982 ceiling of 18 mb/d, had then
increased to 12.5 mb/d. Saudi Arabia's share under the
March 1983 resolution was not specified. However, it was
assumed that, since total OPEC production would be permitted to attain a level of 17.5 mb/d, the Saudi share would be the
residual one, or 5 mb/d. This involved a reduction in Saudi
Arabia's share of 2.5 mb/d in comparison with that allocated
under the March 1982 agreement. The acceptance by Saudi
Arabia of a residual share meant that every member country
was allowed to produce its allocated share except Saudi Arabia, whose production might fall or rise above 5 mb/d according to the prevailing circumstances. But since those circumstances were unfavourable, Saudi production averaged 4.5 mb/d
in 1983, 500,000 b/d less than its assumed share. Although
the role of residual producer assumed by Saudi Arabia in
March 1983 benefited other member countries of OPEC –

since their actual total production had, in the whole of 1983, averaged 12.45 mb/d, only a shade less than the combined quotas – Saudi Arabia suffered alone a loss of 460,000 b/d from its assumed share. That loss went directly to the benefit of non-OPEC producers. Market prices in the autumn of 1984 underwent another bout of deterioration, which prompted OPEC to meet yet again in order to face the growing problem. Subsequently, in October 1984, a meeting was held by OPEC and a lower ceiling of 16 mb/d was adopted. The new quota distribution that emerged accorded Saudi Arabia a share of 4.353 mb/d which involved a reduction of 647,000 b/d from its previously assumed share of 5 mb/d. This reduction also accounted for 43.1 per cent of the total reduction in OPEC ceiling of 1.5 mb/d. Although under the new quota distribution Saudi Arabia officially obtained a fixed share of the total OPEC production ceiling, in a bid to abandon its role of residual producer *de jure*, it continued in fact to perform the same role of residual producer *de facto*, in that it continued to adhere to the official prices of its crude oil corresponding to a price of $28 per barrel for Arabian Light crude. Saudi Arabia adhered strictly to this system of selling on a 'take-or-leave' basis at a time when all other producers within and outside OPEC were selling their crudes on a market-oriented price basis. The outcome of these developments was that Saudi oil became the most expensive crude oil available in the world market. Consequently, its production fell to barely more than 2 mb/d in July 1985 – a dangerously low level, whether looked at from the standpoint of revenue, or from that of adequate gas supplies essential for water desalination and power generation. At this juncture the options open to the Government numbered only two: either to continue its rigid adherence to the OPEC price and bear the consequences of declining revenue, or to abandon the system entirely and adopt, like all other producers, a market-oriented approach. The latter decision was finally adopted, albeit painfully and reluctantly.

While OPEC production, like Saudi Arabian production, was falling, production and exports elsewhere were rising. Crude oil exports from non-OPEC sources, which amounted to 4.6 mb/d in 1979, increased to 5.5 mb/d in 1981 and close to 7.4 mb/d in 1984 and 7.9 mb/d in 1985. Such increases were made at the expense of OPEC exports and substituted for them. In December 1985 OPEC held its seventy-sixth Conference in Geneva and decided to secure and defend for itself a fair share in the world oil market consistent with the income necessary for member countries' development. Nothing was mentioned at that Conference in respect of the price at which OPEC oil might be sold. This meant an inherent abandonment of the official price of $28 per barrel for Arabian Light crude and, thereby, of the entire OPEC crude oil price structure. Also the decision to seek a fair share in the market had in effect put an end to the OPEC official ceiling of 16 mb/d and production became a 'free-for-all'. Historically, in 1982, OPEC member countries, under the pressure of price competition from non-OPEC countries, abandoned the practice of closely adhering to the OPEC official price as, one after the other, they resorted to various measures of discounting which included, *inter alia*, direct discounts, rebates, netback sales arrangements, product sales at market-oriented prices and incentives to equity crudes which belonged to certain oil companies. Saudi Arabia was the last country to follow suit as of September 1985. In the December decision, OPEC conveyed a message to the non-OPEC producers that it would not continue alone to underwrite the crude oil price structure in the world market, since the only beneficiaries from that structure were the non-OPEC producers. To cement that price structure the co-operation of all producers in the world was needed. Non-OPEC producers continued to rely on OPEC for determining the price of oil on a global basis. They made use of this situation in a manner that secured their own interests. They definitely favoured OPEC action and called for it tacitly but did everything possible to undermine it with their lack of co-operation. The false charge that Saudi Arabia is the cause of the world oil price collapse is designed to divert attention from those who refused to co-operate in supporting the official price to which Saudi Arabia had meticulously adhered over the years. Nevertheless, the accusations directed against Saudi Arabia for conducting the netback sales arrangements presented an opportunity to other sellers who sought a scapegoat for the defence of their shortcomings. Between August 1985 and January 1986 the Saudi netback sales generated values for Arabian Light, f.o.b. Ras Tanura, which were very close to the official price and sometimes above it. The price of oil deteriorated in February 1986 and subsequent months in the wake of OPEC's December decision and not before. Organically, therefore, netback sales cannot be the culprit for price collapse. The basic reason for that collapse is obviously the existing over-supply in the world. Again it is futile to attribute the cause of over-supply to OPEC producers alone, because if OPEC production is the alleged cause, then it must be noted that those who hold this contention link their attribution to a certain time frame which began in December 1985. If we go back to 1979 we find that OPEC was producing close to 31 mb/d and non-OPEC (excluding the CPEs) about 17.7 mb/d. In 1984 OPEC production fell to 16.4 mb/d. In 1985 OPEC production fell again to 15.6 mb/d, reflecting a decline of 49.7 per cent from the organization's 1979 level, whereas that of non-OPEC reached 23 mb/d, representing an increase of 30 per cent over the level reached in 1979. Thus, shifting the time frame slightly backward provides the incontrovertible evidence of who the real over-producers were.

The world oil market today is witnessing a very blatant anomaly. The countries with low reserves are producing at much higher levels than those with high reserves. At the end of 1985 the combined oil reserves of OPEC countries amounted to 509.7 billion barrels or 78.9 per cent of total world reserves, excluding CPEs. Their aggregate production had by then reached 5.68 billion barrels, reflecting a share of 40.4 per cent of total world production, excluding CPEs. Their reserves/production ratio thereby reached 89.7 years. This ratio represented an increase of 45.4 years as compared with the ratio that had prevailed in 1980. On the other hand, non-OPEC reserves, excluding CPEs, reached, by the end of 1985, 136.4 billion barrels or 21.1 per cent of total world reserves, excluding CPEs. Their combined crude oil production in 1985 aggregated 8.4 billion barrels, representing a share of 59.6 per cent of total world production, excluding CPEs. Their reserves/production ratio thereby declined to 16.3 years from 18.5 in 1980. This flagrant imbalance in reserves/production ratios implies that non-OPEC countries are depleting their resources continually by over-producing at

fast rates whereas OPEC countries are depleting their resources a great deal more slowly by under-producing. When
this trend began in 1980, it favoured the non-OPEC producers. Depletion was economically warranted by the high returns for both the producing countries and their governments
made possible by high prices. The situation since the beginning of 1986, however, is completely different: the non-OPEC
producers are continuing, as before, rapidly to deplete their
resources – but now they are doing so in a climate of low
prices and low returns. By the time prices start to firm up in
the medium-to-long term, they will be left with reserves so low
that these reserves may not even be sufficient to sustain production for domestic requirements. Consequently, they may
be compelled to import oil from OPEC – the reserves of whose
members, by contrast, are constantly being revised upwards –
at consderably higher prices in the future. Should demand
grow at a rate of 1 per cent per annum between 1986 and the
year 2000, assuming that non-OPEC countries' additions to
reserves (the prevailing low prices notwithstanding) amount
to about 2.5 billion barrels per annum – which may be unrealistic – and assuming further that they will maintain their
high production profile, then their reserves/production ratio
will further decline to about 13.7 years in 1995. But their
production at such a ratio would also fall to about 18 mb/d
from 23 mb/d in 1986. In contrast OPEC may in 1995 be
producing about 26 mb/d. Additions to OPEC reserves were
assumed to grow at 3.7 billion barrels per annum and its
production was assumed to be supplementary to that of non-
OPEC. By 1995 the OPEC reserves/production ratio would
still be a comfortable 45 years. Under these assumptions the
five major producers of the Gulf, including Iran and Iraq, are
envisaged to be producing around 12.6 mb/d in 1990, 17.7
mb/d in 1995 and about 20.5 mb/d in 1997. Saudi oil supplies
may again reach about 7.5 mb/d in 1995 and probably 10
mb/d in 1997. At such production rates, the reserves/produc-
tion ratios for the five countries combined would be 82 years
in 1990, 67.4 in 1993, 56.4 in 1995 and 47.8 in 1997.

    In conclusion, I should like to recapitulate the main points
of my address to you today. I hope I have made it clear that

Saudi oil supply policy revolves around the following objectives:

(a) To produce at levels that correspond to its own interests, a phrase which should be construed as meaning that the Kingdom's production is aimed at reaching levels that provide it with the revenues essential for its development;
(b) To maintain a constant flow of supplies in a diversified manner to the consuming countries, whether industrial or developing, to cope with their energy needs;
(c) To achieve price stability and avoid unnecessary fluctuations;
(d) To control its national resources in keeping with the principle of the sovereignty of the state over its natural resources.

The history of the Saudi oil industry shows that the Kingdom has been highly successful in the attainment of its policy objectives. The revenues it has derived from the export of its oil have been wisely used in developing the economy and in promoting the improvement of the living standards of its citizens. With respect to providing for the essential needs of consuming countries, again our history abounds with events when supply was increased in order to cater for shortages and bottlenecks that emerged during the past twenty-six years. In respect of pricing, it has maintained, throughout its membership of OPEC, a price policy that has taken into consideration the factors of supply and demand in the long term and has always called for determining prices at levels that, to the best of its knowledge, would secure equilibrium in the long term. Saudi Arabia was the only country which, in 1979, predicted the fall in demand and prices during the early 1980s. Its efforts are directed now towards seeking ways and means to ensure long-term stability in the future oil market. In order to achieve this aim it will continue to co-operate with all oil producers, whether inside or outside OPEC, towards reaching a *modus operandi* that is viable and practicable.

9 OPEC AT THE CROSSROADS

Ian Seymour

I want somehow to get under the skin of OPEC and see what has been happening over the past nine months in terms of its decision-making. I think a good and familiar starting-point is the well-known split between, on the one hand, the majority, now numbering nine, who opted for a strategy of improving their market share at the expense of price maintenance through competitive pricing, and, on the other hand, those perhaps now numbering four – Iran, Algeria, Libya and Gabon – who would prefer to see OPEC return to its role as the residual supplier and maintain a much higher price level. This has often been presented as a kind of choice by OPEC, as if strategists got down to look at the options and they had a real choice in front of them to go this way or that way, and they chose the market share rather than the residual.

Of course, nothing like that happened at all. First of all, it would not make sense for OPEC to choose the market share route at the expense of a price fall, since it would lose out financially, at least in the short-to-medium term, and I don't think anybody willingly chooses to incur a financial loss – not collectively anyway. But of course it did not happen like that: it happened because there was no other practical choice. Both outside pressures that reduced the residual market share itself and internal OPEC pressures that militated for higher production by various of its members meant that the residual market share was no longer divisible in practical terms. This was not just a case of people wanting higher quotas for economic or quasi-economic reasons, e.g. Nigeria or the UAE or Ecuador or whoever just wanting an extra quota for various domestic reasons.

This was compounded by one of the fall-outs of the Iraq–Iran situation and I think here you have to go back a little way to consider the March 1983 agreement, which was made

possible because Iraq accepted a quota which, although it
corresponded to its physical capacity at the time, since Iraq
could not physically produce an export volume of more than
1.2 mb/d, was quite out of line as a longer-term quota for
Iraq. This low quota for Iraq in March 1983 helped to make
possible the agreement at that time, but stored up the seeds of
trouble later on when the Iraqis increased their physical export capacity, and therefore wanted a higher quota.

They had always put in reservations at various OPEC
meetings that this level of 1.2 mb/d did not represent their real
quota, but the chickens came home to roost in late 1985 when
the first increment of Iraq's export capacity was about to
come on stream. Not only did Iraq want a higher quota but
also the Iranians took the position that if Iraq was to get a
higher quota, Iran should have an extra two barrels for each
barrel given to Iraq. So really there was a stalemate: the
OPEC residual share could not be divided among the member
countries. The only other possibility open to OPEC was to try
to enlarge its market share to a point where it would be
divisible in some way. This was not a free choice: it was a
course of action that was forced upon them, and I think the
countries that are now pressing for OPEC to return to its role
as the residual supplier are really trying to turn back the clock
in a way that is actually impossible in practical terms.

So now we have to consider the background to this agreement in Geneva in August 1986, which seems at least temporarily to put OPEC back in its role as residual supplier. OPEC,
and particularly the Gulf members of OPEC, seem to be
reassuming the role of swing producer which they swore they
would never take up again. Does this mean, therefore, as Iran,
Algeria and others in the residual camp might argue, that the
market share strategy is dead, that OPEC has finally come to
its senses and reassumed the residual supplier's role? I don't
think so: I think rather that this is a cease-fire or breathing
space. All were agreed that production was much too high in
June and July 1986, and indeed in August, and that some
corrective movement was necessary, whatever happened in
the future. Further, a closer examination of this agreement
reveals that it is not quite as residual as it was made out to be.
The level of 16 mb/d is often quoted, but the fact that Iraq is

left free to produce whatever it likes means that in reality the ceiling moves up to around 17.2 mb/d if you count the war relief crude in with Iraqi production. Furthermore, there will be an overshoot from the UAE of possibly 250,000 b/d, giving a total figure of almost 17.5 mb/d, and that is not really a residual share, particularly considering that production in June, July and August had been getting on for 20 mb/d. Then of course there is a further point about what the others may do given that the agreement has a hair-trigger and if any one party fails to observe the agreement everybody else is released from the obligation to do so, and it is not clear how the UAE situation will fit in there.

Turning now to take a look at how this agreement came about, there are many misconceptions about exactly what happened in Geneva because this agreement was a surprise, even to the participants. The meeting started around Monday 28 July, and by the evening of 1 August it looked as though all efforts had run into the sand. They tried voluntary cuts by simply passing the hat round to see who would cut back and by how much; and there were some offers that were genuine and some that were not so genuine. Some gave a rather elevated figure for their own production and then said they would cut back to roughly what they were in fact producing at the moment. They tried going back to looking at permanent quotas to see if there was any possibility of building on the work they had already done in Brioni in June on permanent quotas. Here there was quite a positive development, which may come up again in the future, which was to admit that the Iran–Iraq situation was impossible and agree to leave the two countries out of the calculations of member countries' shares of the agreed OPEC ceiling, allocating to them something roughly corresponding to what they were thought to be producing but giving them no formal quota and dividing the rest among the remaining members. This proposal did not succeed at the Geneva meeting for various other reasons, but at least that was perhaps the beginning of a fruitful approach for the future.

I think the first intimation that another way was possible in the interim came on Saturday 1 August at a breakfast meeting between the Iranian minister, Mr Agarzadi, and Sheikh

Yamani of Saudi Arabia, at which the Iranian minister first intimated the possibility of a deal whereby twelve members of OPEC went back to their previous quotas under the 16 mb/d ceiling and Iraq was left free to produce what it wanted. When Yamani saw that this was a genuine offer, he seized on this because, first, it showed a way out, and at the same time it had the bonus of a real concession on the part of Iran because this was the first time that Iran had indicated that it was prepared to accept the position as it was and recognize that Iraq was in any case going to produce as much as it could. It was a realistic acceptance of what was happening and also made possible an agreement for cutting back production in the short term from the very high levels that had been reached in June and July. From that moment, Sheikh Yamani put his weight behind this deal and within a couple of days it did in fact come to implementation and signature.

To sum up, it was a deal that gave something to everybody and did not really commit anybody in the longer term. First of all, there was a general feeling among all the OPEC members, whatever their views on strategy, that over-production had gone too far, and that there had to be a corrective movement. Moreover, in the mean time, Gulf spot and netback prices had gone below the $10 barrier to $7–8, and at that point even OPEC begins to tremble because there is a lot of OPEC production whose production cost is in the $5–6 per barrel bracket. A price of $7–8 per barrel does not yield much income on that, and as far as OPEC and its individual members are concerned, however strong the desire to capture additional market share, once the price goes below $10 per barrel people have doubts that a corrective movement will take place. It took place this time and I think it would take place if the price ever went below $10 per barrel in the future, because that is a threshold of pain for OPEC as well as for other exporters.

Secondly, for the Arabian Peninsular producers and Iraq there was the bonus of the Iranian concession of leaving Iraq free to produce what it wanted, which would perhaps not only hold good for this agreement but also lay the basis for some more permanent deal on quotas in the future. The fact that the agreement was temporary in duration – for two months only – meant that it did not prejudice the market share strategy in any way nor prejudice the views of the market share strategists *vis-à-vis* a higher ceiling in the longer term. Nor did it prejudice the claims of various members on longer-term, more permanent quotas. And of course the increase in prices of $5–6 per barrel took prices out of the diaster area below $10 per barrel into a range that was at least more manageable.

The agreement also had something for the group of four, and for Iran in particular, which could present it very much as a diplomatic victory within OPEC. It was a proposal that Iran had made and spearheaded, and which could be presented, at least in the immediate term, as the death of the market share strategy and the victory of the return to the residual share. As I have said, I don't think this really corresponds to the reality.

To go on from here, what is going to happen after the end of October? I think there are only three possibilities: either (a) an extension of the present agreement; (b) a more permanent, longer-term agreement on quotas with a new ceiling and so forth; or (c) a return to the free-for-all.

Taking the first of these, there will clearly be a lot of difficulties in the way of a permanent agreement, so I think that the reaction of a lot of OPEC countries will be to extend this agreement for the rest of the year. I am making the assumption here, which may prove not to be justified, that the agreement will not collapse under its own internal pressures before the meeting of 6 October as a result of its non-observance by one or more of the member countries, but there will of course be a great deal of pressure. The simplest solution is just to roll over the agreement until the end of the year, and I think a lot of the member countries, including some from the majority as well as the minority, will want this to happen. But equally, the Arabian Peninsular producers, and Saudi Arabia and Kuwait in particular, are dead set against this. I do not think that they will agree to it under any circumstances, and there are very good reasons for this. They have been pushed back into the role of swing producer and it is obviously to the benefit of the rest of OPEC to keep them there, but it is not in their interest to remain restricted within the old 1984–5 quotas. They are insisting in fact that this temporary deal can not be extended beyond the end of October; and that it must be followed by a permanent agreement on a new ceiling a good deal higher than the previous one and with a higher share for them within this ceiling. They also feel that if they extend the agreement and take the easiest way out, it will mean the end to any prospect of a permanent agreement on quotas.

The second possibility, i.e. the conclusion of a permanent agreement, does not seem very likely either, since it poses very great difficulties – the same difficulties that have been present all through the year. Every ceiling OPEC tries to divide seems to be indivisible, and there are problems and disagreements about which ceiling to use. The one bright spot is the realization on the part of everyone that they can not do the quota exercise and keep Iran and Iraq within it, so that if there is an agreed ceiling of 18 mb/d, for example, some 4.0–4.5 mb/d must be allocated to Iraq and Iran, but no formal quota. The remaining members must then try to divide the remaining 13.5–14.0 mb/d among themselves. This is the only way to go about it, but there are still very great difficulties in getting individual countries to abide by quota limitations of this kind. There will be an attempt to secure a permanent agreement, but there remain doubts about its chances of success.

The third alternative is the return to a free-for-all, and this of course would have very grave implications for prices for the rest of 1986 and thereafter. I hope it does not happen, but I do not think we can rule it out because, first, the temporary agreement itself is very precarious; secondly, the chances of extending it or rolling it over until the end of the year are pretty slim; and, thirdly, the chances of putting in place a permanent agreement on quotas are also rather slim. We can by no means discount the possibility of a return to the free-for-all in November.

To conclude, I would like to leave you with some food for thought concerning the principle of uncertainty in future prices. There is at present a strong tendency, because stability is such a positive term with a good aura around it, that to question the virtue of stability is rather like impugning motherhood; but looking at it from the point of view of OPEC, and in particular from that of the high-volume, high-reserve producers within OPEC, this seems less certain. The results so far in terms of captured markets have not been terribly impressive. Certainly there has been some voluntary co-operation from Mexico and some now from Norway, and that is worth something but it is not terribly impressive. But the real gain has been in the pre-empting of exploration and development elsewhere which is due largely to price uncertainty. If this really is the major gain that has been achieved as a result of the past nine months, it is due simply to this uncertainty, and it means at least that the incremental demand for oil will go to OPEC and to the Arabian Peninsular exporters in particular. Thus it can be argued that the maintenance of this price uncertainty may in fact be in the best interest of OPEC or a large part of it, since any return to stability would in some measure stimulate more exploration and development elsewhere. It is possible that, just as OPEC exporters do not like to see the price go below $10 per barrel, they may not be very keen to give the rest of the world very clear signals about future prices. It is possible that we will see prices fluctuating up and down within a certain band, and that there will be periods of discipline and periods of less discipline in production, with the price fluctuating accordingly. So perhaps the best idea is not to look at what the price will be on a certain date, but to see what the average is going to be over a certain period, given that fluctuations will take place within a fairly wide margin.

PART III

THE OIL PRICE COLLAPSE AND NON-OPEC EXPORTERS

10 SOVIET OIL

Ed A. Hewett

In this paper I discuss some of the important issues involved in declining and volatile oil prices, the influence they have on the Soviet Union, the alternatives the Soviet authorities have to respond to declining prices, the likely course of action they will follow, and the possible implications for oil markets. When talking about the Soviet Union, it is not only impossible but a flat-out mistake to concentrate discussion entirely on oil. The USSR is so well endowed with oil, gas and coal, and so able to manoeuvre among them, that to some extent it is necessary to consider gas and coal when discussing oil, and vice versa.

To set a context for the problem the Soviets face now and the adjustment problem they had before, in 1983 Soviet exports to non-Socialist countries were approximately $40 billion, of which exports of energy were about $23.7 billion. About $20 billion was oil and other energy sources accounted for the remaining $3.7 billion, so that energy accounted for about 58 per cent of total Soviet export receipts to non-Socialist countries. A figure is often quoted that oil or energy constitutes 80 per cent of Soviet hard currency exports, but that is just to developed countries: for *all* non-Socialist countries the proportion drops to about 60 per cent and that is the best figure to work with. In 1983, which was the last good year, the $40 billion from exports were used to finance imports of about $35 billion, divided roughly equally between machinery and equipment, food, and intermediate products.

To turn now to the oil shock and the adjustment problems that the Soviets face, first of all the oil shock that the Soviets have felt since 1983 came in two parts and really three different ways. The first shock was really felt in 1983–4 in a decline in oil output which was involuntary on their part, unplanned and unwanted. Oil output, which was about 12.35 mb/d at its peak in 1983, fell slightly in 1984 to about 12.2 mb/d and in 1985 was down to 11.9 mb/d, which came as a shock to Soviet oil planners and to many people in the West. Along with that decline in oil output came an decline in oil exports. The peak in oil exports to non-Socialist countries was about 1.6 mb/d net, i.e. net of oil imports which are running in the range of about 300,000 b/d. By 1984, net exports were down to 1.3 mb/d; so they had dropped by about 300,000 b/d net. Since the trough in 1985, oil production has begun to recover and the most recent figures we have are for July 1986 and they are back up to about 12.35 mb/d.

Much of the decline in hard currency receipts in 1985, which was substantial, came from a decline of oil output that surprised them and therefore caused them to decrease oil exports in 1984 and 1985.

In 1985–6 the second part of the oil shock came both in the decline in the price of oil and also in the weakening of the dollar. To give some notion of what the decline in the oil price did to the Soviet economy, if they had exported the quantities of oil they exported in 1983 at the peak, at 1985–6 prices, they would have earned about $7 billion. In fact, exports in 1983 were worth $20 billion, so there was a decline of almost $13 billion in receipts, to be compared with the total export receipts of $40 billion. Another way to think of this is that the effect of the shock, just from the decline in the dollar price of oil, was equivalent to the loss of all imports of machinery and equipment paid for in hard currency.

But the weakening dollar was also important, as it has been to many OPEC countries. To give you some sense of its effect, in 1983–4, with a barrel of oil the Soviets could buy West German equipment worth about DM75. By mid-1986 that same barrel of oil was buying West German machinery worth about DM30. Of that decline from DM75 to DM30, two-thirds was due to the oil price decline, and one-third to the weakening of the dollar, because the Soviet Union is selling oil in dollars and buying goods in West European currencies. This is the harder part to see. In the short run dollar receipts and dollar imports are relatively easily seen, but the increase in the effective price of imports of machinery from Western Europe is harder to track until later when data on the terms of trade become available.

In sum, the oil price shock adds up to a reduction of approximately $12–13 billion in receipts to which the Soviets must somehow respond. The short-term responses available to them are two. First, they can draw down their hard currency reserves but those, to the extent we know them, are only about $12 billion, i.e. enough to postpone the problem for one year. Secondly, they can borrow, and they have been borrowing in recent years. In 1985, which was the first time for about a decade that they actively came on to the market as net new borrowers, they borrowed about $6 billion, and they seem to be active again in 1986. Neither the drawdown in reserves nor the borrowing can close this $12 billion gap if it is going to remain, so that if $15 oil is going to remain for the rest of the 1980s, then Soviet planners must consider somewhat more serious, longer-term responses to the shock.

Soviet planners have six main options available to them. The first three all have to do with increasing oil exports. These are, first of all, just a raw increase in output, throwing more resources into increasing Soviet oil output and exports. The second is gas-for-oil substitution, and the third is conservation. Each of these could have the effect, if managed properly, of increasing oil exports. The other three are: fourthly, increasing exports of manufactured goods to replace lost oil; fifthly, cutting dollar imports; and, finally, working actively to increase the price of oil.

The first of these, increasing oil output and exports directly, is already being put into effect. According to the estimates put together by PlanEcon, a consulting firm in Washington DC that has been following Soviet foreign trade in energy for some time, in 1986 the Soviets will earn approximately $10.7 billion from exports of oil, which is down from the $20 billion earned in 1983 but above the $7.5 billion that would have been earned if they had not increased oil exports above the levels of the 1984–5 trough. This reflects an increase in oil output which started early in 1986 and really has roots going back to late 1985. We do not yet know exactly how they are doing it, but we know they are doing it, and we know where they are doing it.

The Government is throwing tremendous financial and

political resources into West Siberia which is where their problem was in 1984 and 1985. Many First Party Secretaries – the equivalent, approximately, of Governors in the United States but with much more power – have been fired and new people have been put in their place, and it is clear that they have been told directly by the Politburo that their political futures hang on whether or not oil output rises. Considerable material resources have also been allocated to oil. In 1986 the planned increase in investment in oil extraction in the Soviet Union will be about 28 per cent. It is not clear how they are going to get the physical resources out to West Siberia to do this, but the quantity itself is probably not as important as the signal that there is a commitment, and essentially an open-ended commitment, to increase oil output. Those resources are going primarily into bringing out wells that had been allowed to go unrepaired and therefore not to operate, and into new drilling, probably almost exclusively development drilling, which simply exacerbates the problem they have had for some time in that exploratory drilling has been neglected because of the emphasis on development drilling. Resources have also gone into gas injection in the fields because older techniques have not worked so well, and into transportation. There are crews in the European USSR, in the Volga–Urals fields for example, that are now put on an aeroplane, flown to Siberia for three weeks to work a shift, who then come back to rest for a few weeks and then go again. This is a massive military-style operation, similar to the one they launched in 1977–9 after the last threat to oil output, and it is working, albeit at a tremendous cost.

I doubt that it is sustainable since it represents a typical Russian fire-fighting solution to a long-term problem, but it will probably add up to an increase in oil output in 1986 and 1987. It is not sustainable because, first of all, it is focused on development drilling and not on exploratory drilling. It is focused on existing fields and an increasing number of small fields which are far from each other and which have relatively poor access in terms of infrastructure, particularly transportation. There are no large fields to replace Samotlor that have been discovered and that are on the verge of development. Secondly, the investment costs of the increase in production are coming at a time when Gorbachev has set as his highest priority the modernization of Soviet industry – a very expensive proposition – and he wants to do this in the context of a relatively modest growth in total investment inside the Soviet Union. Thus, in 1986 there is a struggle for priority among different sectors of the economy. There is the continuation of an old high priority – energy – and beside that a new high priority coming in – machine-building – and then constantly in the background agriculture and the military clamouring to regain the priority they have temporarily lost. This is not a stable situation, neither politically nor economically, and I suspect that it is the energy sector that will have to give up its very high priority, probably within a very few years.

The second option for increasing oil exports is gas-for-oil substitution. Gas-for-oil substitution is also a policy that has been pursued in the Soviet Union for some time. It has tremendous promise. In power stations alone, depending on the method of counting, there are 1.5–2.0 mb/d of oil that could be substituted by gas. The problem is that this has been understood for some time and yet power station consumption of fuel oil has not been reduced dramatically. There are several difficulties with realizing a desire to substitute gas for oil in the Soviet Union. One of them is, for reasons which remain unclear, that they have not been able to move ahead with plans to build gas storage facilities in the European USSR, so that they do not have the capability now in peak-demand months to draw on gas storage and run power stations that are designed to run on gas all the year round, and therefore in the peak months, say from December to March, they are still forced to use fuel oil.

Secondly, coal deposits, while still rich, are showing declines in calorific content which are long term and substantial. For Donets coal, which is their highest-quality coal, the decline in calorific content is running at 3–4 per cent per annum, and they are having to compensate for that by using oil or gas as a spiking fuel in the power stations in order to maintain fuel inputs. There are some coal-fired stations in the Soviet Union where the primary input is either gas or fuel oil, and that is going to get worse, not better, over time.

It is still possible, if they push ahead with gas storage

facilities, that they will be able to push ahead with gas-for-oil substitution. The Soviets are also interested, and have been for some time, in the easier gas-for-oil substitution possibilities that lie in export policy. They have pushed Eastern Europe, and continue to push Eastern Europe, to accept gas instead of oil. And they are always eager to compete head to head with Statoil and others in the West European market. The gas pipelines from West Siberia to the European USSR are not all dedicated to export, but there is excess capacity and the Soviets are ready to sell gas at quite favourable prices and will be for the foreseeable future. This is partly because the logic of energy development in the Soviet Union is pushing them towards gas as a low marginal cost hydrocarbon fuel, so that any way they can they will penetrate either the export or the domestic market with gas.

The third possible strategy for increasing oil exports is conservation. Conservation has been discussed seriously by the Soviets since the early 1970s, but the results have been meagre. The Soviet Union is one of the few industrialized countries in the world that still has an energy–GNP elasticity above unity. Even in 1981–5, when they were experiencing a rapid escalation in the marginal cost of fuels and when Brezhnev, Andropov, Chernenko and then Gorbachev were all saying that it was critical that fuel conservation become a first priority in industry, the energy–GNP elasticity may have actually risen a little bit.

This reflects a problem with conservation which is easy to describe and hard to resolve. The best conservation measure they could introduce would be an economic reform, which would encourage enterprises to conserve on *all* inputs, one of which would be fuel. They have not done that yet, and there is no prospect they will do it soon. In the mean time, in a system in which output is the most important indicator of success, you are simply not going to see energy conservation successes. The only way you *might* get there would be to impose energy rationing, but the problem with energy rationing in an output-oriented system is that firms respond by cutting output and saying they are doing the best they can. So I regard energy conservation as a real possibility for the Soviet Union in the 1990s or beyond, but not now, so I do not think it is a short-term option to which you can attach a high probability.

To turn to the other three options for dealing with the problems the Soviets are facing, Gorbachev has talked about increasing exports of manufactured goods, and finally moving the Soviet Union into a position in the world economy commensurate with its position as a world industrial and military power. He would like gradually to increase the share of manufactured goods in total exports, and there are some measures being taken in that direction, but there is unlikely to be much success. The only way they might be able to do something would be to convert some of their military industries to producing manufactured civilian exportables. That is the only sector of the Soviet economy that has the potential capability to compete on world markets, but the military programme clearly has first priority at the moment, and I do not expect any change in the near future.

The fourth option, to close some of the $12 billion gap by reducing hard currency import requirements, is already being pursued. In 1985 the Soviets began to show increasing conservatism on large projects, particularly for importing turnkey plants for manufactured goods, and that conservatism continues in 1986. There is a good deal of discussion with Western firms but most of it is reaching no conclusion since there is now a general order in Moscow that no new deals are to be signed and there are likely to be very few exceptions to this rule.

In the long run, the problem here is that Gorbachev's modernization programme will eventually generate very large demands for imports of machinery and equipment. It has not done so immediately because he does not really think that it is necessary. He has a faith in Soviet industry that is shared by very few outsiders and maybe by very few insiders. He has built the modernization programme on Soviet domestic industry and on limited imports from Eastern Europe, but it is not going to work. As he comes to realize that in order to continue this modernization programme imports of machinery and equipment, particularly from the West, must be increased, it is going to be very difficult at that time for the planners to tell him that – for balance-of-payments purposes – he should reduce, not increase, imports of machinery and equipment.

The second major item on the $35 billion import bill mentioned above is food. Food imports in some years can cost as little as $9 billion, but in other years can be $13–14 billion, depending on the performance of the domestic agricultural sector. But reducing the hard currency allocated to counteract the effects of a bad agricultural year would be politically difficult for Gorbachev. The third item, intermediate products, is hard to cut because many imported intermediate products involve production processes that cannot be performed domestically.

Thus cut-backs of hard currency imports into the Soviet Union are not going to be able to reduce the $12 billion gap mentioned above by very much. Most of the change will have to be on the export side, unless there are dramatic changes in the way the Soviets do business.

Finally, the sixth option I mentioned was to raise oil prices, or actively to work to raise oil prices. Historically, the Soviets have been price takers. They have sat on the sidelines, enjoyed high prices and lived through low prices, but not done much about it. As recently as several years ago, when representatives of OPEC suggested to the Soviet Union some co-operation regarding oil prices, they were rebuffed. In 1986, however, the Ministry of Foreign Affairs has announced that it has responded favourably to a request from Iran and has agreed to cut oil exports by 100,000 b/d to show solidarity with the attempt to stabilize the market.

The 100,000 b/d gesture is less significant than it may appear for several reasons. First, since the Soviet Union does not publish oil export statistics and since those of us who guess can easily miss by 100,000 b/d, it does not mean a lot when they announce they are going to cut back by 100,000 b/d. Secondly, 100,000 b/d is not very much. Thirdly, among the many ways that the Soviets have room for manoeuvre there is one that has not yet received much attention. They are selling oil both in Socialist and in non-Socialist trade, and within Socialist trade they are selling oil both for transferable roubles and for dollars. Over time their goal is to reduce the share of oil sold for transferable roubles and to offer Eastern Europe oil for dollars, so that the East Europeans would have the choice of buying from OPEC or buying from the Soviet Union at something like the spot price plus transportation cost, which generally looks like a good deal, if the only choice is to buy for dollars and the question is from where. Because of that, over time Soviet oil exports to Eastern Europe may well stabilize at about the 1.8 mb/d they are at now, but an increasing share will be for dollars which will be difficult for Western observers to monitor. In any particular year, they could increase the share of dollar sales to Eastern Europe easily by 100,000 b/d, while at the same time announcing to OPEC that they were decreasing non-Socialist exports by 100,000 b/d, or even 200–300,000 b/d, when the overall effect on the oil market would be zero. (Potential East European demand for non-Soviet oil would be reduced by 100,000 b/d, which would be covered by the Soviets so that, from the point of view of the market, there would be no change.)

This 'cut-back' is a very good diplomatic move, which explains why it was announced by the Ministry of Foreign Affairs. But it is part of a general, and by past Soviet standards quite dazzling, strategy of a much more vigorous and clever pursuit of foreign policy goals in the world arena. It probably means little for the oil market. Nor does it answer the question of whether in the long run the Soviets might have an interest in trying somehow to join OPEC and other countries in stabilizing the price of oil. Some Soviet officials may talk in such terms and may mean it. But I remain unconvinced that the Soviets will give up their autonomy over decisions on oil output and oil exports. They may be willing to give up some of the appearance of that autonomy, but I think it would be a great mistake to count on them as being a very good player in the game of stabilizing oil prices over time.

Lastly, I would like to indicate the likely course of action and what it will mean for world energy and particularly for world oil markets. In the short run the strategy is to increase oil output and oil exports. Oil exports bottomed at about 1.3 mb/d and in 1986 they will easily be 300–400,000 b/d above that, say 1.6–1.7 mb/d non-Socialist exports. Of my $12–13 billion gap, that only closes about $3 billion at current prices. About $6 billion of the remaining gap will be closed by borrowing in 1986.

To return to the numbers I started with, the Soviets were

exporting $40 billion to non-Socialist countries and importing $35 billion. A major part of the $5 billion difference is Soviet military hardware, which is often exported to Arab countries in exchange for loans, and they may reduce some of that and therefore close some of that gap. That takes care of 1986 and may take care of part of 1987, but if oil prices stay low they will have to shift to other strategies and I believe they will move down my list of strategies mentioned above. Thus, they will increasingly become more serious about gas-for-oil substitution and therefore in 1987–9 we are likely to see an effort to reduce the cost of keeping oil exports to non-Socialist countries in the range of 1.5–2.5 or 1.5–2.3 mb/d by pushing ahead in gas storage and gas-for-oil substitution. Oil output may begin to fall off again, going from 12.3 mb/d back down below 12 mb/d, with oil consumption falling more rapidly, or at least as rapidly, so that oil exports would remain at approximately their current level. There could be some energy rationing as part of the strategy, but they are unlikely to rely heavily on this. They will have to ration to some extent because of Chernobyl, in the European USSR, at least *de facto* through blackouts and brownouts, but also I suspect they will be rationing consciously.

These policies will last until the latter part of the 1980s. Then, in the very late 1980s and 1990s, I expect a shift as part of a serious economic reform towards a more conservationist strategy and, with that, a shift away from such a heavy reliance on energy exports towards a greater emphasis on exports of manufactured goods.

Whether I am right or wrong about the path of these strategies, I am quite sure that for the rest of this century the Soviet Union will be a major force on energy markets. It will be a major exporter of oil, remaining in the range, for non-Socialist countries, of 1.5–2.5 mb/d. It will continue to be aggressive in its efforts to penetrate European gas markets. To the extent it cannot do that, it will simply put more pressure on gas-for-oil substitution in the Soviet Union and push more oil back out into the market.

The difference that Gorbachev makes to this calculus and to my scenario is not so much in the fundamentals, as in the way he sells them, and I take the 1986 announcement to OPEC as symptomatic of that. We may see a much softer visage to Soviet oil policy, but the fundmental framework Gorbachev is working with was there before him and will be there for a long time to come. The basic given in that framework remains in the investment costs of supply side strategies and therefore the growing pressure to move towards gas-for-oil substitution, and finally to conservation strategies.

11   THE OUTLOOK FOR NORWEGIAN OIL

Arve Johnsen

In 1985 Norway produced 38.5 million tons of oil. The relative size and importance of this production in the international market can be illustrated in various ways. It is 1.5 per cent of total world oil production and 20 per cent of total oil production in Western Europe. The conclusion is that Norway is small on the global oil scene, but significant in supplying Western Europe.

Looking at the future, there are four main points to make concerning Norwegian oil production. First, the Norwegian resources of oil are smaller than those of natural gas. At the 1985 production level, the oil reserves would last for almost forty years, while the gas reserves would last for more than 100 years.

Secondly, Norway has been slow in developing the reserves. If we compare the reserves/production ratio for oil with those of other producers, Norway has a high reserves/production ratio. Despite the historically low OPEC production in 1985, countries like Indonesia, Qatar and Nigeria all had lower reserves/production ratios than Norway (see Figure 11.1).

Thirdly, production from the Norwegian continental shelf in the remaining part of the 1980s and the early 1990s is a consequence of decisions taken in the 1970s. Bringing the North Sea oilfields into production is a unique operation, as regards technology, investments and lead times.

The Statfjord field can be taken as an example. The field was discovered and its development decided upon in 1974, production started in 1979, the major field development was completed in 1985 and Statfjord will reach peak production at the end of the 1980s. The production capacity will then be nearly 850,000 b/d. Total investments in the field are about $6 billion. Consequently, as a result of the huge capital investments production tends to be maximized.

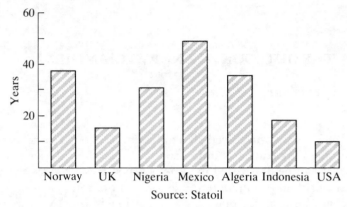

Source: Statoil

Figure 11.1: Crude Oil Reserves/Production Ratios for Various Countries. 1985.

A more detailed look at production field by field shows that the Statfjord field has been the main reason behind the increased production during the last three-to-four years, and has more than replaced the declining Ekofisk output. Statfjord will remain the biggest oil-producing field well into the 1990s. In 1987 the Gullfaks field will start producing. Together with the Oseberg field, which is scheduled for production start-up in 1989, it will make a major contribution to Norway's oil production in the 1990s.

Fourthly, in the 1990s Norway's role in the production and marketing of North Sea oil will increase relative to that of the UK (see Figure 11.2).

Under the assumption that over the next two-to-three years there will be keen international competition between oil producers to defend individual market shares, the market will be unstable and prices may fluctuate around $15 per barrel. However, by 1990 the increased demand for oil may lead to an oil price around $20 per barrel (in 1986 dollars). After 1990 there may be a real increase in oil prices.

Exploration will temporarily fall. On average the annual number of exploration wells drilled between 1980 and 1985 was forty-four. However, the annual average number may be below thirty for the next few years. New production will mainly come from gas fields like Troll and Sleipner. However,

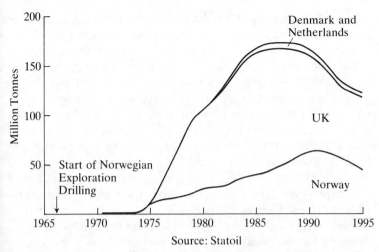

Figure 11.2: Actual and Projected North Sea Oil Production. 1965–95.

these fields also contain some oil, which could be developed in the 1990s, assuming a real increase in oil prices in that decade. Furthermore, satellite oilfields to Statfjord and Gullfaks could be developed.

Research and development will be a vital issue to all companies on the Norwegian continental shelf. Let me offer only a few areas where it will be most relevant.

In exploration, improved and new seismic methods will enhance the value of geophysics and lead to a higher rate of discovery at lower costs.

In drilling and logging, research and development in automation will lead to improved standards of drilling and lower costs. Modern data equipment now makes it possible to reduce drastically the time needed to log a well. That means less lead time before decision-making.

In development and production, new sub-sea production systems, new technology in deviated production wells, and basic research in the area of enhanced recovery based on a better understanding of permeability and porosity in reservoirs will lead to higher production and thereby improve the rate of return on investment.

In transportation, two-phase flow of hydrocarbons over long distances will improve transportation economy and make it easier to develop marginal oilfields with associated gas.

Another important area of research and development is in the field of transportation of LNG. It could well be that in ten years' time a new technology will have been developed making use of liquefied nitrogen to produce LNG based on specialized tankers and terminals. Such a production method would reduce transportation costs and also lead to less energy loss than the presently known methods.

In product development, research in improved qualities of refined products, the conversion of natural gas to gasoline and a higher yield from each barrel of oil may lead to a better competitive position for the oil producers as well as to better products for the consumers.

Probably the most challenging task in the years to come will be the marketing of Norwegian crude oil and refined products. Until now the main markets for Norwegian crude oil and refined products have been in Western Europe. However, whereas this will still be the case in the future, the United States will also become an important market for Norwegian oil in the 1990s and thereafter. In the case of Statoil, downstream integration in Scandinavia has been an important development in the 1970s and 1980s. During the coming years this policy is likely to be extended to include other markets in Western Europe and the United States.

Let me broaden the perspective to illustrate why I feel that the outlook for Norwegian oil is good, irrespective of the short-term volatility in the oil market.

Energy has become an integrated part of the economy in every country on our globe. Therefore production, consumption and conservation of energy are important issues in all camps, whether we are politicians or industrialists, producers or consumers. Oil and natural gas are not the only energy sources to hand. However, these two sources of energy will still play the most dominant role in the world for a long time to come. Therefore, in my opinion it is evident that to continue in the energy industry in general and oil and gas in particular offers a most challenging and profitable opportunity to everyone in this industry.

However, in the energy industry, as in any other industry, some companies will grow, prosper and survive and some will die. The successful companies will continue to recruit and train people within exploration, development, production, transportation, refining and marketing. Individual qualifications will be important, but with the increasing complexity in the commercial development of new projects, management's task will be to develop better team-work with more cross-fertilization between various disciplines within each company.

In a world with a number of economic and social changes, the need for management to understand the signals from consumers, competitors and political decision-makers will become more important than before. Relevant management capacity will be a decisive factor in firms' survival. Such capacity is not only a matter of numbers but also of quality and is not only related to senior management but also to middle management and everyday operations. Within this internationally competitive context, it is my opinion that most actors on the Norwegian continental shelf will not only survive, but even prosper, both at home and abroad.

PART IV

NATURAL GAS AND NUCLEAR POWER

12 THE IMPACT OF RECENT OIL PRICE CHANGES ON THE NATURAL GAS INDUSTRY

Aman R. Khan

Introduction

The precipitous decline in world oil prices since the beginning of 1986 has been a subject of great concern to OPEC and non-OPEC producers as well as the energy industry in general. The average world crude oil price of about $27 per barrel in January 1986 dropped to less than $10 per barrel in the first six months of the year and there were indications that this decline would continue. However, the recent OPEC agreement on production quotas, albeit temporary, may have halted this slide. Nevertheless, this drastic drop in oil prices has had a serious impact on the structure of the oil industry and has also affected other forms of energy which were competitive with oil hardly a year ago.

In 1979, when OPEC increased crude oil prices dramatically, total supply of crude oil (including NGLs) to the non-Communist world was 53.7 mb/d, of which OPEC accounted for 31.6 mb/d or 58.8 per cent. By the end of 1985, with the decreased demand, total supply amounted to 45.5 mb/d, of which OPEC provided 17.2 mb/d or 37.8 per cent. For 1986, OPEC is projected to provide 18.3 mb/d or 39.4 per cent of the total demand of 46.4 mb/d. The average world crude oil price, which had reached a peak of $35.49 per barrel in early 1981, plummeted to $9.62 per barrel by mid-July of 1986 and in some instances spot prices were below $8 per barrel.

During the 1979–85 period, when oil prices were high, natural gas made serious inroads into the market served by oil in some sectors as consumers were lured away by the relatively lower price of gas. However, as oil prices have declined, gas has been subjected to inter-fuel competition in the marketplace resulting in a drop in gas prices as well as a switch back from gas to fuel oil for electric power generation and industrial heat loads. Falling crude oil prices are still affecting the gas price outlook and have had a significant impact on the structure of the gas industry.

Natural Gas Supplies

During the period 1980–85, world reserves of natural gas increased by 26 per cent from 2,744 to 3,452 trillion cubic feet (tcf). Table 12.1 presents the yearly reserves for the period under consideration.

Table 12.1: World Natural Gas Reserves. 1980–85. Trillion Cubic Feet.

	Proven Reserves at Year End	*% Increase*
1980	2,744	–
1981	3,000	9.3
1982	3,109	3.6
1983	3,190	2.6
1984	3,397	6.4
1985	3,452	1.6

Although there was a net addition to reserves every year, it is significant that the proven reserves of natural gas in the world at the end of 1985 had increased by only 1.6 per cent over the previous year as compared with the greater addition to reserves in earlier years. This was largely owing to a decline in exploration and production activity caused by low oil prices. Drilling for gas declined and the number of rigs dropped severely as the oil and gas industry experienced a depression. The number of active drilling rigs in the non-Communist world declined from 3,690 in August 1985 to 1,867 in the twelve-month period. In the United States alone, the number of active drilling rigs has dropped by 1,000 during the first six months of 1986.

Well completions have declined by 26 per cent compared with 1985 and in Canada the situation is no different. This has occurred in spite of a considerable decrease in drilling costs in North America.

Producers are loath to invest in further exploration activity until price stability is restored and an adequate return on investment assured. With the decline in gas prices following the drop in oil prices, certain producers have shut in wells rather than sell gas for less than $1.25/mcf at the well-head.

In the developing countries, there has also been a slow-down in the exploitation of gas reserves, which requires intensive capital investments. The ability to secure this investment has been diminished by the drop in oil prices and the concomitant unwillingness of producing companies to make such investments. In fact, with the large retrenchment by the majors, budgets for overseas exploration have been slashed and exploration for natural gas in developing countries is a low-priority item.

Although natural gas reserves have been increasing more rapidly than oil reserves and are now equal – in energy terms – to 90 per cent of world oil reserves, there is no doubt that the drop in oil prices will further slow the rate of growth. International oil companies are in the midst of a cash crunch. Exploration budgets have been cut to conserve cash and what is available will be spent on lower-risk prospects. In countries with well-developed gas markets, the international oil companies may continue to put some money into gas exploration. But in developing countries, where the gas must be sold to local markets, the return on investment, even if gas is found, may be too low. So even if money is allocated for exploration, it will be spent on areas with likely oil prospects. The government-owned exploration and drilling companies are also having cash-flow problems and will have little money to drill for gas prospects. For the near term, if oil prices do not rebound to reasonable levels, companies will further retreat from gas exploration activities and the yearly additions to gas reserves will continue to decline.

Despite the relatively small increase in world gas reserves, commercial production of natural gas has continued to increase in the world as shown in Table 12.2.

Total production increased in 1985 by 4.3 per cent over the previous year with most of the increase accounted for in

Table 12.2: World Commercial Gas Production. 1980–85.
Trillion Cubic Feet.

	Commercial Production	% Change
1980	54.10	–
1981	54.71	1.1
1982	54.60	−0.2
1983	54.66	0.1
1984	59.94	9.7
1985	62.51	4.3

Europe. Commercial production declined in North America whereas it increased by 16 per cent in the Middle East as more non-associated gas was utilized to make up for the loss of associated gas due to the decline in oil production. Because of the price differential between oil and natural gas, consumption of gas in the developed countries (with the exception of the United States) increased slightly regardless of falling oil prices. At a crude oil price of $10 per barrel ($1.72/mBtu), natural gas still has an edge over oil, and captive markets in the domestic and commercial sectors will not readily switch back to oil. In the industrial sector and for electric power generation, this price is borderline and some fuel-switching may result unless governmental regulations or environmental considerations preclude the move. In the light of the above, it is conceivable that commercial production of natural gas could increase, albeit more slowly in the near term, irrespective of the fluctuations in oil prices. However, it should be recognized that the price of natural gas relative to oil will influence the ability of gas to maintain and increase its share of the market.

Natural Gas Prices

Lower oil prices have recently resulted in widespread reductions in natural gas prices. This is most evident in the United States where, as a result of deregulation and the depressed oil prices, there has been increased competitive pressure to reduce the field prices of natural gas. The average gas price to customers peaked in 1983 and declined thereafter, with field acquisition costs dropping to $2.30/mBtu in 1986 as shown in Table 12.3.

No discussion of the impact of falling oil prices on the US gas industry can disregard other fundamental changes in the industry. Since its inception the gas industry has been comprised of three different industries whose interests have not always coincided. This trichotomy now threatens radically to alter the financial and operational structure of the transmission pipelines and probably many distributors.

Long before the oil price decline, changes were afoot. The national mood to get government out of business created a wave of deregulation which forced an industry long accustomed to government intervention to face competition in the market-place. Advocates of a free market now control the regulatory process and are endeavouring to limit the transmission pipelines to the role of transporters of other people's gas, the intention being to speed the transfer of market signals from the consumer to the supplier, that is, the producer. The transmission industry tried several methods to maintain their historic position in a free market atmosphere. Special marketing programmes and self-help supply programmes forestalled the inevitable, but in 1984 the Federal Energy Regulatory Commission initiated regulatory changes which led to Order

Table 12.3: National Average US Natural Gas Prices. 1973–86.
1985 Dollars per mBtu.

| | Field Acquisition Cost | Retail Price | | | | |
		Residential	Commercial	Industrial	Power Plant	Average
1973	0.46	2.74	2.08	1.17	0.80	1.73
1978	1.25	3.90	3.51	2.99	2.66	3.36
1983	3.08	6.32	5.92	4.82	4.52	5.50
1984	2.96	6.22	5.71	4.58	4.38	5.25
1985	2.53	5.92	5.39	4.16	3.74	4.97
1986	2.30	5.54	4.99	3.70	2.98	4.52

Source: American Gas Association, *Historical & Projected Natural Gas Prices: 1986 Update,* June 10, 1986.

No. 436 setting out its plan for deregulating the industry and providing equal access to all consumers.

Though the plan has still not been fully implemented, it has already wrought significant changes. The simplest way to assure equal access would be to make gas pipelines common carriers, like oil pipelines. But pipeline companies do not want to be common carriers and under existing US law they cannot be forced to do so. So the concept of contract carriage has taken root: pipeline companies must allow equal access, that is they must haul any gas for everyone or no one. Local distribution companies supplied by pipelines that allow access can now buy gas in the field with a reasonable expectation that their pipeline supplier will deliver the gas to their gate station. Large industrial and commercial consumers can also buy directly and may bypass even the distributor. If a pipeline refuses all access, the end-user must look elsewhere for a transporter and there always seems to be someone who will haul their gas. These changes have destabilized an industry which has built its financial base and strength on stability. Falling oil prices can only increase the instability.

One manifestation of this instability has been the emergence of a spot market for gas in the United States. While a spot market for oil has existed for many years, historically the natural gas trade has been governed by long-term contracts between buyer and seller with the transportation link dedicated to such sales. But now, as described above, distribution utilities can shop around and purchase gas directly from supply sources at a lower price and have it moved via the transmission pipelines to their own market outlets.

Spot prices for gas in the United States range from $1.15 to $2.50 per mBtu depending on the region. Average spot prices for natural gas in June 1986 were from $1.48 to $1.70 per mBtu as compared with $1.95/mBtu for No. 6 fuel oil, thus still providing a competitive edge over oil. As oil prices have dropped, spot prices for natural gas have also eroded and quotations have been as low as $1.15/mBtu. Thus, we now have a two-tier gas price system in the USA, representing the prices for tariff and spot gas.

The range of prices paid by local distribution companies in May 1986 for both tariff and spot gas for some regions in the

USA is shown in Table 12.4. In all cases, the spot gas price is lower than the price paid for the traditional gas supply from the transmission company.

The direct impact of the decline in oil prices has forced a gas-on-gas competition as evidenced by the differential in tariff and spot gas prices. The recent volatility of crude oil prices has created almost a daily change in spot gas prices, as the industry has tried to stay competitive with oil in the market-place.

Table 12.4: City Gate Prices in Selected Market Areas. May 1986. Dollars per mBtu.

Region	Tariff Gas Price	Spot Gas Price
New York/New Jersey	2.29–4.10	1.85–2.35
New England	2.42–3.04	2.05–2.27
Western Pennsylvania	2.20–3.60	2.04–2.49
North-east Ohio	2.40–3.60	2.04–2.60
Southern Michigan	2.43–3.47	1.80–2.57
Northern Illinois/ Northern Indiana	2.50–3.47	1.65–2.20
Wisconsin	2.34–3.17	2.01–2.30
Pacific North-west	2.44	1.50–2.25
California	2.23–2.59	1.64

A comparison of natural gas versus No. 6 fuel oil reveals that spot gas prices averaging between $1.48 and $1.70 per mBtu are still competitive with fuel oil at $11.30 per barrel ($1.95/mBtu). However, the commercial price for gas in certain market areas for power generation has exceeded the price of No. 6 fuel oil as shown in Table 12.5. With spot gas prices below contract prices, certain industrial customers are purchasing their own gas directly, rather than from the utility.

Inter-fuel Competition

For the industrial and power plant loads, the relative prices of fuel oil and natural gas have determined the selection of fuel. Because of dual fuel capabilities, these users can switch to

Table 12.5: Wholesale Natural Gas and No. 6 Fuel Oil Prices for Various Cities. Dollars per mBtu.

City	Wholesale Natural Gas	No. 6 Fuel Oil
Chicago	3.60	2.58
Boston	2.85	2.36
Detroit	3.75	2.70
Los Angeles	3.00	1.99
New York	3.50	2.02
Philadelphia	2.70	2.39
San Francisco	3.24	2.02

either fuel depending on the retail price. In the United States, about 52 per cent of current industrial gas sales and 99 per cent of electric generation sales are to purchasers capable of using fuel oil. This dual fuel market, which is price sensitive, imposes pressure on well-head gas prices.

With the decline in world oil prices in the past eight months, one would expect fuel-switching from gas to oil for these loads. This has taken place, but not to the extent one might expect, because of certain intervening factors. These are the lowered costs of pipeline gas purchase, the availability of cheaper spot gas and flexible rates which maintain the competitive position of gas. In 1985, gas markets experienced a net gain of 28 bcf from oil, compared with 40 bcf in 1984, as customers began switching from gas to oil. The projected rate of switching, based on the first quarter of 1986, amounts to 92 bcf on an annual basis with the major replacement being residual fuel oil.

The gas/residual fuel oil price ratio is important in establishing the direction of switch-over from either fuel. In 1986, the switch to oil from gas took place above parity with oil, just as the switch to gas from oil in previous years occurred below parity with oil.

Historically, natural gas has been the dominant energy source for the residential and commercial sector. In the United States, gas accounted for 72.3 per cent of the market in 1984. This declined to 71.7 per cent in 1985 with oil picking up the loss primarily in new building starts on the East Coast.

Although there may be some loss of gas loads in the home heating market with the lower prices of No. 2 fuel oil, it is reasonable to expect that gas will maintain its share of the residential and commercial market in the near term in spite of depressed oil prices.

In summary, the impact of falling oil prices on gas demand has been offset in some measure by the deregulation of gas, the creation of a spot market for gas and the existence of a captive domestic and commercial market. However, if oil prices continue their downward slide, this will have a detrimental impact on the gas industry and result in further erosion of the gas market.

International Trade

On the international scene, the decline in oil prices has had serious repercussions on the gas trade. This is particularly true for the LNG trade and to some extent also for pipeline exports. Most of the LNG export contracts were tied into parity pricing with a basket of crude oils or fuel oil at the port of delivery. An example of this is the LNG export contracts between Pertamina of Indonesia and Japanese buyers. In the contract formula applicable since 1977 for the first project, the f.o.b. price was indexed for 90 per cent with the price of Minas crude, with the remaining 10 per cent increasing by a compound rate of 3 per cent per annum. To this were added the transportation costs at the rate of $0.39/mBtu in 1979, $0.45/mBtu in 1980, $0.55/mBtu in 1981 and $0.60–0.70/mBtu at present, to provide the LNG prices delivered to Japan as shown in Table 12.6.

However, if the formula were observed strictly, then the Indonesians would have a problem since the price of LNG sold to Japan based on their own crude oil tax-reference prices, which are linked to current spot crude prices, would be below $2.70/mBtu c.i.f. Japan. The official LNG price versus spot-adjusted price would be as in Table 12.7.

About 75 per cent of the LNG imported by Japan serves as fuel for power generation and is therefore competing with low-sulphur fuel oil and coal, which are presently below the LNG c.i.f. price. However, environmental considerations and

Table 12.6: Prices of Indonesian LNG c.i.f. Japan.
    1978–86. Dollars per mBtu.

	Price
1978	2.80
1979	3.45
1980	4.69
1981 (Jan)	5.78
1981 (Jul)	5.07
1982 (Jan)	6.00
1982 (Jul)	5.49
1983	4.95
1984	4.74
1985 (Nov)	4.90
1986 (Apr)	4.43

Table 12.7: Official and Spot-adjusted Prices of Indonesian LNG Exports
    c.i.f. Japan. April–June 1986. Dollars per mBtu.

	Official	Spot-adjusted
April 1986	4.43	2.55
May 1986	4.40	2.65
June 1986	4.48	2.68

the desirability of diversifying energy sources together with a $0.17/mBtu extra tax on crude and fuel oils effective from 1984 maintain the acceptability of the relatively higher-priced LNG. The application of the spot-adjusted prices shown in Table 12.7 would result in an f.o.b. price of LNG of about $2/mBtu which would be unacceptable and uneconomic to the LNG producer.

For the time being, both parties recognize their mutuality of interests in not disrupting the trade, and negotiations are proceeding on a floor price with an indexing system that would guarantee a return on investment irrespective of volatile crude oil prices.

About 70 per cent of world LNG production is purchased

by Japan with supplies originating in Abu Dhabi, Alaska, Brunei, Indonesia and Malaysia. Since the decrease in oil prices, the price of LNG delivered to Japan has declined in all cases and current contract prices from various sources are shown in Table 12.8.

Table 12.8: Contract Prices for Japanese Imports of LNG. 1986.

Source	Contract Price $/mBtu	Gas Oil Equivalent $ per Barrel
Abu Dhabi	4.81	27.90
Alaska	4.01	23.26
Brunei	4.09	23.72
Indonesia	4.43	25.69
Malaysia	4.86	28.19

On an oil equivalent basis, the LNG prices are considerably higher than the spot prices of $17.34 per barrel for gas oil in the Tokyo market. LNG sellers are therefore under heavy pressure to renegotiate their existing agreements.

Algeria, which supplies LNG and pipeline gas to Europe, is being subjected to similar pressures owing to the drop in oil prices and the availability of supplies of pipeline gas from the USSR and Norway. Algerian LNG exports to Europe (France, Belgium and Spain) have been based on a contract price f.o.b. in 1985 of $3.85/mBtu indexed against quarterly averages of OPEC crudes. Pipeline exports to Italy were based on a price at the Tunisian border of about $3.49/mBtu. With the slide in oil prices, European customers have been demanding a price cut to stay competitive with oil products in the market-place.

Recently, Algeria agreed to an f.o.b. price of $3.18/mBtu for supplies to France and Spain, equivalent to crude oil at $18.44 per barrel. However, Algeria has encountered problems in settling contract prices with Belgium and Italy. Assuming the existing crude oil market base price, both customers would pay as little as $2.36/mBtu f.o.b. for the gas. On the other hand, assuming OPEC official selling price levels for crude oil, the f.o.b. price for LNG would then be $3.80/mBtu.

Algeria's stance in the past on pricing LNG at parity with crude oil on an f.o.b. basis was opposed by its customers and considered unrealistic at a time of high oil prices. As oil prices drop, it is obvious that this philosophy will result in lower revenues for the exporter and lead perhaps to one good result – a recognition by Algeria that a mutuality of interests between buyer and seller requires a flexible and acceptable contract that keeps the gas flowing.

Apart from the existing LNG projects in the world, the near-term prospects for LNG are limited to the Pacific basin, with contracts for additional LNG supplies to Japan from Australia, and with South Korea and Taiwan as the new entrants into the LNG import business. Considering the plunge in oil prices and consequent reduction in gas prices, the USA will probably not be a contender for LNG supplies for quite some time.

The only LNG imported into the United States in the past year has been from Algeria by Distrigas of Massachusetts and this was for peak-shaving customers. With the availability of domestic gas at the relatively low prices caused by the oil price decrease, a buyers' market prevails. Presently, Distrigas has had problems obtaining customers for imported LNG and is in bankruptcy court. Distrigas is hopeful that an agreement can be reached with the Algerians whereby spot purchases of LNG can be made for the 1986–7 winter period. For the long term, imports of LNG for peak-shaving purposes may continue, but base-load imports will be dictated by competition from domestic supplies and pipeline imports from Canada and Mexico.

With respect to the international gas trade by pipeline, the future is brighter. The recent agreement between Norway and six European buyers guarantees gas supplies from the Sleipner and Troll fields well into the next century. The total quantity of gas sold will be about 16 tcf over a period of twenty-seven years. Significantly, the selling price of gas under this deal is end-market competitive and will be adjusted in accordance with energy prices and not just against an arbitrary marker such as crude oil. However, the sellers are optimistic that oil prices will increase in the 1990s and that European gas demand will continue to rise.

Elsewhere in the world, developing countries with domestic gas resources that are presently being utilized have not been affected to a great degree by the drop in oil prices. Examples are Thailand, Pakistan and Bangladesh. Domestic gas is still cheaper than imported oil but exploration activities for additional gas reserves have been hampered by the lack of interest and capital on the part of foreign oil companies. Those countries with known gas reserves that are dormant may suffer a set-back in their timetable of gas development, and it is probable that utilization of domestic gas will not occur until crude oil prices climb back up to the level of $15–20 per barrel. Some projects such as the export of pipeline gas from Malaysia to Singapore have been shelved pending the restoration of oil prices.

The Gas Industry Outlook

In the present period of fluctuating oil prices, it is difficult to predict the outlook for the energy industries. The gas industry has changed considerably and faces even more challenging times. In the United States, which is still the largest consumer of natural gas, the industry has undergone structural changes. There have been mergers and acquisitions of companies as the industry has faced deregulation and been forced to compete with other energy forms in the market-place. Competition among gas suppliers has been fierce in many markets and has resulted in the creation of a spot market for gas. Prices for gas, which were already declining on the spot market, have dropped sharply as oil prices have collapsed and revived competition between gas and oil. A new era of open-access transportation for inter-state pipelines has emerged permitting the end-user to move away from traditional suppliers and make arrangements directly with the producer. It is estimated that this kind of arrangement alone accounts for over 6 bcf/d of gas in the United States, equal to the total gas consumption of West Germany or the United Kingdom.

In the United States, falling demand has also had serious implications for the contractual relationships between producers and their traditional customers, the transmission pipelines. In the late 1970s some pipelines had contracted to buy gas in the field at very high prices, which in many cases now exceeded the burner-tip value. In the rush to tie up gas supplies they agreed to high take-or-pay commitments which, if enforced, could consume their capitalization. In an effort to relieve the pressure some were able to renegotiate contracts. But others invoked 'market out' provisions, refusing gas that they deemed unmarketable, or claimed *force majeure* and abrogated their contracts. Obviously, producers will be careful in their future contracts to avoid such breaking of agreements.

With the current downward pressure on gas prices, every drop in crude oil price of $1 per barrel requires a corresponding fall of $0.17/mcf in the gas price in order for gas to compete with fuel oil for the marginal load. Reduced gas prices and a reduced gas market decrease the netback to producers, thereby curtailing drilling and exploration activity.

Undoubtedly, competition between gas and residual oil in the industrial sector will influence the price of gas in the coming years. Nevertheless, various projections indicate that natural gas consumption will increase world-wide. According to the Energy Information Administration, natural gas consumption in the market economies (i.e. excluding CPEs) will grow at an average rate of 3.3 per cent per annum from 38.1 tcf in 1985 to 45.5 tcf in 1990 and 52.7 tcf in 1995. This is based on the assumption that economic growth in these countries will average 2.9 per cent over the next ten years and that real world oil prices will decline initially and then increase to $30 per barrel in 1985 dollars or $50 per barrel in current dollars by the year 1995.

What are the prospects for the gas industry in North America and around the world? If oil prices continue at low levels, gas prices in domestic and international markets will also be depressed. Exploration will be limited, reserves additions will continue to decline and as price-induced demand rises the reserves/production ratio may drop. A moderate oil price recovery, perhaps to the $20–25 per barrel level, could stimulate exploration and stabilize the supply/demand balance. In the mean time the industry will have to contend with yet another set of transitional problems:

(a) In gas surplus countries such as Argentina, Bangladesh and India, the cost of marketing already discovered gas will be less than the cost of alternative fuels so development will continue at a reasonably rapid pace, so long as the capital is ploughed back into gas industry development and not siphoned off to replace the decline in oil revenues.

(b) In countries where gas development is in its initial stages – Thailand, Brazil and Colombia for example – growth may be slowed until the netback value becomes high enough to support more exploration as well as field development and pipeline construction.

(c) In the countries where the gas infrastructure is highly developed but supplies are limited – the United States is probably the best example – things may get worse before they get better. Supply will decline and demand will increase. This will put more pressure on the limited supplies and captive customers who cannot quickly switch to oil may face shortages. Unfortunately the political response in the United States to gas shortages is all too clear – more regulation. It is not unreasonable to expect that the regulatory pendulum will swing back in the not too distant future and that the gas industry will once again be faced with the transitional problems of shifting from deregulation to regulation.

(d) International trade will continue, but new projects will probably be postponed until a measure of price stability is restored. One of the fortunate fall-outs of the oil price decline has been a better understanding of the need for contractual flexibility, on both sides. This can lead to better understanding between buyers and sellers in the future and, in the long run, more stability.

13 NATURAL GAS IN WESTERN EUROPE: FACING THE OIL PRICE UNCERTAINTIES

Burckhard Bergmann

The Impact of the Fall in Oil Prices

The uncertainties of predictions and forecasts have recently been confirmed again by the slump in the price of oil in 1985–6 which has, of course, implications for gas marketing, since oil products, and more particularly gas oil and heavy fuel oil, are the main competitors of gas in the various sectors of the energy market. The market environment in which gas operates is therefore to a large degree determined by oil product price developments, and gas will not be able to hold its own in the market-place unless its price follows the price of these oil products. Oil price uncertainties are thus also uncertainties with regard to the development of the price of gas (see Figure 13.1).

It is therefore necessary to examine how gas would fare if no medium-term recovery of the price of oil were to occur and if the long-term oil price level were to be substantially lower than energy price forecasters still thought in 1984. This low oil price scenario is by no means a more probable model of the future than other scenarios, but realistic planning must also study the implications of such an eventuality for the gas industry.

The short-term implications are demonstrated by the evolution of the energy market between November 1985 and July 1986. The price at which gas is sold is adjusted at monthly or quarterly intervals. The adjustment reflects heavy fuel oil and gas oil prices, and sometimes also coal prices, about six months before the date of the adjustment. Even though in Western Europe the time-lag in some gas sales contracts with consumers is shorter than six months, the delayed operation of the price indexation mechanisms causes the price at which gas

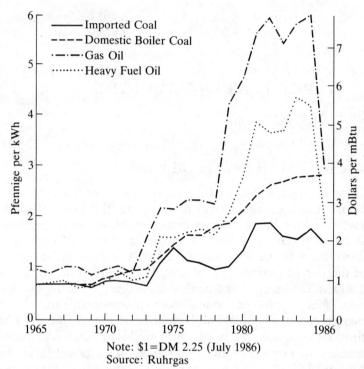

Note: $1=DM 2.25 (July 1986)
Source: Ruhrgas

Figure 13.1: Prices of Fuel Oil and Hard Coal in West Germany. 1965–86.

is sold and the price at which oil products are offered to differ substantially during a period of rapidly declining oil product prices. In the industrial sector, where the time-lag is normally shorter than in the residential and commercial sector, users who had the necessary facilities substituted oil products very quickly for gas, in so far as their gas contracts allowed, in order to benefit from the price differential due to the time-lag between the oil product price decrease and the corresponding gas price decrease. In some countries, the gas industry responded by offering temporary gas price discounts. This process has not yet come to an end. Ruhrgas, for instance, offered a more rapid gas price adjustment to counteract the impact of low oil prices. Numerous industrial users have now accepted this offer. In fact, though, the time-lag does not operate to the detriment of gas users, since the loss suffered at a time of falling oil prices is made up by corresponding benefits as a result of the delayed increase in the price of gas when oil prices are rising.

In the residential and commercial sector, the time-lag effect did not cause clients to switch from gas to oil, because residential and commercial users do not operate dual-fuel plants and the price differential due to the delayed adjustment of the gas price is temporary in nature. However, the rate at which existing space-heating installations are retrofitted for gas firing has slowed down. In most instances, this slow-down of conversion to gas may be attributed to a delay in the replacement of an old boiler rather than the purchase of a new oil-fired boiler which would commit the user to gas oil. Further progress by gas in this market would therefore seem to have been merely delayed rather than curbed. In the new dwelling space-heating market, gas continues to hold a share of more than 50 per cent.

In effect, the gas industry has investigated whether gas oil users who are able to decide when they purchase the gas oil needed to fill up their tanks have actually been able, over a protracted period of time, to buy gas oil more cheaply than consumers who must buy their fuel at the price ruling at the time when the fuel is needed. The study showed that the average gas oil user did not benefit from the free choice of the time of purchase over the period from 1979 to 1985.

In Western Europe, the short-term implications of the oil price slump for the gas industry seem to be less serious than in the United States. This difference is, however, explained by the fact that the percentage of industrial users with dual- or multi-fuel switching capabilities is twice as high as in Western Europe and that gas-to-gas competition does not exist in the same form in Western Europe.

The short-term effects of the fall in oil prices again raise the question of whether gas prices should be adjusted more rapidly to the prices of competing sources of energy. It seems remarkable that a more rapid adjustment is advocated by institutions that in 1985, in view of abundant gas supplies, were still demanding that fuel oil price indexation should be abandoned and that gas should develop its own independent price. Minimization of the time-lag between oil product prices and the price of gas would seem appropriate in cases in which users can switch fuel at very short notice. A reduced time-lag would also appear reasonable in the case of industrial customers. In the residential and commercial sector, however, less frequent gas price adjustments help to make the price of gas more steady. Users do not suffer any losses from the delayed adjustment of tariffs and know at the time at which the gas is received the price that must be paid. Last, but certainly not least, the time-lag allows private consumers to plan their household expenses more easily, since consumers can not react to energy price changes by immediate changes in consumption as in the case of gasoline prices, where the annual mileage is influenced by the price of gasoline as the 1986 increase in automobile usage again demonstrates.

At the supply end of the market, the low oil price level has hardly any short-term impact. Gas prices are falling, with a certain delay, in line with the prices of oil products. Some sellers are, within very narrow limits, willing to negotiate temporary special terms to counteract temporary load reductions attributable to the time-lag problem. Gas availability is entirely unaffected, since long-term agreements do not generally allow an adjustment of the quantities of gas to be made available and to be offtaken. Such an adjustment would, in any case, be premature or even entirely unnecessary.

The implications of a long phase of depressed oil prices would be quite different. To show the effects, the assumption could be made that the price of oil will remain in the range of $10–15 per barrel for several years and will not return to $20 per barrel (in real terms) until the mid-1990s.

Even in the case of this low oil price scenario, energy consumption in the residential and commercial sector would probably not accelerate. For replacements and new installations, most energy-efficient appliances, such as low-temperature boilers, equipped with electronic controls and thermostats, are also an economic choice at an oil price level of $15 per barrel. High-cost technologies, such as gas-fuelled heat pumps, would, however, not pass the break-even point. In addition, the energy consumption of new installations would continue to be curbed by regulations imposed to promote energy conservation, such as thermal insulation rules and rules for the regular inspection of burner adjustment. Finally, past investments in energy conservation, for example by the retrofitting of improved thermal insulation material or improved space-heating systems, are irreversible. It is more difficult to assess how far consumer behaviour could change as a result of low energy prices. Users could well decide to heat additional rooms or to heat their rooms to higher temperatures. Such changes in consumer behaviour could easily add up to an increase in residential and commercial energy demand of 5 per cent, equivalent to the overall demand growth predicted for this sector for the remainder of this century. However, any rise in demand that was attributable to such behavioural changes would be volatile, and would be reversed as and when energy prices increased again.

As long-term gas supply contracts warrant that gas will remain competitive even if the price of oil products is low, the overall standing of gas in the residential and commercial energy market would be slightly improved because production costs do not allow some of the competitors of gas – electricity and district heating – to align fully to such a downturn in energy prices. On the other hand, the replacement of existing boilers and, hence, the conversion to gas would be slowed down. The decision whether or not and when to replace an existing boiler, which must be taken in the next few years for some 5 million boilers in West Germany, for instance, will again essentially be determined by the life of the equipment rather than by the economics of fuel saving achieved by an early replacement.

In the industrial sector, gas sales are substantially determined by the structure of industry and the output of the different branches. It is very difficult to predict the impact of low oil prices on industrial output. It will probably be small and may be limited to a certain oil price-induced boost to economic growth in 1986. Further, in spite of an economic climate favouring investment, industry may delay the purchase of energy-efficient plant and equipment, and the exodus of energy-intensive branches of industry to overseas, low-cost energy regions may be slowed down. However, specific energy consumption will continue to decline as old plants are replaced by more efficient new installations. In sum total, final industrial energy consumption may be slightly higher than it would be if oil were more expensive, and the position of gas in this market sector will probably be strengthened relative to coal and electricity.

In the power station market, a low oil price scenario could delay the substitution of coal and perhaps nuclear energy for fuel oil and gas in some West European countries such as Italy, Belgium and the Netherlands. In West Germany, nuclear power stations presently in operation or under construction and lignite-fired power stations remain unchallenged, since their variable costs are lower than those of gas-fired power stations. Low oil prices would not entail a revival of gas at large base-load or medium-load power stations because large new quantities of natural gas would have to be available at prices that would allow gas to compete against imported coal. Even if gas could be sold under long-term arrangements at a substantial premium over imported coal because of lower handling and flue gas treatment costs, if would be impossible to purchase such additional volumes of gas under long-term agreements, since the gas would have to be supplied from sources involving development costs higher than the break-even price. Furthermore, such base-load electricity generation projects would boost demand in a manner that would affect international gas pricing for other market sectors. The Chernobyl incident has so far not changed the outlook for gas.

Low petroleum prices could, on the other hand, stimulate the use of gas for small co-generation, since the economics of power production by the combined generation of electricity and thermal energy would be improved relative to the purchase of grid electricity.

In toto, a protracted period of depressed hydrocarbon prices would slightly improve the position of gas in energy markets. This position would, however, be furthered only marginally by low-priced oil supplies. Naturally, this analysis assumes that governments will not introduce new or increased energy taxes which substantially offset the decline in the price of oil or distort inter-fuel competition.

Regarding supplies, long-term contracts provide, of course, for an automatic adjustment of gas prices to changes in oil product prices. In principle, this mechanism warrants that gas prices will remain competitive in relation to gas oil and heavy fuel oil, even if oil product prices fall. However, it will be necessary to discuss below the extent to which present price indexation clauses in international contracts must be reviewed.

Some may wonder whether long-term supplies under these conditions will be adequate to cover the predicted level of demand. The gas industry has no reason for concern. Firm supply contracts give West European pipelines sufficient flexibility to serve even a slightly larger market until the end of this century, assuming, of course, that agreed contracts will be honoured. This assumption appears justified, since production under existing contracts will remain an economic operation in the large majority of cases or at least a stoppage of supplies would be more costly than continued contract performance. Further, most international contracts do not contain any provisions allowing an adjustment of contract quantities. However, West German onshore production and indeed UK and perhaps Italian offshore production may be lower than was predicted when oil prices were higher, although, in the cases of West Germany and Italy, such a decline would hardly affect overall supplies.

The economics of new distant gas projects needed to boost supplies after the year 2000 appear more critical. However, the issue would seem to be a matter of the phasing-in of projects rather than a point of principle because even low oil price scenarios predict oil prices for the early years of the next century that could make these projects viable.

Price Irritations

International gas trading can not be equated with international oil trading. Gas trade across borders is equivalent, expressed in energy terms, to only 12 per cent of total world oil exports and less than 25 per cent of the exports of the OPEC countries. Further, the long-term nature of gas contracts conditioned by the capital intensiveness of all gas operations, combined with tight competition in the market-place, does not allow independent gas pricing. In spite of these economic principles underlying international gas trading, gas pricing mechanisms in international contracts have for many years been a controversial issue in public discussions which have sometimes even taken on almost ideological dimensions.

During the first half of the 1970s, fuel oil price indexation made its breakthrough in West European cross-border trading, as parties agreed to adjust gas prices almost entirely, and sometimes even exclusively, in line with the ups and downs of the price of heavy fuel oil in the various end-user markets. Under the conditions of the 1970s, this was an appropriate substitute for perfect competition in the various market sectors. This concept of the fuel oil price adjustment principle became the corner-stone of a reliable gas pricing system equitable for both parties. It warrants that the buyer will always receive the gas he is committed to take under long-term arrangements under competitive terms and conditions while the seller will always receive the true market value for his gas. The need to correct the price formulae of the 1970s in the wake of the 1979–80 oil price hikes does not reflect inadequacies in the design of such pricing systems, but indicates only that their mechanisms were unable to translate such extraordinary jumps in the price correctly. The operation of the price adjustment equation would have widened the margin earned by importers beyond the modest level with which importers had previously been satisfied. It was also necessary to realign the basket of competitive energy prices to which the price of gas was pegged, since gas oil had become a stronger contender on the energy market while heavy fuel oil had had to concede substantial market shares. The necessary changes were agreed, partly by renegotiation under the existing price review clauses and partly by means of a more fundamental renegotiation of the terms of the contracts themselves.

In the course of these price review negotiations conducted in the early 1980s, some sellers demanded crude oil parity pricing. They argued their case by maintaining the false claim that fuel oil price indexation clauses were no longer operable, and pursued a strategy of cutting the cord between the price of gas and oil product price quotations published in the consuming countries. The objective of this strategy was to bring the gas price formation mechanisms to a more aggregated level that would not be subject to possible influences in the consuming countries. However, it is impossible for the producers simultaneously to reap the benefits of more integration and secure the true market value of the commodity. For this reason, crude oil price indexation has never gained a foothold in Western Europe and is now a remnant of wishful dreams.

Today's issues are quite different. Oil product prices have returned to the pre-1979 level. Some may wonder whether price adjustment formulae must be restored to the same status. In fact, new corrections are called for but the wheels of price adjustment cannot be turned back to pre-1979 conditions because:

(a) Gas serves different outlets today from the markets in which it was sold ten years ago;
(b) The costs of gas transmission and distribution have risen and the increase has been only partly offset in some market segments by economies of scale;
(c) The price of coal is higher than in the late 1970s and nuclear power has become a serious competitor, at least in some countries.

The response to these fundamental changes in circumstances and the need for adjustment will be the subject of the price review negotiations still to be held under various contracts in 1986 and mainly to be conducted in 1987. The importers need a substantial improvement of their margins, which the oil price slump has reduced dramatically on the basis of the present price formulae. Although the criteria agreed for these reviews are market value oriented rather than production cost oriented, importers can not expect their margins to remain unaffected by the oil price slump and the corresponding reduction in the end-user market value of the gas, and producers will not be able to ignore the substantial rise in the cost of gas production since the 1970s. Nor will the uncertainties of the fate of oil prices during the course of the next three years facilitate the negotiations. On the other hand, these uncertainties do not justify delays. Nevertheless, the gas industry is confident that this new challenge to the long-term reliability of gas supply contracts will again be mastered by adequate adjustments to current pricing mechanisms agreed by exporters and importers.

Another issue of international gas pricing will emerge, stimulated by low oil prices. Exporters of gas have wanted, and until now been able, to sell their gas at equivalent prices at the borders of different importing nations, taking upon themselves the transit costs incurred, in order to expand their markets. As oil prices have slumped, the netback differentials associated with this policy will be felt more painfully. However, as experience shows, suppliers have a particular interest in a geographic expansion of their markets only in periods of limited demand in existing markets.

In this connection the question may also be raised whether, in view of the diverse structures of the gas markets in the various nations, pricing mechanisms should be tailored to fit the specific structures of inter-fuel competition of the individual importing countries more closely.

Irritation and confusion are presently characteristic of the public discussion of gas pricing, since the underlying issue, i.e. the adjustment of the price formulae to reflect the oil price slump and the fragmentation of sales markets, is obscured by a flood of data on monthly changes in the prices of gas imported under operational projects which are distorted or made incomparable by differences in the currencies, the reference periods, the load factors and the other terms and conditions, as well as in the points of delivery to which these prices relate. In addition, the relevance of spot gas sales and spot gas prices is a new element in ongoing discussions, although spot gas sales play a negligible part in the West European gas trade while they have become an important feature of the US gas market.

Market Hierarchies

The oil-induced changes in the energy market environment faced by gas are not limited to the slump in oil prices but also include a shrinkage of the gas oil/heavy fuel oil price differential. Whereas gas oil was still about DM320 ($132) per tonne more expensive than heavy fuel oil on the West German energy market of 1982, the difference between the two prices had fallen to approximately DM100 ($47) per tonne in July 1986 (see Figure 13.2). Some argue that, in view of this trend,

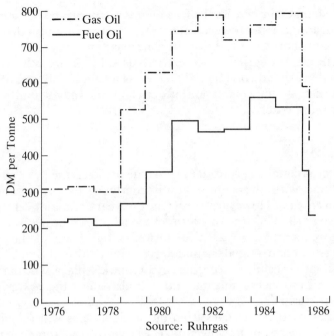

Figure 13.2: Gas Oil/Fuel Oil Price Differential in West Germany. 1976–86.

the hierarchy of target sales markets for gas should be reshuffled, since net income from gas sales to users in the residential and commercial sector, where gas oil is a main competitor, is lower than net income from sales to industrial users, whose alternative option is heavy fuel oil if the differences in transmission, distribution and storage expenses are taken into account. However, nobody can be positive today that this small differential between the prices of these two oil products will be a long-term feature of the energy market. Nor is it possible continually to adjust marketing patterns for short-term income optimization. The sale of gas will always remain a long-term business.

Finally, criteria other than short-lived netback profits must be applied in the definition of marketing strategies and target market hierarchies. One vital criterion is the continuity of demand by the residential and commercial market, which contrasts with the elasticity of industrial demand in response to changes in the level of economic activity and structural transformation. However, the present experience also demonstrates that it would be an ill-conceived and unhealthy long-term marketing policy to restrict gas sales principally to the residential and commercial sector. As at the supply end of the market, the diversification of outlets is the only sound long-term approach.

Conclusion

International gas contract arrangements keep the price of gas in line with the somewhat disorderly pattern of oil price movements. However, as during the years of major oil price rises in 1979–80, the weakness of the oil price now necessitates the redefinition of gas price formulae by means of the concerted action of sellers and buyers in 1986 and 1987. The dramatic decline in returns in the market-place will mainly curtail producers' income, but will also affect the rewards of all performers.

Taking its price cues from oil products, gas will remain a strong player, or may even take a larger role as some participants will not be able to maintain their market shares in competition with the low-cost gas. However, it would be unfounded optimism to hope for these reasons to attract a much wider market since a low oil price scenario would also discourage the boosting of supplies from high-cost sources of production.

14   NUCLEAR POWER AFTER CHERNOBYL

Ryukichi Imai

As of the beginning of 1986, i.e. before the Chernobyl accident, the world nuclear power industry was fairly well organized, with a share of about 20 per cent of world electricity supplies.[1]

Table 14.1 illustrates the following main points:

(a) The industry's strong growth in France, the USSR and Japan has continued, and equally strong future programmes are planned.
(b) The USA still remains the world leader, but its future is very much in doubt. Having sufficient primary energy resources of its own, the USA ceased to maintain interest in nuclear power after the rapid growth of the nuclear industry in the 1960s. The technological strength of the civilian sector is probably backed up by the strongly nuclear US navy and by other military-related activities.
(c) The same applies to the UK which, at one time, was the unquestioned standard-bearer of nuclear power. The general economic situation, consideration for coal, and more importantly for North Sea oil and gas, have changed the boundary conditions for UK nuclear power.
(d) Several countries including West Germany, Sweden, Belgium and Switzerland are already close to the operational (grid) maximum of nuclear electricity at the level of 30–40 per cent. Unless a very strongly pro-nuclear leadership emerges, these countries are not expected to experience significant development in the near term.
(e) The prospects for nuclear power are limited to the technically advanced countries. Although much is heard about Egyptian, Turkish, Chinese or other programmes, they

---

[1] This paper is based on information publicly available as of 20 August 1986.

Table 14.1: The World Nuclear Power Industry in December 1985.

	In Operation		Under Construction		Electricity Generated	% of Total
		MW(e)		MW(e)	TWh	
USA	93	77,804	26	29,258	385.7	15.5
France	43	37,533	20	25,017	213.1	64.8
USSR	51	27,756	34	31,816	152.0	10.3
Japan	33	23,665	11	9,773	152.0	22.7
West Germany	19	16,413	6	6,585	119.8	31.2
UK	38	10,120	4	2,530	53.8	19.3
Canada	16	9,776	6	4,789	57.1	12.7
Sweden	12	9,455	–	–	55.9	42.3
Spain	8	5,577	2	1,920	26.8	24.0
Belgium	8	5,486	–	–	32.4	59.8
Switzerland	5	2,882	–	–	21.3	39.8
South Korea	4	2,720	5	4,692	13.9	22.1
Finland	4	2,310	–	–	18.0	38.2
Czechoslovakia	5	1,980	11	6,284	10.9	14.6
South Africa	2	1,840	–	–	5.3	4.2
East Germany	5	1,694	6	3,432	12.2	12.0
Bulgaria	4	1,632	2	1,906	13.1	31.6
World-wide	374	249,625	157	141,942		

Source: IAEA, 1985 Annual Report

are not expected to account for a significant proportion of energy supply. Despite the somewhat biased and exaggerated picture painted by prospective suppliers of nuclear components, the financial and industrial infrastructure needed to make nuclear power truly operational is not really in place in these countries. Talk about an Arab nuclear project seems to have subsided.

The world-wide nuclear generating capacity of 250 million kW, with another 140 million kW under construction, supplying a total of 21 per cent of OECD electricity as of the end of 1985, was already an impressive performance.

A good deal of this development can be attributed to the advanced countries' changed energy policies after the oil crisis of the 1970s. Table 14.2 shows that coal and nuclear power were the largest contributors to new energy supplies in the

Table 14.2: Percentage Shares of Primary Fuels in OECD Electricity. 1974 and 1985 (at Year-end).

Source	1974	1985
Nuclear	6	21
Hydro/Geothermal	24	20
Coal/Other Solid Fuel	34	42
Gas	12	10
Oil	24	7

Source: OECD/NEA Report, July 1986

non-OPEC world. This situation developed against the background of the relatively high ruling prices of hydrocarbons and the expectation that these prices would continue to rise. The development of alternative energies (with the possible exception of the Brazilian ethanol project) was limited to the OECD countries which have the necessary industrial infrastructure to switch sources of energy.

According to one study quoted in *PIW* (April 7, 1986), non-OPEC supplies of energy rose by 23 mboe/d between 1972 and 1986, of which 12.4 mboe/d (54 per cent) was accounted for by nuclear, coal and hydropower, 7.6 mb/d (33 per cent) by non-OPEC, non-Communist world oil, and 2.8 mb/d (12 per cent) by Soviet oil. In addition, conservation measures eliminated some 19 mboe/d of potential demand, thus indicating the significant roles played by conservation and by immediately available alternative energy sources.[2] Coal liquefaction, solar energy, large-scale wind power and fusion were too remote and too expensive to show any effects.

The financial and social problems faced by the nuclear power industry cannot be underestimated. The very important issue of nuclear non-proliferation seemed to have lost momentum as was indicated by the rather uneventful Third Non-Proliferation Treaty Review Conference of September 1985. Difficulties in the financing of major nuclear projects (power generation or fuel cycle) under conditions of low

[2] *The Crash In World Oil Prices* and *A Return To The Age of Oil?*, US Committee for Energy Awareness, Washington DC, 1986.

growth, delays in licensing and environmental approval, and the problem of radioactive waste were the three main outstanding issues. It is well understood that, when people are relatively unconcerned about shortages in energy supply, they become more concerned about the possible adverse effects of energy supply. In particular, it was in the field of energy that supply problems and environmental concerns surfaced together in a very major way in the 1970s. This is why the two main events of early 1986, the fall in the oil price and the Chernobyl accident, had such significant effects for the assessment of the future of nuclear power. Serious doubts were raised about the economics and safety of nuclear power generation.

In the pre-Chernobyl forecasts, such as the one undertaken by the OECD and the NEA in spring 1986, nuclear power would be producing 26.2 per cent, or 2,125 TWh, of total electricity in the year 2000. This would correspond to roughly 10 per cent of the world's total energy requirements. In fact, it could be argued that nuclear power based on fission, and on the reactor technology currently available, would reach a saturation point at this 10 per cent level. Something very new and different would have to happen in order to increase the proportion of energy supplied by nuclear power, particularly if it were to displace the shares held by oil and gas. In view of fuel cycle costs, the current state of technology, use practice, radiation problems, etc., the general consensus has been that 10 per cent is a well-balanced goal for the year 2000, unless a very different energy supply and demand picture should emerge in the mean time.

Table 14.3 shows the same pre-Chernobyl story in terms of the demand and supply of enriched uranium looking to the year 2000. Many projects of very large enrichment capacities once talked about in the 1960s and 1970s for the USA, France, URENCO and others have disappeared simply because the level of projected demand is so low. Today enrichment continues to be a buyers' market, with newcomers with new technology (laser enrichment in particular) concerning themselves only with the possibilities arising in the very long term. The use of plutonium as a fuel in fast breeder reactors remains mostly at the stage of research and development, while some

Table 14.3: Supply and Demand of Enriched Uranium in OECD
Countries. 1984–2000. Thousand Separative Work Units.

	1984	1985	1990	1995	2000
Supply					
France	10,800	10,800	10,800	10,800	10,800
URENCO[a]	1,250	1,650	3,000	4,500	6,000
Japan	50	50	250	1,200	2,800
USA	19,500	19,500	19,500	19,500	19,500
Total	31,600	32,000	33,550	36,000	39,100
Demand					
Belgium	450	700	700	830	830
Finland	260	260	260	320	430
France	4,500	5,300	6,600	8,000	9,300
West Germany	2,100	2,200	2,600	2,800	3,000
Italy	115	115	320	970	1,650
Japan	4,700	2,800	6,200	7,700	9,500
Netherlands	70	70	70	210	350
Spain	350	714	687	757	1,171
Sweden	800	850	850	850	850
Switzerland	370	370	370	370	460
Turkey	0	0	240	91	91
UK	660	670	730	1,190	1,640
USA	8,820	8,300	10,300	11,100	12,400
Total	23,195	22,349	29,927	35,188	41,672

Note: (a) West Germany, the Netherlands and the UK.

countries are ready for commercial demonstration, but with
little prospect of viable commercial operation. Needless to say,
there is today excess production capacity of natural uranium.

It is worth noting that the nuclear industry had stopped
talking about demand and supply in the twenty-first century,
and this is in keeping with the recent practice in all other
energy areas. The past record of five- or ten-year energy
predictions have been nothing but a nightmare for most experts.

Exactly what happened at the Chernobyl No. 4 reactor at
1.23 a.m. on Saturday 26 April 1986 is neither well known nor

properly understood. With the given system of operation and safety control, and the design of RBMK (graphite moderated, tube type, boiling water) reactors under critical review within the USSR, there must have been several factors that contributed to make the scale of the accident the worst in history. Whatever experiment was conducted on that day, it could not by itself have led to the scale of accident that in fact occurred, especially considering that reaction time constants are larger for graphite reactors. With some of the real-time operational record at the main control room apparently lost in the confusion, and the very centre of the accident, the reactor core, now covered by 5,000 tons of dirt, cement and boron, there is no way that a precise post-mortem analysis can be carried out beyond the extent of the report made available to the IAEA. The early information from the Chernobyl site was very confused, indicating that some of the post-accident emergency measures were less than adequate. The incident must have been due to a combination of design faults and human error, as is the case with most major industrial accidents, and, according to one Soviet official, it has produced a level of environmental contamination equivalent to one-third of a major nuclear weapon attack.

As a consequence of the Chernobyl accident, radioactive material and fission products spread far and wide across national boundaires and covered much of northern Europe. Whenever a reactor accident leads to the core being depressurized to atmospheric levels, it is to be expected that a large volume of radioactive noble gas, representing roughly 10 per cent of contained radioactivity at the time, will be released, forming a plume carried by high wind, and spread over a wide area downwind. Noble gases are not usually absorbed by living organisms, and are not soluble in water. Thus, after the initial gamma radiation, they disperse and disappear into the earth's atmosphere. The initial radiation level experienced in Scandinavia (downwind) must have been due to the effect of these noble gases. This is a one-shot affair, and the principal danger associated with it (if any) is the accumulated long-term effect on the earth's atmosphere.

At Chernobyl, where the graphite moderator temperature was high and had a positive coefficient of reactivity in which many manually operated safety protection features failed to operate, the entire core started to burn. This means that the graphite, zirconium alloy tubes and uranium oxide fuel were all red hot, and were discharging a very large quantity of fission products upward through the broken building and contaminating the environment, including crops as far as 2,000 km away. Fission products include such radio isotopes as ^{131}I (which has a half-life of 8 days), ^{129}Te (34 days), ^{137}Cs (30 years), ^{106}Ru (1 year) and other non-volatile material, all of which have a chance of being absorbed into the human body through inhalation or through food contamination. Fortunately, many fission products have short half-lives, while materials with long half-lives such as uranium and plutonium would be most unlikely to escape from the core to the atmosphere.

No one seems to be sure to what extent the available primary information has been disclosed to the IAEA by the Soviet authorities. It is estimated that approximately 10 per cent of the long half-life fission products, i.e. several million curies, has been released into the atmosphere, and that about 130,000 people around the station had to be evacuated and still can not return home. If we had more information about the readings of radiation levels in the Ukraine, we would have a much better understanding of what has happened and would be much better able to assess the probable long-term effects upon the soil, the water table and plant life. In any event there is no question that it was a major accident, far worse than that at Three Mile Island in 1979, in that the dissemination of radioactive material to the general public was several orders of magnitude larger. At the same time one should be careful not to exaggerate: the capacity of nature, which is by definition highly radioactive, to absorb additional and inadvertent radioactivity should not be underestimated. It was widely predicted that Hiroshima would be uninhabitable for a long period of time, but the result is very different today.

The effect of Chernobyl on the world nuclear industry as a whole is difficult to assess, and seems to depend very strongly on what happens in the Soviet Union, Japan and France.

The Soviet Union is showing every indication of its intention to rectify the problem and go ahead with its nuclear programme. Since shutting down all reactors of the RBMK type would represent the equivalent, in energy terms, of losing 430,000 b/d of hydrocarbons, it is not a realistic choice. The shift from plutonium-producing reactors to more modern and container-equipped PWRs will be accelerated, but the overall plan of relying on nuclear power, particularly in remote industrial areas, and releasing as much oil and gas as possible to be exported for hard currency is so central to Soviet energy policy that it is hard to envisage how any major revision could take place. The series of punitive measures taken against the officials responsible for the nuclear industry, from Deputy Minister level down, indicates Gorbachev's determination to streamline the system and resume the programme more vigorously than before. Repeated Soviet overtures to involve the IAEA in international accident management also indicate an effort to open up the management of the Soviet nuclear industry's internal problems to external criticism. It is difficult to assess the extent to which this attempt will succeed as more and more details become known to the world. Soviet nuclear reactors currently in operation and under construction are listed in Table 14.4.

A similar trend is reflected in other East European countries, which rely on Soviet technology and services. Bulgaria, Czechoslovakia, East Germany and Hungary have all laid great stress on accelerating their nuclear construction programmes.[3]

While it may be premature to draw conclusions about Japan, there are indications that the Japanese feel relatively unaffected by the accident. First of all, Chernobyl is a distant and unfamiliar place in the Ukraine, and no Japanese have been directly exposed to radiation. The type of reactor is very different from those in operation in Japan. In particular, it lacks the usual concrete container structure which proved so effective in containing the release of radioactivity at Three Mile Island where, despite a serious melt-down, the container retained most of the fission products (other than noble gas) pressurized within the reactor building. Secondly, there may

---

[3] All the nuclear power plants presently under construction in Eastern Europe are PWRs, unlike the RBMK reactor at Chernobyl.

Table 14.4: Soviet Nuclear Reactors. 1986. Megawatts.

		In Operation	*Under Construction*
RBMK			
23.9 million kW	Siberian	100×6	
	Beloyarskii	100, 175	
	Leningrad	1,000×4	
	Kursk	950×4	
	Smolensk	950×2	950×2
	Chernobyl	950×4	950×2
	Ignalina	1,450	1,450
	Kostroma		1,450×2
PWR			
30.5 million kW	Novo-Voronezh	265, 338, 410 410, 950	
	Kola	440×4	
	Oktoberyan	400×2	
	Rovno	440×2	950×2
	Nikolayev	950×2	950×2
	Kalinin	950	950
	Zaporozhe	950×2	950×2
	Khmelnitskii		950×3
	Neftekamsk		950×2
	Volgodonsk		950×2
	Odessa		900×2
	Belakhov	950	950
	Aklash Krimia		950×2
	Nizhnekamsk		950

be a feeling that the operators of Soviet plants do not apply such high standards of safety as their Japanese counterparts. Thirdly, the pace of the Japanese reactor construction programme has been slowing down somewhat in any case, particularly when compared with the once-popular target level of 60 million kW by 1985. The Japanese nuclear industry had an operating capacity of less than 24 million kW at the end of 1985, and the current pace of construction is not very high, but still regarded as adequate. It is currently expected that by the year 2000 nuclear power will provide 370 TWh of Japan's electricity, or 39 per cent of the total. At the same time, preparations for investment in fuel cycle facilities and fast breeder development are continuing at a characteristically Japanese slow-but-steady pace. It is worth noting that most electrical utilities are enjoying very healthy financial conditions as a result of the decline in the price of oil and the strength of the yen, and are willing to make extra expenditure to be better prepared for any future energy crisis.

The extent to which France can physically add nuclear power plants to its electricity grid is a very intricate subject. With 64.8 per cent of total electricity already coming from nuclear power, any further additions will require a significant increase in load-following capabilities. Standardized plant design has the advantage of economies of scale, while its obvious disadvantage is that a common failure mechanism may develop. These matters have been topics of discussion for some time, and it is not very clear whether the incident at Chernobyl has added anything or not. The French nuclear programme has in any case been approaching a saturation point, especially given the *de facto* restrictions on overseas market possibilities.

The UK, on the other hand, will potentially be strongly affected, according to those responsible for the UK nuclear industry. The development of North Sea oil and the strength of labour unions in the coal-mining industry seem to be the principal factors affecting the UK's energy position. While there has been much talk about a switch from advanced gas-cooled reactors (AGRs) to PWRs, it is becoming increasingly difficult to find sites for new PWRs. The current level of AGR production capacity is sufficient to any replace the now ageing Magnox reactors, and the case for new investment in PWRs and the associated fuel cycle can not be very strongly argued in the post-Chernobyl atmosphere.

It is clear that Sweden has given up nuclear power, despite the excellent design and performance of Swedish PWRs. Whether the same thing will happen to the PWRs in West Germany is one of the major political questions facing Europe, especially in the era of nuclear arms negotiations in which attention is focused on the medium-range nuclear missiles on Europe's central front. In the case of West Germany, nuclear power is much more than an energy issue, and it is well known that Chernobyl may be one of the major issues in the coming federal election in January 1987.

It is too early to talk about the final effects of the Chernobyl accident: indeed, we have not yet really come to any final conclusions regarding the effects of the Three Mile Island accident of 1979. At the same time, we know very well that the initial excitement usually has a half-life of about six months. The lessons from Three Mile Island, namely the need to devote more attention to training, to design precautions for unanticipated events, and to revise the radiation source terms for accident analysis because of the ability of containment domes to retain fission products, are becoming very clear and are being taken into account in the design and operation of new plant. Similar reactions in response to Chernobyl are unlikely, partly because the reactor is of a different type but also because it seems that much valuable information was lost in the initial confusion. There will be some universal lessons to be learned concerning the value of international co-operation in dealing with accidents, but it will not be easy to integrate the various national review procedures because there is no agreed international standard for the assessment of nuclear plant accidents. I have tried to describe some early indications of the effects of Chernobyl on the world nuclear industry as a whole, but it is difficult to extrapolate from them into the future, especially as regards the development of nuclear power in the Soviet Union.

It has been forecast for some time that the nuclear power industry will grow to account for roughly 10 per cent of the world's total energy requirements by the turn of the century, and no major change in this growth is to be expected, so long as Japan, France and the USSR remain on their present course. As has been pointed out already, developing countries, including China, are unlikely to have much in the way of nuclear power. Changes in the price of oil will not affect the development of nuclear power, especially when electric utilities are both able to gain from the fall in oil prices and determined to be better prepared for any possible future oil crisis.

In my view, unless there is another major reactor accident, this time involving a light water reactor made by one of the world's major manufacturers, the current pace of construction of nuclear capacity will not change by more than 25 per cent. Unless we run into such a misfortune, and as long as we refrain from trying to predict the pattern of world energy production in the twenty-first century, we should not expect the total picture of the world nuclear industry to change very much.

PART V

**THE OIL PRICE COLLAPSE AND THE
INDUSTRIALIZED OIL-CONSUMING COUNTRIES**

15   PROSPECTS FOR THE OECD AREA ECONOMY

John Flemming

Initial evaluations of the marked fall in the oil price and the
large movements in exchange rates that have taken place since
the start of 1985 led to the emergence in early 1986 of what
seemed to be a fairly bullish consensus among forecasters
about global economic prospects. This consensus has
weakened of late as a result of rather disappointing data on
output and trade, and a keen debate has developed as to
whether we are witnessing merely a pause in world growth or
some more fundamental slow-down.

According to the OECD the major seven industrial countries had been enjoying an upswing for three years by the end
of 1985.[1] Real growth for this group averaged around 3.75 per
cent per annum in that period, somewhat less than in previous
upswings and insufficient to produce any overall reduction in
the prevailing high level of unemployment. For this reason,
one might not want to describe this upswing as a phase of
cyclical recovery. Inflation was steadily declining, with the
overall policy stance generally remaining cautious. Thus, and
with recent falls in primary product prices and the realignment of exchange rates, conditions would have seemed
reasonably propitious for continuing, non-inflationary expansion. Does this conclusion stand up to closer scrutiny, particularly after the rather weak performance to date?

In tackling this question, it may be instructive to look into
the background of the latest upswing in a little more detail.
The policy stance in industrial countries has differed from that
in previous cycles which can in turn perhaps be best understood by examining the different reactions to the oil price
increases of 1973 and 1979.

---

[1] *OECD Economic Outlook*, No. 39, p. 20.

Each of those oil price 'shocks' imposed an unavoidable loss of real income on the OECD area and gave an immediate inflationary impulse. After the 1973 increase some industrial countries adopted a relatively expansionary fiscal stance in order to fend off the recession, which otherwise seemed bound to set in as a result of real income loss (via the terms of trade) and the unlikelihood of oil-exporting countries quickly adding sufficiently to world demand to offset it. Those expansionary policies are nowadays judged to have been misguided. They fuelled inflationary pressures, which were already lurking as earners sought compensation for oil and other commodity price increases. Surging price levels, typically accompanied by rising current account deficits, depreciating exchange rates, or both, then required the brakes to be applied. As a result it was 1978 before a broadly balanced pattern of growth appeared to have been re-established within the OECD, but even then the OECD inflation rate was still around 8 per cent.

Inflation had indeed not been conquered when oil prices surged for the second time, in 1979. On this occasion, however, restraining monetary policies were more uniformly maintained in order to prevent second-round inflationary consequences. In this respect the approach clearly achieved considerable success, but at no small cost in terms of economic activity and employment in the short term. Thus the overall cost to OECD countries, in terms of real income, of coping with the second OPEC price shock in the chosen manner was not much different from that of coping with the first, despite the first being bigger in terms of the percentage increase in the real price of oil and despite the OECD being less (and prospectively even less) dependent on net imports of oil in 1979 than in 1973. But the post-1979 strategy succeeded in bringing OECD inflation down markedly – to below 5 per cent and still falling even before the assistance of last winter's sharp reversal in oil prices.

Given the major stagflationary consequences of the two big oil price increases for the OECD economy, both directly and through associated policy responses, it is plainly relevant to assess the likely impact of the recent price fall on present economic prospects. I hardly need remind this audience that, even after the recent recovery to around $15, the oil price on the spot market has halved in dollar or sterling terms from what it was last autumn, and the decline is much greater in terms of currencies such as the yen or D-mark. Although there had been a fair amount of talk about oil being overpriced before the collapse, the markets did not appear to be expecting anything so sudden or so large. Thus we would be justified in regarding the drop, in the jargon of economics, as 'news', being largely an 'unanticipated shock'.

For analytical purposes we are dealing with a substantial sudden shift in relative prices between oil and other goods. It is possible to argue, on the basis of a number of simplifying assumptions, that in the very long run shifts in relative prices imply shifts in the global distribution of real income and wealth but do not affect the eventual level of global welfare in the aggregate – although, to the extent that the recent oil price fall is associated with a move away from a cartel towards freer competition, it might be regarded as welfare-increasing. The long run, however, may be a very long way off, and in the mean time the relative price movement opens up policy choices, including the option of doing nothing, which effect welfare losses during the adjustment period.

Vying with recent oil price developments for the limelight, over a slightly longer period, has been the transformation in exchange rates. By the time it peaked in spring 1985 the dollar had been rising with few interruptions for four-and-a-half years, by a total of almost 70 per cent in effective terms from its average 1980 level. As the dollar climbed there were mounting predictions of a downturn, so that when the turning-point came it was probably a surprise only in its precise timing. Moreover, while as substantial a realignment as has subsequently occurred may have been seen as necessary, it was certainly not expected: the effective rate has fallen by 30 per cent in the eighteen months since the turn, and is now only 18 per cent above its 1980 average (about 13 per cent in real terms). Certain bilateral rates have moved even more sharply, most notably the dollar/yen, with the dollar losing 72 per cent since the 1985 peak. To some extent these exchange rate developments may therefore be categorized alongside the oil price collapse as a recent 'shock' to the world economy.

If I appear to have laboured the classification of shocks it is because I believe that unanticipated shocks, including those with apparently neutral or even expansionary medium-term characteristics, may carry a deflationary bias in the short term. Just because sudden oil price increases turned out to be stagflationary, one can not assume that an oil price collapse will be unequivocally stimulatory. And the same is true of exchange rate shocks.

We are dealing essentially with a situation where there is a sharp and probably largely unanticipated movement in relative prices in the world – whether between commodities (oil and others) or between currencies – with consequential impacts on real income and wealth. There are some rather obvious reasons for believing that those who find themselves better off are likely to expand their spending less quickly than those who are worse off cut theirs. First, one is likely to become aware of a deterioration in one's financial circumstances more quickly, perhaps abruptly, than one is of an improvement. Next, even if the desired response is symmetrical (for example, if both sides wish to maintain existing real expenditure), those who are worse off may face financial constraints either because financial markets do not recycle smoothly or because there are justifiable doubts over creditworthiness. Moreover, sudden price changes are likely to engender a degree of uncertainty, as to whether, for example, the new trend is likely to halt, continue or reverse: given the usual presumption that economic agents are on balance risk averse, the shock is likely to delay spending decisions until things settle down.

These considerations cast doubt on whether the immediate impact of the lower oil price on the world economy as a whole will be beneficial; and they suggest that even for a net oil importer, such as the OECD, the benefit to real income from the terms-of-trade improvements may be transformed only slowly into increased activity.

A major factor determining the reaction of the OECD economy to recent oil market developments is likely to be the policy response in the major countries. Given that the overriding preoccupation has for many years been the defeat of inflation, a windfall reduction in the price level has given governments a choice between, at one extreme, tightening the nominal stance of policy so as to ensure both that the immediate disinflationary gain is permanent and that the pressure for further gains is sustained; or, at the other, leaving the nominal framework untouched, thereby allowing scope for an expansion of real activity, with the inflation outlook certainly no worse than it was before the windfall and in the expectation that it might be better, if pay settlements were to respond favourably to the initial drop in prices.

In practice, no government has chosen the first of these extremes. Most have veered towards the second, although some have taken the opportunity to raise indirect taxes (thereby partially offsetting the effect on the price level of cheaper oil) in order to improve their budgetary position. Reduced inflation and lower interest rates, both now in evidence, should, together with improved profitability, provide a stimulus from the supply side to supplement any demand effects. The overall effect will be the greater, the more confident people have become about the sustainability of the present phase of disinflationary expansion.

Turning now to exchange rates, the realignment amounts to a sizeable relative price shift within the OECD, together with a probably modest favourable shift in the OECD's terms of trade *vis-à-vis* the rest of the world, more countries of which will have moved down with the dollar than up with the yen or the D-mark. Within the OECD, the benefit of the realignment is likely to be progress towards a more sustainable pattern of current accounts. Improvement will not be immediate because of the J-curve. Nor can the realignment be expected necessarily to redress present imbalances completely: it is widely acknowledged that other adjustments, such as a reduction in the US fiscal deficit and a correction in Japan's domestic savings/investment imbalance, are also needed. But the realignment does help, and any move towards better external balance among the major countries should be conducive to lower interest rates and steady growth.

Let me now summarize what I have been saying so far. The OECD economy has, at least until quite recently, been enjoying steady, if unspectacular, growth since 1982, with inflation declining more satisfactorily than unemployment. The cautious tone of current policy accounts for this performance.

The lower oil price should further depress inflation and, along with the new pattern of exchange rates, should serve to stimulate activity, although the immediate impact effect on activity could go the other way. Let us now turn to consider recent performance and the actual outlook in a bit more detail.

In a number of forecasts released during the second quarter of 1986 (e.g. those of the IMF, the OECD and the Bank of England) there has been a broad consensus that the OECD area outlook has improved somewhat since the autumn of 1985, particularly in the sense that the various and substantial risks surrounding the central case forecasts are considered to have been reduced. For the seven major countries the consensus suggests real GNP growth of 3 per cent per annum for both 1986 and 1987, with inflation falling below 3 per cent. These forecasts were based on oil price assumptions around $15–20 per barrel; and if they had, say, been conducted on the basis of an oil price steady at around $10 per barrel, it seems likely that the growth forecast might have been closer to 4 per cent per annum and that for inflation well below 2 per cent. The optimism at that time in regard to activity stemmed not only from oil and exchange rate developments *per se*, but also from the associated recent reductions in interest rates. Together with the fall in the dollar, falling interest rates significantly improve the positions of indebted countries. And those not exporting oil may be able to increase their imports further. But the forecasts contained little prospect of the major external imbalances within the OECD being corrected: at best the US current deficit might mark time (unless the Administration effected more sizeable reductions in the fiscal deficit than are currently in prospect) while the surpluses of Japan and West Germany would grow in the short term as a result of terms-of-trade and J-curve effects.

There are no more recent major forecasts available for the major countries as a group but you will probably, like me, have sensed an air of disappointment at some of the activity indicators for various countries that have been released over the summer of 1986, by implication casting doubt on the likelihood of realizing 3 per cent growth this year, let alone 4 per cent. In this vein a number of individual country forecasts have also been less bullish of late.

In the United States, growth was at an annual rate of only 2.5 per cent in the first half of 1986, with expenditure in the energy sector down sharply, net trade not yet showing much response to the more competitive exchange rate, and some investment spending perhaps being delayed until the promised tax reform package became clearer. None of these factors is likely to be a continuing depressant to the rate of growth, but there is concern that prospects are hindered by slow growth of demand from other countries despite the more competitive dollar. The US Administration seems confident that, helped by the exchange rate, cheaper energy and lower interest rates, growth will be stronger in the current half-year, although the earlier forecast of 4 per cent for the year as a whole has now been reduced to 3.2 per cent. The Federal Reserve is somewhat less optimistic, suggesting 2.5–3.0 per cent for the year. Official forecasts for growth in 1987 range from 3 per cent to 4.25 per cent, with the likelihood of some pick-up in inflation as exceptionally favourable factors recede and dollar depreciation works through.

In Europe, too, there is no firm reason to believe that the shortfalls from forecast activity in the first half of 1986 have been due to other than temporary influences, such as the severe winter weather that hit West Germany in particular. But these set-backs mean that earlier forecasts for the year as a whole may not be achieved: to expect West German growth of 3 per cent year on year appears, on present evidence, to require a highly optimistic view of the second half.

The evidence from Japan is also rather disappointing. The Japanese economy is driven very much by exports. When export growth fades, as it appears now to be doing under the influence of the sharp appreciation of the yen, domestic demand is not easily induced to fill the gap in domestic activity, nor to provide the much needed stimulus to imports. Of course, lower interest rates, already in place, may help.

On balance I tend to share the feeling that emerges from the preceding remarks, that 1986 as a whole may turn out to be less buoyant for the OECD than forecasters earlier predicted. The surplus optimism stemmed, I suspect, partly from failure to appreciate the magnitude of the potentially adverse impact effect of shocks, in particular their various financial effects, and partly perhaps from a failure to allow sufficiently for the normal time-lags between oil deals and deliveries, for divergences between quoted spot prices and average effective prices. But the set-back to the OECD economy might even now be behind us, with the prospect of reasonable growth into 1987 and beyond still intact. We simply do not know.

But in looking beyond the fairly short-term horizon one moves on from facing essentially conjunctural issues to addressing some fundamental structural questions. The importance of a particular oil price or exchange rate constellation recedes.

In this somewhat longer-term context one is inevitably confronted with questions about the sustainability of present external imbalances (notably those of the USA, Japan and West Germany) and their domestic counterparts, the savings/investment imbalances (negative in the USA, largely on account of the public sector, positive in Japan and West Germany, largely on account of the private sector), and whether these pose a threat to the broader world economy. It is one thing to identify weaknesses in the world economic situation, but quite another to find a remedy or, in particular, to determine what contribution active policy can or should make.

A continuing focus of criticism is the US fiscal deficit. It has been identified as a significant factor explaining high real interest rates around the world, in that the associated strong dollar has forced other countries to raise interest rates to limit the depreciation of their own currencies. Nominal rates, especially long-term ones, have fallen under a US lead over the past year or so, but much of the fall reflects better inflation prospects and the fall in real rates may be rather modest. To the extent that real US rates have eased, it may reflect their increased determination to tackle the fiscal deficit, but markets will wish to see words converted to action before too long if the tendency for lower real rates is to persist. At the same time, however, one can sympathize with the US view that, whatever the rights or wrongs of the underlying situation, the correction of their twin fiscal and external deficits needs help from abroad in the guise of stronger demand for US exports. Depreciation alone may not suffice, so the USA is understandably looking for buoyancy in other economies.

As I noted earlier, the apparent slow-down in the OECD area in the first half of 1986 may turn out to have been no more than a pause. If, however, it transpires that we are really moving into a prolonged recession, the question of appropriate policy responses will increasingly come to the fore. Few would nowadays dispute the desirability of continuing to set policy in a medium-term framework designed to minimize inflation and essentially to allow the private sector, by fulfilling its potential, to lead the way in growth. This philosophy, preached more than pursued by the US Administration, rejects fine-tuning in a short-term context, but does not rule out – indeed it requires – adjustments where necessary to keep to designated medium-term paths. The problem is, of course, to identify whether a particular departure from the selected path of a fiscal or monetary indicator is a random element that should be ignored, a lasting deviation that needs correction, or a signal of some structural or institutional change that requires that indicator to be either reset or discarded.

It is within this sort of framework that one should analyse the many calls currently being made on the governments of West Germany and Japan to stimulate their economies. Have their fiscal positions become unintentionally tight? Has West Germany's target monetary aggregate become aberrant for some structural reason (as with UK and US experience) with the result that monetary policy is unintentionally tight? I do not believe there is enough evidence to support affirmative answers to these propositions, but we are now entering a critical period during which a clearer picture should emerge. In sum, in an era when we are all preaching fiscal rectitude and monetary caution it would be both unwise and hypocritical to urge a general administered stimulus at the first sign of slow-down, unless it could assuredly be accomplished without jeopardizing counter-inflationary objectives.

Turning aside from macroeconomic policy, it is widely acknowledged that structural factors at the microeconomic or even the social level often present major inhibitions to efficiency and growth. Typically, and rightly, these are normally regarded as supply side influences, but in Japan – by way of example – there are micro factors that appear also to inhibit the much desired expansion of demand and of imports from the demand side. Examples are tax biases that favour excessive savings, and non-tariff barriers in trade and commerce. But whether demand or supply oriented, there is a strong international consensus to the effect that economic prospects will be at least as dependent in the longer term on the removal of such rigidities as on any acts of macro policy. Given the positions of economic strength in which the West Germans and the Japanese now find themselves, there may be no better time for them to launch an assault on their own micro rigidities and biases, whether or not they succumb to pressures to reflate at the macro level.

I have singled out the USA, West Germany and Japan for special mention for the simple reasons that they are the largest economies and that each has its own rather obvious problem of a huge external imbalance and, in West Germany's case, its share of Europe's enormous unemployment. They are certainly never short of gratuitous advice. But none of us is spotless. Here in the UK we would be able to make a greater contribution to world growth if we had more success in bringing down pay inflation. The UK Government's response is a mixture of non-accommodating macro policies and efforts to improve the supply side of the economy.

I mentioned earlier that the period since 1982 is distinctive in its falling inflation rate, for which the maintained cautious stance of policy could take credit. I have also alluded to a second distinctive feature, namely the unprecedented attention being given to the supply side. I now note a third feature, which has emerged most recently – the renewed acknowledgement of the interdependence of the world economy and the resultant attention to matters of policy co-ordination and mutual surveillance. It is too early to say what fruits any of this may ultimately bear, but the general atmosphere is one of considerable determination to resolve co-operatively both the near-term and longer-term problems of the world economy – both of the OECD and beyond.

**THE IMPLICATIONS OF THE OIL PRICE
SITUATION FOR CONSUMING COUNTRIES**

Pierre Desprairies

Introduction

In order to determine the implications of the oil price situation
for consuming countries, we must first of all state the price
situation to be considered as a hypothesis for such a reflection.
First, oil prices will remain low or very low and will fluctuate
strongly, probably between $15 and $10 per barrel (in 1986
dollars) and perhaps even lower, until about 1990. Secondly,
they will then rise slowly to a level of $18–20 around 1995 and
stabilize between $20 and $25 between 1995 and 2000. The
reasons behind this choice are as follows.

Prices will remain low as long as the enormous surplus
production capacity – currently 10 mb/d or 40 per cent of the
international market in 1986 – has not been sharply reduced.
It will take between five and ten years for this surplus capacity
to disappear. This will stem more from the reduction in expensive non-OPEC production caused by the decrease in
prices than from any upswing in world demand, which should
be little more than 1.5–2 per cent per annum. The surplus
capacity will stay at this level longer if prices settle on the
higher side.

As long as the surplus remains large, the downward price
trend will remain very strong because, in the next ten years,
there will also be surpluses of natural gas, coal, and hydraulic
or nuclear electricity struggling to hold their own and creating
great competition among energy sources. In short, during the
next ten years there will be too much of everything on the
energy market. An agreement among the leading producing
countries and the major oil companies on what behaviour
should be adopted to raise oil prices should not be impossible
if prices settle below $10 and cause upheavals in some

producing countries and an increase in US imports. If such an agreement comes about, it will be a fragile one.

Except for the minority group of countries of low population density and high oil production, the world community as a whole is greatly in favour of the price reduction to revive world economic growth and hence to reduce poverty and unemployment.

The market will begin to stabilize when the demand for OPEC oil attains 21–23 mb/d some time after 1990.

Current oil prices are showing a temporary downward excess which is linked to the production surpluses caused by the excessive rise that had gone before. This is the backlash of the oil shocks of the 1970s. After five or ten years, the market will have found its footing again as well as a new equilibrium, with a price compromise reached between the various economic and political forces, half way between the crest and the trough. The price will be one that will neither kill off the market as it did between 1973 and 1983, nor eliminate production outside the Middle East as it is doing in 1986. In brief, it will be around $20 or slightly higher, a level that everybody now quite miraculously agrees to be a reasonable goal.

Is the Geneva agreement of 4 August 1986 a harbinger of the coming stabilization of the market? This is still uncertain. At any rate, the agreement can not be conceived of as a victory for Iran and the smaller OPEC producers over Saudi Arabia and the countries around the Gulf. The North Sea producers have not changed their stance. But Saudi Arabia achieved most of what it was seeking by raising its production in June–July and by threatening to push the price down to $5. By this I mean the quota agreement reached by the thirteen OPEC members, made possible by Iran's backtracking instead of continuing to block such an agreement, by the absence of a quota for Iraq, Saudi Arabia's ally, and by the maintenance of a quota of 4.3 mb/d for Saudi Arabia. The most important concession has been accepted by Iran because it is hard pressed by financial needs.

Obviously, neither the Gulf countries nor the leading oil companies that are the non-OPEC producers can have a drop in prices as a long-range goal. They can only wish for a profitable margin. Their continuing confrontation results from an occasional concordance of their medium-range interests. For the Gulf countries, this means winning back a reasonable share of the market by weakening their main competitors, i.e. the oil and gas producers in the industrialized countries. For the oil companies, confronted with the collapse of prices, this means opportunities to buy up reserves in the ground at a low price and then waiting to produce them when the situation gets better. In this way, both sides are aiming at the same target, i.e. the independent producers in the United States and Europe. The Gulf countries want to take over their outlets, the companies their reserves.

If this *de facto* alliance of the leading Southern and Northern enterprises to force expensive production off the market involved only economic forces, the situation might result in two-to-three years of very low prices – enough time for independent enterprises to resign themselves to letting go of their assets. Fortunately for them, political factors will probably intervene to take off some of the pressure, as was the case in August 1986. The Gulf countries can not risk either forcing their OPEC allies to the verge of bankruptcy or revolution or themselves facing the risk of oil import taxes. Their lasting interest is in the maintenance of reasonably high prices. If excessive concentration in the oil industry becomes worrisome to public opinion or if the increase in imports awakens the reflex of self-sufficiency in energy, the US Government will have to come to the aid of independent oil companies by means of tax or customs protection.

The outcome of the Geneva meeting will probably be an episode of stabilization in the chaotic years of surplus production capacity. The reabsorption of this excess capacity will be accompanied by jumbled and unpredictable interventions by economic and political forces acting sometimes in parallel and sometimes in opposite directions, pushing prices sometimes downwards and sometimes upwards. At any rate, this outcome seems probable. Unless governments decide to protect the most costly fields, which would prolong the period of over-production, these fields will be mothballed in the years to come. Their shut-down, combined with the progessive increase in demand, should result in bringing world prices to an equilibrium level.

Consequences of this Situation for Consuming Countries

(a) *Immediate Consequences.* There is great joy as a result of the current price drop in the oil-consuming countries, namely nine out of ten countries. This is justified in the short run. Each of the next few years will see $60–80 billion disappearing from the fiscal revenues of the producing countries as compared with the 1985 revenues, which should help the economic situation of the consuming countries, which will find obvious advantages such as an improvement in their balance of payments, which will be particularly welcome for the developing countries which will then be in a better position to pay off their debts to Western banks – one of the major problems facing the world economy. The benefit will also be great for the industrialized countries. As long as the price of oil remains around $15 per barrel, their oil bill will be halved, which for the European Community represents 1 per cent of aggregate GNP. Inflation rates and interest rates will thus tend to improve. For the industrialized countries as a whole, it is expected that the drop in oil prices should enable economic growth to become stabilized at a rate of 3 per cent per annum. International trade should be encouraged by this good growth rate, as should the demand for oil, which is the result hoped for by the producing countries.

Likewise, the drop will improve the profit margins of the refining sector. However, the improvement in this sector will not be sufficient to offset the losses of production, and the competition on the market for end products made possible by netback contracts in their present form should not lead to any lasting revival of the downstream market.

At first sight, the results thus appear to be very positive, but the reality is more complex. The drop in oil prices is a windfall in the purest form for the poorest countries, those that can be called consuming countries in the purest sense of the term, and which are condemned to remain so for a long time owing to their lack of even the most minimal natural energy resources, geological hopes of finding any, or financial resources to exploit them. But this category of almost desperate poverty concerns only a minority of countries in terms of their number, their population and their influence on the world economy. Most consuming countries have invested or plan to do so to make better use of energy, to diversify their energy sources and to exploit their own national resources. Such is the case for all the old industrialized countries, for all the new industrialized countries such as Brazil or Mexico, and for the majority of the other developing countries. The drop in oil prices will affect them from the standpoints of their demand and supply of energy, their national economic balances and, in the longer run, the independence of their supplies.

It seems certain that the drop in oil prices will help to bring about a general revival of the world economy; but it is not certain that the $60–80 billion per annum that the producing countries will stop receiving will be compensated to the same extent by the growth of international trade. The majority of the oil-exporting countries are developing countries, and most of their oil revenues are used for equipping these countries, in the form of orders from abroad. For four-fifths of them, the sum transferred goes to the industrialized countries for the simple reason that they are the main buyers of the oil sold on the world market. Most of this money will be used by the industrialized countries within their national boundaries. An industrialized country produces most of its own services and capital goods together with the consumption in which it engages. Hence, it is the domestic economies of the industrialized countries rather than international trade that will be stimulated. A large share of the reduction in pressure obtained by the drop in oil prices will doubtless also go towards reducing budget deficits and financing the wiping out of unemployment.

Likewise, some large consuming countries are also producing countries. The United States and the UK have worked out forward-looking economic balances according to which the losses that their petroleum industries undergo will be more than compensated by profits from the economic revival and the growth of exports. This is probable provided that prices do not fall too much below $15. But their petroleum industries are deeply affected by the drop, and the equipment and service industry is in the front line. The number of oil wells drilled in the United States in 1986 will be less than half the number drilled in 1985, and less than one-fifth of the number drilled in the exceptional year of 1981. The south-western states are in an economic quagmire that is striking for all visitors. Petroleum activity accounts for 8–10 per cent of the US economy. In the UK, oil and gas account for only 5–6 per cent of fiscal revenues; but a prolonged drop in oil prices would probably have an unfavourable effect on trade accounts and on the exchange rate. In Norway, where oil has grown to account for 15–20 per cent of economic activity, the drop in prices is being felt hard and has already caused one change of government. The Soviet Union seems to be by far the most affected by the drop in its export revenues, of which oil accounts for 60 per cent.

It is too early to make a full assessment of the effects of the price drop that occurred in early 1986 because of payment and accounting delays. The effects of the price drop will not be fully felt by producing countries and industry until 1987.

Will the drop in oil prices cause a reduction in world production? A survey of twenty-one US oil companies made by the API in April 1986 indicates that a price of $15 per barrel would result in a 2.7 mb/d drop in production in 1991, namely 30 per cent of the 1985 output. At the same time, natural gas production would drop by 23 per cent. In the near future, many wells will be shut in, but this will affect only small amounts of oil, and these shut-downs will not be permanent.

Other estimates coming from the world oil industry on the basis of a price of $15 per barrel are less pessimistic and call for smaller decreases in production of about one-half of these figures, i.e. 2–3 mb/d for production outside of OPEC between now and 1990, half of which will be in the United States.

The lack of accuracy is just as great concerning the effects on demand resulting from the drop in prices. A recent survey by the EEC forecasts that a price of $15 in 1990 could cause a 7 per cent increase in energy consumption over and above current forecasts, and that the increase in oil consumption should be from 7 to 14 per cent, resulting in an increase in imports into the EEC region of 1.0–1.5 mb/d. On a world-wide level, the estimate of the increase in the demand for oil between now and 1990 varies between 2 and 7 mb/d according to the experts, with the higher figures corresponding to the assumption that petroleum products will not be taxed in the consuming countries. This assumption seems rather optimistic given the size of the budget deficits expected in the next five years. Excise taxes on oil products will probably reduce demand. For the developing countries, which make up the largest potential oil market, the low level of the price of raw materials and the extent of their indebtedness will probably act as effective limits to their demand.

Other factors will probably limit the increase in demand. The market now offers only low-consumption and efficient cars and furnaces. Producers of natural gas and coal will not allow oil to take over their share of the market without reducing their prices. They have already done so in Europe and the United States. A probable effect of the drop in oil prices will be that competition among energy sources, and particularly between oil and gas, will become more intense. The competitive ability of natural gas is great in markets situated relatively close to production sources, i.e. less than 1,000–1,500 kilometres from fields, especially if transport systems already exist. The marginal cost of gas production is much lower than that of oil, i.e. about $2/boe, whereas it is $5–7 per barrel for oil outside the Middle East. If the transporter, often a subsidiary of the producer, agrees to a reduction in his profit margin, the field will probably be able to continue producing at $2.50/mBtu (c.i.f. the consuming country), i.e. $15/boe. However, if the gas price is $1.50/mBtu, as is now the case in the United States, there is no point in trying to develop new fields.

The industrial consumers that switch to gas during these years of turmoil will keep their fuel oil tanks, and will be equipped to use dual energy supplies, thus helping to prolong the instability of the oil market. At the present time, the only significant increases in oil consumption resulting from the drop in prices are the result of increased demand from installations already equipped for dual-fuel operation, i.e. cement works, electric power plants, steel mills and other large industrial consumers. The increase in oil demand resulting from low prices appears limited and unstable.

The marginal cost of nuclear electricity is such that all existing nuclear power plants should stay beyond reach because nuclear power stations supply to power plants at a price of about $5/boe. However, lower prices for heavy fuel oil and heating oil will limit any further industrial and residential development of electricity. All the same, if the price of crude oil is between $10 and $15, and hence that of fuel oil is between $8 and $12, the reconversion of fuel oil-fired electric power plants to coal will be delayed and the use of coal rather than fuel oil in various existing coal-fired power plants will be ruled out. Here again the gains of oil will not be durable. Coal from Australia and South Africa is very competitive. On the shores of Western Europe, its price is around $8/boe.

The 40–60 per cent drop in oil prices, which will probably be attenuated somewhat by taxation in the years to come, should therefore not bring about any dramatic upheavals in the energy market in the next four or five years.

With regard to consumption, energy policies will probably not be as strongly emphasized by governments as in the past. The drop in oil prices clearly shows that these policies have now attained most of the goals set in 1973–4. The restoration of normal prices for oil and gas is a basic element in deciding upon an energy policy. When the new prices are felt to be stable ones, the decisions taken twelve years ago will have to be reconsidered. But, as far as the near future is concerned, the equipment, habits and state of mind of consumers have changed in the last thirteen years: present practices will continue without the need of much stimulation. Consumers have become economical and wary with regard to oil, and there will probably not be any far-reaching change in the growth rates of energy and oil consumption.

With regard to production, the drop in the production of non-OPEC countries caused by the price drop should be slow. Between now and 1990 a gradual upswing can be expected in the demand for OPEC oil, which may rise back up to between 21 and 23 mb/d around 1990, but no revolution can be expected in the market. All in all, from a world-wide standpoint, the short-term drop will probably have largely favourable effects for all the consuming countries. It is by looking at the long-range effects that the wider consequences of the change in prices are to be seen, stemming from the reduction in investment in the production of oil and other energy sources.

(*b*) *Long-term Effects of the Drop in Oil Prices.* The drop in prices has already caused oil companies to reduce their expenditures for exploration and for development that has not already begun, since a large number of fields already discovered have a cost price of $10–12 per barrel. In the North Sea and elsewhere, ongoing projects are being pursued; but the price of oil would have to rise back up towards $18–20 for the exploration for and development of new fields to be resumed, and it would have to be higher than $20 for any return to an investment rate comparable with that prevailing in 1985.

Already in 1986, exploration and development expenditures by the oil industry have been cut by 33 per cent, according to a poll taken in June 1986 by Salomon Brothers among 147 world enterprises whose budgets for this sector had been reduced from $49 billion to $33 billion. What is even more bothersome and is illustrative of the durable nature of these decisions is that the majority of these enterprises have made slashes in their exploration and production crews. At the annual meeting of the American Association of Petroleum Geologists in Atlanta in early July 1986, it was feared that some 15–20,000 of the 55,000 members of the Association might find themselves unemployed by the end of the year.

At the same time, there is hardly any company in good financial health that is not more or less openly talking about the possibility of buying up reserves in the ground belonging to small companies that find themselves in difficulty because of the drop in prices, especially in the United States.

During the coming five or ten years of low prices, the petroleum industry seems to be tempted today, as it had been in 1983–4, by what was referred to as 'drilling on Wall Street'. There is some cause to hesitate when, in relation to a production cost for new reserves which is often higher than $10 per barrel in the early years, it appears possible to buy up reserves in the ground at $5 per barrel or less. Most of these reserves will probably begin to be produced again only after prices have gone back up.

Such a trend would be doubly regrettable for the world economy. The money spent in buying up reserves would not be spent on discovering new ones: the same reserves would simply change owners. The renewal of reserves outside the

OPEC area would be halted – reserves with short lifetimes of about 10–15 years.

The attitude of governments in various consuming countries with serious hopes of oil or gas discoveries seems to be different from that of the oil companies. Brazil and India, for example, having learnt from the tough experience of the price rises in the 1970s, have given priority to the development of their domestic energy resources, especially of oil or gas, often under difficult technical conditions, involving drilling in very deep water offshore Brazil for example. The same drive has led the Norwegian Government to push ahead with the development of the large Troll gas field, a daring gamble which will succeed only if the price of oil is higher than $20–22 per barrel in 1996.

However, action by several governments will not make up for the back-pedalling of the oil companies in their exploration and development activities caused by low prices. It is estimated that between 1.5 and 2 mb/d of potential production capacity could be lost between now and 1990 in the Western countries provided that the price does not rise above $15.

Likewise, a prolonged slump in oil prices will certainly slow down the development of non-oil energy sources: hydroelectricity, natural gas, coal and renewable energy sources. This is already the case for various national projects such as alcohol production in Brazil and the construction of dams or the development of gas fields in a number of African countries. This will also be the case for gas projects aiming at the international market that are not near enough to their potential outlets. It is only in the Soviet Union that this may not apply. Following the Chernobyl accident, the execution of the Soviet nuclear power programme risks being delayed by the measures being taken to improve safety equipment, and the current levelling off of domestic oil and coal production leaves the Soviet authorities little choice but to develop natural gas production for the domestic and international markets. This is one of the reasons that leads one to suspect that the struggle for the export market of gas and oil could be acute in the coming years.

Around 1995, if the price of oil has not risen above $15 per barrel, it seems ineluctable that, because of the non-renewal of reserves in most countries in the world, the Middle East will again become the unrivalled centre of world oil production. Will the dependence of consuming countries on the Middle East again reach the level of 65 per cent as it did in the early 1970s, leading to the crisis of 1973? What seems probable today is that the return to this dependence will take place gradually and that it will not appear until shortly before 1995. Between now and then, the consuming countries will have enough time to see how the new situation develops, and decide what to do.

What Should be Done?

If dependence on the Middle East reappears during the 1990s, it will be different from that in the early 1970s. Let us suppose that, in the autumn of 1992, demand for OPEC oil has risen to around 23–24 mb/d, for a production capacity of 27–28 mb/d, and that the organization decides to raise the price from $22 to the 1985 level, $28, in a single jump or by stages spread out over one or two years. Things would not turn out as they did in 1973.

First of all, with a price of $28, oil production would increase quickly. A careful distinction must be made between the *production surplus*, which is the amount in fact sold over and above the normal demand, estimated today at 2 mb/d, which is the visible tip of the iceberg, and the *surplus of production capacity*, which is the submerged portion, currently 8 mb/d, corresponding to closed faucets on equipped fields. If the production surplus decreases because the demand increases, or because the lifetime of some fields has ended, then everything is fine, because the iceberg is melting. But if the decrease comes from the discipline of a cartel or from a drop in prices that shuts the faucets, the surplus of production capacity increases by an amount equal to that of turned-off production: the iceberg has sunk but has not melted. It will melt, and the market will be durably straightened out, only when the production capacity decreases. A surplus of production capacity should last until around 1995 at the rate now forecast for supply and demand. Between now and then, a price rise would cause various wells and fields closed down in 1986–8 to be opened up again because they would again be profitable, and various delayed exploration and development projects would be resumed. Non-OPEC production as a whole would increase.

On the other hand, as soon as the price of oil began to increase, its replacement by gas, coal and in some areas primary electricity for use as a fuel would begin to speed up. We must never forget that about one-third of all oil consumed outside the Third World is still used as a fuel that can be replaced by other energy sources, and this proportion will still be 25 per cent of total oil consumption in the year 2000.

In short, if oil prices increase too much, the machinery to reduce oil consumption and to increase its production will start up again, almost by itself.

The producing countries know all this very well: indeed this is why several of them feel that it is in the collective interest of producers to maintain moderate prices.

Thus, henceforth, market forces alone can bear the brunt of the price and reliability of energy supplies. Non-OPEC oil, natural gas and coal can effectively act as policemen for the market. Should not market forces alone be left to ensure the reliability of prices for oil supplies without any government intervention?

For another fifty or hundred years at least, oil will remain the most important raw material for the survival of nations. It will become more and more precious as time goes on, as it comes to be reserved for those uses for which it is irreplaceable. Common sense tells the consuming countries to limit the risk of putting all their eggs in one basket by relying too heavily on a region that is constantly disturbed by wars.

Pragmatism must be exercised in accepting a few minimal interventions by governments, not to counter natural movements of the market, but to soften any wild price fluctuations, to protect the solid nucleus of national oil, gas and coal industries, to limit industrial concentration in the oil industry if it results in the creation of too strongly dominant positions, to make use of taxation and mining rights to create or maintain national production levels at reasonable cost, to take advantage of low prices to fill up inventories, and to continue to encourage the use of energy-efficient equipment; in short, to prevent any return to excessive dependence on imports; and lastly, to maintain relations with OPEC, which are natural and necessary between a major supplier and a major customer for an essential raw material, both of whom would do well to try to harmonize their decisions when faced with a crucial situation.

Conclusions

To sum up, during the next five-to-ten years, the drop in oil prices will be a great asset for all consuming countries and for the world economy. In the longer run, if prices settle below $15, the drop would risk making the consuming countries once again overly dependent on the Middle East. But this risk would be limited if, after two excessive jumps upwards and then one downwards, the price should become stabilized at around $20, a level that would enable non-OPEC production to continue together with the necessary development of non-oil energy sources. If necessary, the governments of the consuming countries should encourage the progress of the market in this direction.

17 THE IMPACT OF LOWER OIL PRICES ON IMPORTING COUNTRIES

Edward R. Fried

When oil prices started their fall in December 1985, financial markets reacted positively, if not euphorically. This was not surprising. Most forecasts suggested that a sharp reduction in the price of oil would be a strong plus for the economies of the oil-importing countries. Lower interest rates, stronger aggregate demand and improved business confidence were all in prospect. To be sure, some thorns would be mixed with the roses – havoc in the domestic energy industries, weaker markets in the oil-exporting countries and additional pressure on those banks closely associated with oil industries and countries. And for the future, security of supply questions would be more troublesome. These were serious concerns, but even so, the net economic effect of a sharp fall in oil prices, taking all factors into account, looked promising and the financial markets reacted accordingly.

Nine months later, in September 1986, this promise does not seem to have materialized, at least not on the surface. The outlook for the industrial economies has weakened, not strengthened. Indeed, when OPEC arrived at its August 1986 production restraint agreement and prices began to recover, Wall Street and equity markets elsewhere paradoxically seemed to cheer once again, or at least to heave a sigh of relief. Was the earlier analysis seen to be wrong, or was price instability a destabilizing influence, or were other, offsetting, factors dominant?

To address this question, I propose to review what was expected to happen at the beginning of 1986 and compare that assessment with what has happened so far, trying in the process to sort out the reasons that might explain the difference. Following that, I intend to consider whether the experience of the 1986 oil price collapse sheds any light on the respective interests of exporting and importing countries and on the relationships between them, as these might affect oil markets in the future.

The Impact of the Price Collapse: Prospect and Reality

From December 1985 until August 1986 oil prices are estimated to have averaged $17 per barrel, some $10 per barrel or almost 40 per cent less than the average for 1985. Since the value of oil production constitutes 4.5 per cent of world GNP, so large a change in its price would be expected over the course of a year not only to bring about a sizeable redistribution of income between and within countries but also significantly to affect all the major indices of economic activity. Looked at from the viewpoint of the oil-importing countries, this was a sizeable economic event – the more so because it took place over a relatively brief period of time.

Compared with 1985, a $17 oil price would transfer $75 billion per annum from oil-exporting to oil-importing countries. Some $60 billion would go to industrial countries and $15 billion to oil-importing developing countries. The terms-of-trade gains would equal about 0.75 per cent of their GNP. It is also useful to recognize that, in the aggregate, income transfers from the oil price collapse would amount to only one-third the size of those that followed the price jumps of 1979–80, in the opposite direction.

What is less widely noted is that an income transfer turbulence of roughly similar magnitude would take place *within* the oil-importing countries. Consumers of oil and other forms of primary energy would gain while domestic energy producers and governments (through lower tax revenues) would lose. Here the incidence varies widely. The United States alone, as a major energy-producing country, would account for about half of this internal redistribution of income. The impact would also be substantial within the UK, Canada and Norway. On the other hand, countries such as Italy, France, Japan and West Germany would be virtually unaffected by this aspect of the new oil situation.

Inflation would be significantly reduced. The direct impact on consumer prices would be of the order of 1.5 per cent.

Prices of competitive fuels – notably coal and natural gas – would also decline, but by smaller amounts. Furthermore, the depreciation of the dollar, under way since March 1985, would mean still lower oil prices and a still larger reduction in consumer prices in countries whose currencies are not tied to the dollar. Also, cost-of-living adjustments in wage settlements would be lower. After all these changes worked their way through the system, the total reduction in OECD inflation stemming from the oil price collapse might total 2–3 per cent at the end of two years.

Interest rates would also fall, depending on monetary policy. Certainly the dampening of inflation would provide monetary authorities with more leeway to permit interest rates to decline.

Taking these factors into account, this type of analysis argued strongly that the collapse in oil prices would mean higher economic growth. Just as the earlier upward price shocks were likened to a giant excise tax imposed from without, so a price collapse should be seen as a tax cut. However, there would be offsetting effects.

A sharp reduction in sales to oil-exporting countries as their exchange earnings decline would be the principal demand-depressing offset to the stimulus from higher incomes in the oil-importing countries. Without going into the details, I estimated earlier in the year that the decline in export sales to these countries would offset 60 per cent of the demand stimulus from lower oil costs in importing countries. Stronger markets in oil-importing developing countries would take up some of this slack.

Another possible offset is the effect of the oil price collapse on the debt problem. Pressures on oil-exporting debtor countries would worsen; those on oil-importing debtors would improve. Both groups would benefit from the reduction in interest rates and from stronger export markets in the OECD countries. Any net assessment on the problem as a whole is bound to be a guess. My own view has been that lower oil prices would improve the debt problem in the sense that the direct and indirect foreign exchange gains to the high-debt oil-importing countries would significantly exceed the foreign exchange losses of the high-debt oil-exporting countries. This apparent net improvement in the position of debtor countries as a group could, however, be misleading. Intensification of pressure on several high-debt oil exporters – of which Mexico is the recurrent and dominant example – could threaten new crises that could put the international financial system – and hence economic growth – at risk. Or at the least, financial uncertainty could weaken business confidence. Averting such crises would in any event require strong, co-ordinated, international support on a continuing basis.

All in all, a decline of $10 per barrel in oil prices was expected to increase economic output at the end of two years by roughly 1 per cent over what it otherwise would be. This is about half as much as might have been expected if the effects were symmetrical, in the opposite direction, from what occurred in 1979–80 when oil prices suddenly jumped. Differences in OECD macroeconomic policies and in the size of the trade offsets in the two periods account for this substantial disparity.

In any event, at the end of two years most of the adjustments to a lower world oil price would have been made and in these respects the elements for the resumption of trend economic growth would be back in place. The effects on the different oil-importing countries would vary widely. Output gains would be expected to be much higher in Japan and the West European oil-importing countries than in the United States. Compared with the United States, oil imports into these countries are larger in relation to GNP and any fall in world oil prices, which are denominated in dollars, would lead to a greater fall in these countries' domestic oil prices, because of the appreciation of their currencies against the dollar. As net oil exporters, the UK, Norway and Canada would be losers on the oil account, along with the oil-exporting developing countries and the Soviet Union.

How do these expectations compare with reality? While the economic performance of the OECD countries so far in 1986 shows little evidence of an oil stimulus, the explanation lies elsewhere. A review of what has happened suggests that the main lines of the analysis are more or less intact.

Inflation is certainly down, much as had been anticipated. In the first half of 1986, the rate of increase in OECD consumer prices fell by 1.5 percentage points. Factors other than oil prices were certainly at work, especially reductions in food and other commodity costs and greater restraint in wage settlements. None the less, the drop in oil prices, despite lags before becoming fully effective, has been a major force. While a few countries have increased energy taxes, the general approach, most notably in the United States, has been to permit lower oil prices to pass through fully to final users.

Interest rates have fallen dramatically, by about 2 per cent since the end of 1985. While they are still high in relation to inflation compared with post-war norms, monetary authorities did not reduce money supply targets during this period to accommodate the decline in oil prices. Thus the new oil situation was permitted to exert its effect on interest rates as well as on prices in general.

None the less, economic performance in the OECD during the first six months of 1986 has been disappointing. Why have the benefits of cheaper oil and lower interest rates not been more manifest?

Time is one explanation. The process of disinflation and of realizing terms-of-trade gains works through the system only gradually. Furthermore, a downward oil price shock, much like an upward one, has its disruptive consequences to which adjustments, sometimes costly ones, must be made. Beyond that the explanation must be sought in other developments, most importantly in how effectively macroeconomic policies in the OECD countries, and the interconnections between them, are dealing with the enormous imbalances that continue to trouble the international economic system. A brief review of developments in the three largest OECD economies, focusing on the impact of oil in relation to some other factors, serves to illustrate these points.

In the United States, economic growth was satisfactory in the first quarter and then came to a virtual standstill in the second. Consumer spending was not the problem. In fact it strengthened, aided no doubt by the continuing income-improving effects of lower energy prices. Non-residential fixed investment, however, declined principally because of the drastic cut in capital spending in the oil industry. And in some areas the energy industry's problems spilled over into local construction markets, detracting from the housing surge stimulated by the fall in interest rates. In all likelihood, the bad news from oil has been front-loaded in the first half of 1986 with the effects from here on out looking more positive. The enormous US trade and current account deficits, however, continue to exert their major dampening effect on output, which greatly outweigh the stimulus from oil.

In West Germany, negative growth in the first quarter was followed by a strong rebound in the second. Growth prospects for the year are reasonably good, although not as exuberant as had been anticipated at the end of 1985. West Germany's benefits from the fall in oil prices are magnified because it has not had to face a slash in domestic oil investment expenditures and because the appreciation of its currency has magnified the effect of the oil price decline on consumer prices. These oil price benefits have contributed to the strength of domestic demand, which for the present has replaced exports as the engine of growth.

Japan's economic performance may be the poorest of the three largest OECD economies, even though, like West Germany, it stands to benefit greatly from the fall in oil prices. Economic growth was negative in the first quarter and may have improved very little in the second. Private consumption seems to be holding up, again in part reflecting the oil stimulus, but that has not been enough to counteract the depressive effect of currency appreciation on the foreign trade sector. Thus far, the Government has not moved aggressively enough in fiscal and monetary policy to take up the slack. It is possible that Japan's economy in 1986 may show the poorest results since the oil-induced recession of 1974–5.

In sum, OECD economic performance in the first half of 1986 would have been even more disappointing had it not been for the oil stimulus. Oil prices, after all, are but one factor in the total equation and even then their full effect, because of lags, has still not been felt. It can equally be said, moreover, that OECD policies failed to take full advantage of the growth possibilities from the fall in oil prices. An enormous US current account deficit, and its twin, an equally enormous US budget deficit, continue to hang over the international economy. Decisive US actions are necessary to whittle down these imbalances to manageable size and, at the least, such actions are now in strong prospect. If they are to succeed without causing a world recession, however, more aggressive growth policies are needed elsewhere in the OECD to absorb their dampening effects. The oil-induced falls in inflation and interest rates facilitate pursuit of such policies but so far have not assured their adoption.

A Free Fall in Oil Prices: Too Much of a Good Thing?

While the fall in oil prices has been an economic plus for importers, would this conclusion still apply irrespective of the magnitude of the fall? At the beginning of 1986 some economists scoffed at that proposition. One view is that because large oil price increases brought harm to the OECD economy, price falls, however large, can only do it good. Does the experience of 1986 provide any useful insights on this question?

When oil prices seemed to be in a free fall in the middle of the year, heading – some suggested – to the marginal cost zone for a large bloc of production, discomfort spread well beyond the energy industry. In the United States, the call for an oil import tax became more insistent, if not urgent. It is not difficult to understand why.

Experience has shown that industrial economies can not cope effectively with large, sudden, external shocks. This was clearly demonstrated in 1973–4 and 1979–80. In both instances, the sharp increases in the price of oil caused large losses in OECD output. This loss of output was much larger than, and over and above, the loss of income associated with the adverse movement of the terms of trade.

The fact is that the industrial economies were neither politically able nor economically knowledgeable enough to make quick, optimum adjustments to the sudden jump in oil prices. As a result, the loss in aggregate demand could not be made up by fine-tuning macroeconomic policies. The inflation engendered in the system could be wrung out only slowly, the more so because wage rates were not flexible. And capital equipment became prematurely obsolescent, requiring huge costs for investments to improve energy efficiency.

A price collapse, although an esssentially benign event for

importers, can have similar short-term costs. In 1986, governments in the USA, the UK and Norway in effect sheltered oil companies from a large part of the impact of falling oil prices, down to \$20–22 per barrel, through lower oil taxes. None the less, rig counts plummeted early on and the domestic energy industry, along with suppliers of equipment and services, went into its private recession. As prices threatened to go through the floor, uncertainties about the debt problem, domestic and foreign, particularly in the United States, cast a shadow, if not a pall, over otherwise buoyant financial markets. More generally, extreme oil price volatility and concern about a quick bounce back of oil prices and the resurgence of inflation grew more disconcerting.

At what point these negatives could outweigh the positives is difficult to estimate, but the possibility that they could at least exists. More importantly, and as a general case, experience to date suggests that more gradual price changes rather than price shocks or collapses are likely to require less costly adjustments for the losers and to produce larger net gains for the winners.

Relations between Exporters and Importers

To suggest that both exporters and importers of oil would benefit from gradual rather than violent changes in the price is not to argue that they can do much about it through joint action. Two major obstacles lie in the way. In the short term, a conflict over economic rents places their interests in opposition. Agreement on a price, let alone the means for sustaining it, looks on the face of it like an impossibility. Secondly, the longer-term supply price of oil is difficult if not impossible to determine. Attempts by governments to fix such a price path are bound to go wrong, and to be costly. Market forces, despite their imperfections, are considerably better for this purpose than the alternatives.

These two factors alone rule out an exporter–importer commodity agreement for oil. Anyway, the record of other commodity agreements does not indicate promise for such an approach. An agreement on oil, which in size alone would be unique, would never get off the ground. Nor should it.

Are there other, more limited possibilities for joint or co-operative actions to avoid or dampen potentially extreme price movements?

The systematic exchange of information between organizations representative of the two groups would obviously be useful. Going a bit further, understandings or better information might help to avoid situations such as that which led to the recent price collapse. If exporters had some assurance that price reductions would pass through to final users and thus increase demand, might they have moved more opportunely to reduce prices? Had oil prices fallen earlier and more gradually, would investment and financial reactions have been less drastic and in that sense less costly?

As to upward price shocks stemming from supply interruptions, the main defences lie in the timely use of emergency stocks held by importers, the avoidance of panic reaction by the industry, and a willingness of exporters with spare capacity to act quickly to reduce the shortfall. Effective use of these defences will require co-operation between exporters and importers, implicit if not explicit.

At the least, these avenues are worth exploring. They would neither constitute a grand design nor call for new instruments of government intervention. More than a decade of experience has demonstrated that oil pricing is important to the performance of the world economy and that relative price stability is preferable to volatility. It has also made clear that for the foreseeable future the marketing of oil will be influenced by oligopolistic forces on the supply side and by government measures – for budget and security reasons – on the demand side. These aspects of the oil market point to potentially important areas of joint inquiry to avoid unnecessary costs and to improve gains for both groups over the longer term.

18 JAPANESE PETROLEUM POLICY

Masahisa Naito

In this paper I intend to focus on Japan's petroleum policy, but I should like to begin with a brief review of the historical changes that the petroleum market has undergone, and then discuss the impact these changes have had on Japan's domestic economy.

Historically, petroleum was a commodity in over-supply owing to the discovery of large oilfields. It appeared to be a commodity with a downward price rigidity because first the major oil companies, through a cartel, controlled almost all oil production, and afterwards OPEC employed a distribution system by using the buy-back system of major oil companies. Following sharp price increases in 1973 there was a structural decline in the demand for petroleum by consuming nations. Since the beginning of 1986 we have witnessed a plunge in the price of petroleum. Today's situation is quite different in nature from that in the past, when price fluctuations were due to the continual discovery of new oilfields. Now fluctuations are being caused by the structural decline of demand rather than by over-supply. It has even been suggested by some observers that the oil market has reverted back to the situation that prevailed at the beginning of the century, i.e. that petroleum is once again a commodity governed by the market, and many are welcoming this change. There are many reasons, however, why the destabilization of the oil market should be a cause for concern. Destabilization of the petroleum market threatens to destabilize the economies of petroleum producing countries, creates confusion in the international monetary system by further exacerbating the debt problems of oil-exporting developing countries, and is also a serious threat to the sound development of the world economy.

For Japan, the destabilization of the world oil market threatens to create acute problems, and its experience since the first oil crisis of 1973 makes Japan wary of making long-term commitments in an unstable market. That Japan's economy is particularly sensitive to changes in the world petroleum market is evidenced by several facts: Japan is the largest importer of crude oil, the second-largest importer of petroleum products, and, after the United States and the Soviet Union, the third-largest consumer of petroleum in the world.

Petroleum is the primary energy source for Japan, accounting for 57 per cent of the energy supply, while coal and nuclear power supply only 19 and 9.5 per cent of Japan's needs, respectively. According to one Government estimate, in the year 2000 petroleum will still account for 42 per cent of Japan's energy consumption. Furthermore, Japan's petroleum supply base is extremely fragile and highly vulnerable to disruption since it imports 99.7 per cent of its crude oil and most of it comes from a limited number of geographic regions.

The experiences of the first and second oil crises highlighted the fragility of the energy supply and demand structure in the Japanese economy and made us aware of the danger this poses to sound economic development. Overcoming this vulnerability in the near future, therefore, is of the greatest importance to Japan.

Thus, it is clear that price trends in the petroleum market pose a serious threat to the Japanese economy. Since the sharp rise in petroleum prices following the first oil crisis in 1973, Japan has attempted to overcome its inherent energy limitations. Between 1973 and 1984, Japan's GNP increased by 53 per cent and the index of industrial production increased by 38 per cent while the increase of total energy demand remained at 7 per cent and energy demand in mining and manufacturing industries decreased by 11 per cent.

This record was accomplished both through nation-wide conservation, and through the efforts of industries to improve energy efficiency and thereby conserve energy. Other factors that contributed to the decline in energy demand were a shift away from energy-intensive industries and the development of energy-saving industries such as high technology and service industries.

In 1970, energy-intensive industries accounted for 17.9 per

cent of industrial production, but in 1984 that figure dropped to 14.5 per cent. In comparison, energy-saving industries such as the electronics and information industries and service industries increased their share of the industrial sector from 42.7 to 53.7 per cent.

Although these efforts towards structural conversion have brought results, energy prices continue to be one of the major factors, along with wages, that regulate the direction of economic activities in Japan. From our point of view, violent price fluctuations create confusion in the economy and jeopardize the well-being of the entire society. On the one hand, excessive price hikes of petroleum give rise to considerable adjustments in cost, in terms of employment, in both the national and regional economies, since they have an impact that can not be dealt with on a short-term basis by industries with high energy consumption. On the other hand, excessive sluggishness in crude oil prices tends to undermine the goal of the conversion of the industrial structure, since achieving the latter requires time.

A further problem is that a decline in petroleum prices accelerates the pressure towards a stronger yen, reflecting Japan's strong dependence on imported petroleum. At the same time, major price declines have a destabilizing effect through the increase in Japan's trade surplus which results from a reduction in the amount paid for imported crude petroleum.

I think it is clear from what I have said so far that I believe that stabilization of the petroleum market is indispensable for creating and maintaining a sound industrial structure and hence a sound economy in Japan. Having said this, however, I do not subscribe to the view that the lower the price of petroleum the better. There are three reasons why a long-term unreasonable decline in petroleum prices is not desirable:

(a) Low prices reduce the incentive to develop new petroleum supplies.
(b) Low oil prices tend to cause stagnation in the development of alternative energy sources.
(c) Low prices gradually generate conditions of uncertainty and volatility in the supply and demand of petroleum.

Some argue that if the price of oil drops then demand will recover naturally, and an equilibrium will be achieved through the substitution of petroleum for other energy sources. Today in Japan, however, reserve conversion to petroleum does not always follow despite the fact that the competitive price against coal is said to be between $8 and $16 per barrel on a c.i.f. basis in the electric power sector, and in major fields of the industrial sector such as cement, steel and paper pulp.

There seem to be various reasons for this, but one crucial factor is the lack of confidence on the part of businesses regarding the stability of future oil prices. The uncertainty surrounding future petroleum prices is limiting the fixed investment of enterprises for conversion back to petroleum. Instead, businesses are maintaining their long-term purchasing contracts for coal. Unless confidence in the stability of the market is fostered, the recovery of demand for petroleum will not be as large as the fall in its price might suggest. We can not hope for stabilization of petroleum supply and demand without the future expectation of a stable, or at least predictable, price trend.

Today, the price of petroleum is low, but the supply/demand relationship is unstable, and therefore the price must be considered to be volatile. Over the long run, the inevitable depletion of petroleum resources means that the price must eventually rise. How this upswing occurs is the important economic policy question.

In the past, the major oil companies could manage and moderate price movements. In the 1970s their power to manage market adjustments dwindled, and the governments of oil-producing countries emerged as the price setters. More recently, the structure of the world oil market has changed because of the marketable surpluses of supplies. Now, the market seems to be more influenced by national policies. Each of the governments of the oil-producing countries now does business according to its own perception of the national interest, and in accordance with domestic political considerations. The supply side of the market is determined by the cumulative effect of the policies of governments around the world.

In other words, market forces are operating within constraints imposed by governments. It is a situation very similar to that of world agricultural markets, where the agricultural policies of governments of food-producing countries determine world trade prices as well as prices of food products within national markets. Despite the efforts of many governments over many years, no good solution has yet been found to reduce the role of governments in world agricultural trade, and to liberalize world markets. Likewise, there does not seem to be any easy way to make oil markets work more efficiently so long as governments play such a major role in managing world supplies.

Because the interests of governments vary so widely, there is no common point of perspective from which they could manage the market successfully, on a continuing basis. It is currently very difficult for producer governments to manipulate the market with a common objective. Therefore, we must continue to rely heavily on market mechanisms to balance supply and demand, but in doing so, we must recognize that normal market forces may often be distorted by the cumulative effect of varying, and often inconsistent, national policies.

What this means is that it is not enough for governments to say that the market mechanism can be relied upon, because the market is subject to varying national purposes, and varying national political configurations – characteristics that tend to change from year to year in every nation.

In other words, market forces can be relied upon to clear the markets in the short term, but it is doubtful whether market forces give the right long-term signals.

Thus we must think about how to improve the long-term economic efficiency of the market, and this will require an improved dialogue with the governments of oil-producing nations. There must ironically be more intergovernmental consultation if we really want markets to work better. Otherwise, the market mechanism will be dominated by perceptions of present and potential government policies. Private interests will act differently when there is a recognition that governments are a major factor in determining prices, and that government policies are subject to continuing and often unpredictable changes. This means that more close intergovernmental consultations are necessary.

Japan recognizes that we must co-operate in order to find complementary policies that will enable the market mechanism to function properly. For example, it is my personal view that what is needed is a series of periodic exchanges of opinions on economic matters by the ministers of the major oil-consuming nations. Then, if approval can be obtained from other oil-consuming countries, these discussions may form the basis for continual dialogue with the oil-producing states, and provide each group with accurate information and ideas on the market situation. Of course, this is by no means to suggest the formation of a commodity agreement, which would never be successful.

Furthermore, in view of the extremely important role that timely and accurate information plays in the stability of the market, it may be useful to institute a system to make possible the provision of objective and accurate information on exploration activities, production, demand and inventories. Obviously, co-operation between the consuming and producing nations is a prerequisite for this. Japan is willing to deal constructively and flexibly with this issue by co-operating with other consuming nations. By doing so, we might be able to achieve the goal of a comparatively orderly managed market price.

Thus far my discussion has centred on international oil supply and demand considerations. Let me now turn to a review of Japan's domestic petroleum policy. The basic principles guiding Japan's oil policy are to obtain stable and reasonably priced supplies of petroleum during peacetime and, at the same time, to secure the availability of petroleum during periods of emergency while maintaining a system that allows adequate and expedient allocation to consumers.

To secure its petroleum policy objective, Japan pursues several policies.

First, we believe that, in order to obtain a reliable and reasonably priced supply of petroleum during peacetime, it is essential that suppliers view Japan as an attractive and dependable market. As the world's largest importer of crude oil, consuming some 20 per cent of the amount traded internationally, Japan would seem to be in a position to exercise substantial influence in crude oil market conditions through its procurement practices. But the current situation is that oil market conditions are set in Europe and tend to be presented to Japan as given, thus discouraging any Japanese contribution to a market realignment.

None the less, Japan wishes to co-operate with oil-producing countries in order to achieve and maintain a stable market. Moreover, Japan recognizes that stabilization of the crude oil market can not be realized without socio-economic stability in the oil-producing countries. In view of this fact Japan has sought to establish a wide range of long-term co-operative relations with oil-producing countries in an effort to contribute to their economic development. In the oil-producing countries, however, there is some misunderstanding of Japan's policy goals and actions. It is my hope that we can achieve greater mutual understanding in the near future.

Another means by which Japan has recently sought to enhance its market attractiveness is through integration with the international market in petroleum products.

Japan has been adopting a so-called 'onshore refining system', that is a system in which crude petroleum is imported and refined to suit domestic demand. Although naphtha, heavy oil and LPG have been imported to supplement domestic refining, gasoline, kerosine and diesel/gas oil had not been imported, until recently, for two reasons:

(a) The scale of the petroleum products trade done in the international petroleum market around Japan is very small, and is not sufficient to provide a stable supply to Japan.
(b) The quality of these petroleum products is not good enough to satisfy the demands of Japanese consumers.

However, it is important to recognize that the conditions surrounding the Japanese petroleum industry are changing, and that the trade in petroleum products, such as gasoline, is expanding despite the slump in the international oil market in recent years. This expansion is taking place against the background of the completion of export-oriented oil refineries, which are expected to increase the export capacity of petroleum products by oil-producing countries. An agreement on a common approach was reached at the Ministerial meeting of the IEA in July 1985. This approach is to maintain or create conditions such that imported refined products can go to the markets of the different IEA countries and regions on the basis of supply and demand as determined by market forces without distortions. The Provisional Measures Law on the Importation of Specific and Petroleum Refined Products was formulated in order to cope with recent major changes in the trade of these petroleum products and provides conditions to promote the import of gasoline, kerosine and gas oil.

This law was implemented on 6 January 1986. The first ship with imported gasoline arrived in January. As of the end of July 1.418 million kl of gasoline, 1.152 million kl of kerosine and 468,000 kl of gas oil, that is about 6–7 per cent of Japan's domestic consumption, have been imported. These amounts are much higher than was originally estimated. Such a prompt response by the Japanese Government has been greatly welcomed by the governments of the USA, the EEC countries and some Middle Eastern countries.

Secondly, realization of Japan's petroleum policy also rests on establishing a firm base for its petroleum industry. Like the major companies in the West, the petroleum industry in Japan started out with a development division. The Japanese petroleum industry has a long history, beginning in the 1880s. Traditionally, however, it refined imported petroleum and imported petroleum goods. It did not succeed in developing domestic or overseas projects. This trend continued after World War II, and the ability to deal only with downstream processes became obvious. In addition, the petroleum industry's structure has no vertical integration since other enterprises specializing in development were put in charge of overseas development. Furthermore, financial arrangements in the Japanese petroleum industry are extremely complex because, in many cases, domestic capital and major oil companies are closely linked.

The industry also has a tendency towards excessive competition because of the large number of companies, especially in the distribution process. The number of gas stations, for example, has reached about 60,000. In addition to these factors, the management base of the industry has become extremely fragile because of a large excess of refining facilities caused by a slump in the demand for petroleum in recent years.

For these reasons, Japan is stepping up improvements to the petroleum industry through making some linkage between upstream and downstream companies, the rationalization of refining divisions, the grouping of both refiners and wholesalers, and the rationalization of the distribution system.

The third means by which Japan seeks to secure a stable supply and a reasonable price level for oil during peacetime is the steady promotion of petroleum development.

The world oil reserves that can be ultimately exploited are plentiful. None the less, since petroleum resources decrease with production, continued discovery of new reserves worldwide is indispensable for the long-term stabilization of oil supplies and prices. We believe that this is our responsibility in the twentieth century to our descendants in the twenty-first century.

As the third-largest petroleum consuming nation in the world, Japan intends to make reasonable contributions to this goal by utilizing her industrial, capital and technical power. To realize this, the Japanese Government is currently searching for fiscal and financial measures to encourage the promotion of projects deemed economically efficient. We are doing this in view of the reduction in petroleum development projects in the private sector. In doing so, we hope to create an environment in the oil-producing countries that fosters development, which tends to suffer in such adverse conditions, and to achieve improved benefits for both producing and consuming countries through a revitalization of the private sector.

Japan's petroleum policy is also designed to ensure that reserves are available in times of emergency.

Up to now, Japan has stockpiled more than ninety days' worth of petroleum reserves through the Petroleum Reserve Act, which prescribes that the private sector should provide ninety days' worth of reserves. We have also been promoting increased national reserves with a target of 30 million kl by 1988. As of the end of July 1986, there was a total of 142 days' worth of reserves on the basis of domestic consumption, which consisted of 105 days in private reserves and thirty-seven days in national reserves. Since the supply and demand of petroleum might be disrupted by political turmoil, steady promotion of reserves is essential. With low prices of petroleum and the consequent low purchasing costs of crude oil, now is a prime opportunity to promote reserves. From the standpoint of contributing to the stabilization of international supply and demand, Japan is also planning to increase her stock by 3.5 million kl in fiscal 1986.

Finally, the development of alternative energy sources for petroleum is a long-term component of Japan's energy policy.

For this reason, MITI has decided to implement policies such as developing technology and promoting the introduction of domestic and foreign alternative energy resources, as well as promoting the utilization of nuclear power, by investing approximately 230 billion yen of Treasury funds in fiscal 1986 despite severe national financial conditions. In addition to these measures for alternative energy, we also think it is important to develop and introduce a 'flexible energy system', which will enable consumers to have wider choice in selecting primary energy sources according to their price. Thus, this policy will contribute to the stabilization of petroleum supply and demand through the recovery of elasticity in the petroleum and energy market. It is in our interest to promote by all means the development and introduction of such a system, hopefully with co-operation from overseas.

I have sought to outline the main components of Japan's petroleum policy. Japan intends to continue the development of a flexible petroleum policy in order to stabilize the petroleum market, but this cannot be achieved by the efforts of Japan alone.

PART VI

THE PRICE COLLAPSE AND THE ARAB WORLD

19 THE IMPACT OF THE OIL PRICE DECLINE ON ARAB ECONOMIC RELATIONSHIPS

Ibrahim B. Ibrahim

Introduction

It seems rather odd to speak on the impact of an oil price decline after getting used to hearing about the impact of oil price increases, or the price 'shocks', as many authors refer to the sharp increases of 1973 and 1979.

Now that the oil price has declined very sharply in 1986, are we, to be consistent, going to refer to this development as the third oil shock? Most probably not, as many authors have already started using more neutral terms such as the crash, the plunge, the collapse or simply the sharp decline.

More importantly, would we be able to utilize the abundant existing literature on the impact of oil price increases to assess the impact of the oil price decline? Not entirely. More research and investigation are needed because of the lack of symmetry in the two cases. For one thing, the countries that would benefit from the oil price decline are in many cases extremely different from those that would benefit from an oil price increase in terms of their resource endowments and the state and mode of their economic development. For another thing, the impact of the oil price increase on one country will not be a mirror image of the impact of the oil price decline because of institutional and behavioural factors that change the conditions of reversibility for energy and oil utilization or for other impact variables.

This paper intends to assess the impact of the oil price decline on the economies of the Arab countries utilizing a large system of econometric models developed by OAPEC and ENI and which will be referred to from now on as the Interdependence System.[1] The paper will link the simulations

---

[1] *The Interdependence Project*, OAPEC/ENI, Rome, 1985.

run to a general theoretical background to enhance the value
of the results. Owing to the fact that Arab countries are
developing countries, and considering that they have varied
energy positions, it is hoped that the results presented here
will provide useful information on a broader category of developing countries with similar positions.

Initial Winners and Losers

A significant change in the oil price would have an impact on
the economies of most countries in the world because each is
either a net oil importer (NOI) or a net oil exporter (NOE).
The main direct impact stems from transfer of wealth, which
affects both welfare and income. Based on this impact alone
we can make a crude statement that in the case of an oil price
decline, net oil exporters would lose and net oil importers
would benefit. The opposite would be true in the case of an oil
price increase.

Considering energy production levels, its consumption, and
its trade patterns in the last five years, it can be said that
NOEs represent a significant percentage of world population.
Among the developed countries, the Soviet Union, the United
Kingdom, Canada and Norway are NOEs with a combined
population of about 360 million.[2] It is interesting to note that
while the United States is an NOI, it is the second-largest oil
producer after the Soviet Union. Further, it is estimated that
NOEs represent slightly less than 50 per cent of the total
population of the developing countries.[3] Among the Arab
countries, twelve countries are NOEs with a combined
population of 119 million or with 65 per cent of total Arab
population.[4]

While the oil trade position of a country may affect the
direction of the impact of the oil price decline, the significance
of this position in relation to this country's level of economic
activity determines the magnitude of this impact, especially

---

[2] *The World Bank Atlas*, World Bank, Washington DC, 1986 and *International Financial Statistics*, IMF, Washington DC, 1985.

[3] *Energy in the Developing Countries*, World Bank, Washington DC, 1980, p. 50.

[4] *Unified Arab Economic Report*, Arab Monetary Fund, Abu Dhabi, 1985.

for an NOE. Based on this criterion alone, Arab major oil exporters (AMOEs) would be among those most affected by the oil price decline.[5] The value added of oil is estimated to be about 50 per cent of their total GDP (with the exception of Algeria) despite its steep decline since 1980. Non-major Arab oil exporters would be less affected but, because of additional factors (which will be discussed later), the impact of the decline on their economies could be severe. Table 19.1 shows the ratios of oil GDP to total GDP for selected Arab net oil exporters (ANOEs).

Table 19.1: Ratios of Oil GDP to Total GDP for Selected ANOEs. 1975–85.

	1975	1980	1985
Saudi Arabia	0.72	0.64	0.46
Kuwait	0.81	0.70	0.48
UAE	0.75	0.63	0.49
Libya	0.72	0.65	0.47
Algeria	0.37	0.28	0.24
Egypt	0.10	0.21	0.24
Syria	0.20	0.13	0.08
Tunisia	0.12	0.12	0.09

Source: OAPEC/ENI, 1985

For NOIs, the intensity of the impact of the oil price change would be constrained by a structural relationship between energy consumption and GDP such that the main variations in the ratio of imported oil bill to GDP between one country and another stem from the availability of domestic energy supply and the state of economic development. It is true that this relationship is physical and not monetary as is the oil import bill, but price elasticities of demand, of substitution, and of imports would ensure that the monetary relationship is tied to the physical one.

---

[5] We usually refer to all the Arab members of OPEC as AMOEs, but for the purpose of this paper specific figures and results for AMOEs will refer to Saudi Arabia, Kuwait, the UAE and Algeria – the countries investigated.

Table 19.2 shows the ratios of imported oil bill to GDP for major industrialized countries between 1973 and 1984. This table enables one to make two points. The first is that, during a period of extreme change in oil prices, the ratio of imported oil bill to GDP changed at most by about four percentage points for Japan and Italy. Between 1975 and 1984 the change did not exceed two points for any of the countries mentioned. Of course, these changes are not insignificant but in no way can they be compared with the changes in the ratios of the value added of oil to GDP for AMOEs in a comparable period.

Table 19.2: Ratios of Imported Oil Bill to GDP for Major Industrialized NOIs. 1973–84.

	1973	1975	1980	1981	1984
Japan	1.6	4.2	5.5	4.9	3.7
Italy	2.4	4.3	5.1	6.1	3.8
West Germany	1.6	2.8	4.3	4.6	4.0
France	1.4	2.8	4.0	4.2	3.2
USA	0.6	1.7	3.0	2.7	1.6

Note: For Italy, West Germany and France, only crude oil is included. Thus the ratios are somewhat underestimated.

Source: IMF, 1985

The second point to be made is that the differences in the ratios among the countries in Table 19.2 can be explained to a large extent by the availability of their domestic supply.

Using the ratio of oil imports to total energy consumption as an indicator of the availability of domestic energy supply, we find that in 1985 these ratios were 59 and 55 per cent for Italy and Japan respectively. If we add to the numerator natural gas imports, whose price is closely associated with oil, the ratios become 69 and 64 per cent respectively. For West Germany and France, these ratios are 41 and 43 per cent respectively. On the other hand, this ratio is only about 10 per cent for the USA.[6]

---

[6] *BP Statistical Review of World Energy*, 1986.

Among net oil-importing developing countries, we find even wider variations. It is estimated that, in about 50 per cent of these countries, oil imports represent 25 per cent of total commercial energy consumption or less, and, in about 24 per cent, oil imports form more than 75 per cent of total energy consumption.[7] These ratios, of course, decline significantly for some countries if we add their non-commercial energy consumption.

All Arab net importing countries would fit in the last category as their domestic energy supply is virtually non-existent.

The Mechanism

So far the impact of the oil price has been discussed based on a country's energy trade position which leads to an initial transfer of wealth when the oil price changes. However, the final impact is determined by a variety of factors that could differ greatly between one country and another. Some of these factors will be discussed below.

(*a*) *Net Oil Exporters.* The decline in oil prices results in an automatic reduction in GDP by decreasing the level of oil exports. This in turn will lead to a decline in investment and consumption. The severity of the decline in these variables depends to a large extent on:

(a) the initial change in oil exports;
(b) the marginal propensities to invest and to consume;
(c) the accumulated wealth;
(d) the relative importance of foreign transfers.

The greater the first two factors, the sharper the decline, while the greater the last two factors, the smaller the decline. For AMOEs, as we have seen, the initial change in oil exports would be extremely high. However, because their marginal propensities to invest and to consume are relatively low, the decline in investment and consumption would be relatively smaller, and for those who accumulated a significant amount of wealth, the reaction would be delayed and reduced further.

---

[7] *Energy in the Developing Countries.*

These factors, it should be emphasized, play only a moderating influence on the extreme pressure facing these countries from the reduction in their oil exports.

For other Arab oil-exporting countries, such as Egypt, Syria and Tunisia, the initial decline in oil exports would have a smaller impact on GDP but the rate of decline in investment and consumption would be greater, given the same decline in GDP, because of greater marginal propensities. However, this may be partially offset if certain import restriction procedures do not stiffen or if net transfers and net factor incomes do not decrease. Whether any of these outcomes materializes or not can not be determined a priori, but there is sufficient evidence that they would. In this case, the severity of the decline could be even greater.

The decrease in investment and consumption would have a negative effect on the value added in the non-oil sector though this would be less than proportionate to the decrease in the value added of oil, thus increasing the ratio of non-oil GDP to total GDP.

On another front, the decline in oil exports would worsen the trade positions of oil exporters, which might lead to further pressure on investment and consumption, especially for countries with chronic balance-of-payments deficits.

The decrease in oil prices should, however, lead to a higher world oil demand which in turn would trigger a specific supply response depending on the production capacity of the oil-exporting country and its cost of oil extraction. Here we may distinguish three different types of responses:

(*i*) *Higher quantity supplied.* This response is expected in countries with largely unsatisfied production capacities and with relatively low extraction costs.[8] AMOEs fit into this category even though most may not wish to produce up to their maximum capacities owing to oil conservation policies. The increase in the quantity of exported oil would partially offset the initial decline in oil exports, especially in the intermediate and long terms.

---

[8] Note that the chronology could be first an increase in oil production and then a decline in oil prices without changing the nature of the analysis.

(*ii*) *Relatively constant quantity supplied.* Countries that were producing up to their maximum production capacities before the oil price decline would be able to increase the quantity of their oil exports only marginally in response to higher demand. The decrease in GDP would lead to a lower domestic energy consumption leaving a slightly higher amount of oil for exports.

(*iii*) *Lower quantity supplied.* The discussion in the above two cases applies to countries with unsatisfied supply or with vertical or backward-sloping supply curves. In countries with satisfied upward-sloping supply curves, the decline in oil prices would lead to a reduction in their oil production and thus to a lower quantity available for export. The movement in response to the oil price is not expected, however, to be down the same curve but rather down a new and less elastic supply curve. This is so because, in the new curve, fewer types of costs may be considered as variable costs.

(*b*) *Net Oil Importers.* A decline in the price of oil would lead initially to a transfer of wealth which would affect welfare and only partly reflect on GDP. The increase in GDP would in turn raise the levels of investment and consumption. In addition, the decrease in the bill for imported oil, by releasing a portion of the previously committed foreign exchange, could stimulate investment and consumption further, especially in developing countries with balance-of-payments problems. The intensity of these changes depends to a large extent on the relative importance of the initial impact which, as has been said before, is mainly determined by the availability of domestic energy supply.

The impact of the above developments on domestic demand and supply of energy in general and oil in particular becomes more significant in the intermediate term. The decline in the oil price would put a double pressure on the energy position of an oil-importing country through an increase in the demand for oil and a decrease in the production of domestic energy resources.[9] This means a higher bill for imported oil that

---

[9] The analysis assumes that the decline in the price of oil is not offset by increases in taxes, subsidies or tariffs. To the extent that this happens, the impacts would be different.

partially offsets the initial decline. The impact of the increase in oil demand on GDP depends on two main factors: the portion of the increase going to industry in relation to that going to households, and the marginal rate of substitution with other factors of production. The higher the former and the lower the latter, the greater the increase in GDP.[10]

Previous research on the subject had the objective of testing whether energy consumption could be reduced without affecting GNP or GDP. One of the approaches followed is to use the so-called Sim test for causality. This can be done by regressing GNP on energy consumption including lagged and future variables. The presence of future coefficients that are significantly different from zero implies a causality running from GNP to consumption. A similar procedure can be used to test for causality from consumption to GNP by regressing energy consumption on GNP. The results of these studies appear to be inconclusive, but tend not to reflect causality from one variable to another.[11]

As the data used were for the United States and as different results may be expected in the case of developing countries, we performed a similar test for five developing countries that differ in the degree of their development and in their energy positions. These are India, Brazil, the Philippines, Morocco and Kenya. Published United Nations annual data from 1965 to 1982 were used for this purpose.[12]

Utilizing the F test for the difference between the residual sum of squares for the restricted and unrestricted regressions, a causality from energy consumption to GDP was found only in the cases of India and Morocco. For the other three countries, a causality from GDP to energy consumption was found. While these results require more investigations that are

[10] See Morici, Peter Jr., 'The impact of higher oil prices on economic growth in the industrial economies' in Askin, A. Bradley (ed), *How Energy Affects the Economy*, Lexington, 1978, pp. 35–49.

[11] Kraft, John and Kraft, Arthur in 'On the relationship between energy and GNP', *The Journal of Energy and Development*, Vol. 3, No. 2, Spring 1978, pp. 401–403, find a causality from GDP to energy consumption. Their results are refuted by Akarca, Ali T. and Long, Thomas Veach II in 'On the relationship between energy and GNP: a re-examination', *The Journal of Energy and Development*, Vol. 5, No. 2, Spring 1980, pp. 326–331.

[12] *1982 Energy Statistics Yearbook*, United Nations, New York, 1984.

beyond the scope of this study, they do confirm, at least for some developing countries, that higher energy demand leads to higher GDP, and vice versa, contrary to the evidence presented in the studies quoted.

The oil price decline would also cause an automatic decrease in the GDP deflator by reducing the price index of imports. But whether this decrease would trigger a further decline is not very clear, though it can safely be assumed that the chain effects, if any, would be minimal and that the final impact would be smaller in magnitude than in the case of a price increase. This is a result of the inflexibilities in the downward movement of prices and wages and the lack of pressure on the monetary authorities to accentuate the initial price impact by a tighter policy.

So far the direction, though not the magnitude, of the benefits to NOIs from a decline in oil prices has been fairly predictable. However, including the indirect effects could make the picture less clear. Some of these effects are discussed below.

(*i*) *The impact on exports.* The impact of oil price decline on exports is a complex one. It depends on the nature of the product exported in terms of its energy content and its elasticity as well as on the mechanism of the general price level in the country involved. This is if exports are to another NOI. The exports to NOEs, however, would no doubt suffer because of the decline in their purchasing power. The extent of the decrease in exports depends on the strength of trade relations with NOEs. Some NOIs with strong trade relations with NOEs could be affected greatly.

Table 19.3 contains the average annual growth of exports of selected NOIs to the major OPEC countries (MOEs) and to the rest of the world during the years 1973–81, a period characterized in general by an increase in oil prices. This table shows that these countries' exports to MOEs grew much more than they did to the rest of the world or to other developing countries. It further shows that exports to MOEs represent about 10 per cent or more for all of these countries and about 15 per cent or more for many of them (including Europe). By inference, one would expect that these countries' exports to

Table 19.3: Annual Average Growth of Exports of Selected NOIs to MOEs and Other Groups. 1973–81. Percentages.

Country/Region	To MOEs	To Rest of World	To Other Developing Countries	Exports to MOEs/ Total Exports
Brazil	34	24	15	10
Cyprus	45	24	11	32
Europe	46	21	17	14
Greece	42	17	12	19
Hong Kong	29	23	19	10
India	26	15	13	21
Japan	31	18	18	15
North Korea	60	33	17	21
South Korea	56	35	25	13
Malta	27	20	20	10
Thailand	29	18	20	11
Turkey	58	14	12	32
USA	25	18	15	9
Yugoslavia	45	16	17	12

Source: IMF, 1980 and 1984

MOEs would decline significantly in a period of oil price decline.

(*ii*) *The impact on net transfers and factor incomes.* These funds are very important to many developing countries including some NOEs. While they come from different sources, many developing countries benefited greatly from net transfers and labour remittances originating in MOEs, especially AMOEs. Table 19.4 shows the development of these funds in relation to total exports for some Arab countries including oil exporters.

It can be seen that, as late as 1980, the two sources combined were greater than total exports for Jordan and Yemen AR or total non-oil exports for Syria. For Egypt the ratio of net transfers to total non-oil exports declined sharply after 1975 owing to political reasons, but that of net factor incomes, which is only partly due to labour remittances, increased significantly. It is estimated that in 1985 most of these ratios declined owing to the decline in AMOEs' income. If the price

Table 19.4: Ratios of Net Transfers (NT) and Net Factor Incomes (NIKL) to Total Non-oil Exports (X) for Selected Arab Countries.[a] 1975–85.

	1975		1980		1985[b]	
	NT/X	*NIKL/X*	*NT/X*	*NIKL/X*	*NT/X*	*NIKL/X*
Jordan	1.18	0.54	0.85	0.44	0.59	0.60
Morocco	0.24	−0.69	0.33	−0.29	0.39	−0.48
Yemen AR	10.60	0.52	6.26	0.79	3.81	0.50
Syria	1.32	0.16	1.64	−0.18	0.88	−0.17
Egypt	0.49	−0.02	0.12	0.34	0.07	0.23

Notes: (a) For Jordan, Morocco and Yemen AR non-oil exports equal exports.
(b) The 1985 figures are estimates.
Source: OAPEC/ENI, 1985

decline in 1986 is to remain, these ratios are expected to decline further.

(*iii*) *The impact on capital movement.* A sharp decline in the oil price is expected to change the trade and current account surpluses in favour of certain oil-importing countries. In the Interdependence Study,[13] it was found that the shift in the current account would be mainly towards some European countries and Japan in the long term.

The deficits of the rest of the world on the other hand would remain high. It should be recalled that, following the price increases of 1973 and 1979, despite the increase in the current account surplus of MOEs, a shortage of capital never materialized because of the recycling of the surplus funds. Whether the same situation would exist if the pattern of the surplus were to shift in the other direction is anybody's guess. This is not an insignificant problem because our investigation shows that, unless new capital is channelled to developing countries, their development progress will remain at a low rate.

(*iv*) *The impact on interest rates.* In the aftermath of previous major oil price increases, monetary authorities in Western

---

[13] OAPEC/ENI, op. cit.

industrialized countries in general acted in a conflicting manner. After the 1973–4 increase, a relaxed monetary policy was followed and the real interest rate reached a very low level and was negative in some instances. The reverse policy was followed after the increase of 1979 leaving the real interest rate extremely high.[14]

While it can not be said that this behaviour is mainly in response to oil price changes, it is a fact that it had a great impact on the economies of oil-importing developing countries (OIDCs). For instance, between 1981 and 1983, the bill for imported oil of the OIDCs declined from $61.4 billion to $51.5 billion while their debt service obligations increased from $71.7 billion to $95 billion.[15] Considering that the debt problem of OIDCs is not going to decline in the foreseeable future, it would be necessary to include the behaviour of the interest rate when assessing the impact of a change in oil prices.

(*v*) *The impact on domestic energy supply.* As has been said before, domestic oil production may decline in response to a decline in the oil price, though the downward movement would be on a new supply curve. This would also have a dampening effect on the production of competitive energy resources as their prices are expected to follow that of oil. The final result would be a transfer of wealth from energy producers to energy consumers, releasing unused factors to other sectors of the economy. Whether the released factors would lead to more efficient production or to higher unemployment depends on the ability of the economy to accommodate these resources without a long-delayed adjustment.

The Simulation Runs

Although the above analysis does not cover all the variables that would be affected by the oil price decline or their interaction, we believe it illustrates the complexity of the problem

---

[14] See McColl, G. D., 'Capital needs for energy supply', *Energy Policy*, Vol. 12, No. 4, December 1984, pp. 395–408.
[15] MacKillop, Andrew, 'Adjustment and energy: dangers of a demand-side obsession', *Energy Policy*, Vol. 12, No. 4, December 1984, pp. 380–394.

and the need for models to quantify the impact variables. It should be emphasized, however, that models have their own limitations and can at best provide estimates of the most important impact variables. The models used for the present simulation are no different. They are macroeconometric models for the countries investigated. They consist of up to eighty equations and are estimated in general for the period 1970–82 as part of the Interdependence System. These models are built with comparable structures and in general with similar endogenous and exogenous variables, a treatment that enhances their usefulness for comparisons among countries. The scenarios utilized to assess the impact of an oil price decline were formulated for the purpose of the present investigation.

The main assumption about the oil price was made in relation to a scenario in the Interdependence System called the Trend which is a fairly pessimistic scenario about world economic performance and international and regional co-operation. In this scenario, the oil price was assumed to remain at $27 per barrel until 1987, and then to increase by 5.7 per cent in nominal value annually to reach $42 by 1995. In the present scenario, a sharp decline from $27 to $12 is assumed in 1987 and an increase in nominal value by a rate of 6 per cent per annum thereafter. Accordingly, nominal oil price trajectories would be as in Table 19.5 in both scenarios.

The impact of the above development in the oil price will be assessed for three groups of Arab countries:

(a) Arab Major Oil Exporters (AMOEs). The oil production of the AMOEs is expected to increase in response to higher world oil demand and to compensate for some cut in the

Table 19.5: Nominal Oil Prices for Alternative Scenarios in the Interdependence System. 1985–95. Dollars per Barrel.

	1985	1986	1987	1990	1995
Trend	27	27	27	30	42
Decline	27	27	12	14.3	19

Source: OAPEC/ENI, 1985

production of certain regions in the world. In the Interdependence System, a detailed production schedule for countries or regions was formulated for different scenarios taking
into consideration reserves, production capacities, production
costs and declared production policies. The exception was
Saudi Arabia, whose production was derived after estimating
world oil demand. Based on this analysis, the production
schedule assumed for the national macro models in the Trend
scenario is given in Table 19.6. The same table includes the
production schedule assumed for the oil price decline. While
world oil demand was not estimated for this scenario, it can be
said, on the basis of other scenarios where world demand is
estimated, that the assumed production schedule for the oil
price decline case is attainable. This of course applies to the
total production and not to each individual country's production as the distribution could vary from the one assumed.

Table 19.6: Oil Production of Selected AMOEs in the Two Scenarios.
1990 and 1995. Million Tons.

	Trend		Decline	
	1990	*1995*	*1990*	*1995*
Saudi Arabia	360	400	480	560
Kuwait	55	55	75	80
UAE	55	58	70	75
Libya	60	77	70	80
Algeria	22	18	22	18

Source: OAPEC/ENI, 1985

Other exogenous variables such as investment and non-oil
exports are left unchanged. We believe this treatment is justified as the growth rates of these variables are assumed to be
low in the Trend scenario. However, if any bias arises from
this assumption, it will be an upward bias.

The results of the simulation for the GDP growth rates are
shown in Table 19.7 with those of the Trend scenario and the
historical period 1975–80. This table illustrates the use of
GDP to assess economic performance at its worst.

Table 19.7: Annual GDP Growth Rates for Selected AMOEs in both Scenarios and in 1975–80 Historical Period. Percentages.

	1975–80	*1985–90*		*1990–95*	
		Trend	*Decline*	*Trend*	*Decline*
Saudi Arabia	7.0	6.2	8.4	4.0	4.4
Kuwait	−1.2	2.7	4.3	3.1	2.1
UAE	1.9	2.2	4.4	2.2	2.0
Libya	6.3	2.1	2.5	4.8	3.0
Algeria	7.8	3.0	1.1	4.0	4.4

Source: OAPEC/ENI, 1985

The annual growth rates for the period 1985–90 are greater for the oil price decline scenario than for the Trend (with the exception of Algeria) despite the fact that the only major change is a decline in the purchasing power of exported oil, estimated at about 40 per cent in 1990. Similar inconsistencies can be detected by comparing the second and the first fore-casting periods and by analysing those for the high period performance of 1975–80, especially for the growth rates of Kuwait and the UAE. These inconsistencies are expected during a period of extreme fluctuation in oil prices as is the case in the oil price decline scenario or in the period 1975–80. A more appropriate measure would be the adjusted GDP where the real oil value added is derived by dividing the current value by an import price index while real non-oil value added is derived as usual. Thus real adjusted GDP = current oil value added/import price + real non-oil value added. Applying this criterion we get the results in Table 19.8.

These clearly show the severe impact of the decline in oil prices on the economies of the AMOEs. The annual growth rate of real adjusted GDP is negative for all during the period 1985–90 (except for Algeria). The smaller negative growth for Saudi Arabia is due to the assumed sharp increase in its oil production. However, if the relative change in both scenarios is considered, the loss would be around five percentage points or more for all except Algeria, whose economy is less depen-dent on oil. This is despite the fact that these countries would be selling about 3.3 mb/d of oil more by 1990. Adding that the

Table 19.8: Real Annual Adjusted GDP Growth Rates for Selected AMOEs in both Scenarios and in 1980–85 Historical Period. Percentages.

	1980–85	1985–90		1990–95	
		Trend	Decline	Trend	Decline
Saudi Arabia	−3.3	5.1	−0.6	6.9	6.6
Kuwait	−3.8	1.8	−3.9	4.1	2.6
UAE	−4.6	1.1	−3.6	3.1	3.1
Libya	−7.0	1.3	−3.6	5.4	3.1
Algeria	−1.9	2.9	0.3	4.4	4.6

growth rates during 1980–85 were also highly negative points to the extreme difficulties that AMOEs could face from a sharp decline in the oil price. The simulation provided detailed results about other economic variables, but analysing them would not be feasible given the time and space allocated to this paper.

(*b*) *Minor Oil Exporters.* For other Arab oil-exporting countries such as Egypt, Syria and Tunisia, the factors that determine the magnitude of the impact and distinguish them from AMOEs may be restated briefly. First, as oil exports represent smaller percentages of their total exports and of their GDP, the initial impact would be relatively smaller. Secondly, they can not offset the loss from the oil price decline by exporting substantially more oil because they would be producing up to capacity. They may be able to increase their oil exports only slightly owing to the lower oil consumption that would be brought about by the decrease in the GDP growth rate. Thirdly, a loss from a decline in net transfers and factor incomes is expected to be added to the loss of revenues and, as we have seen, this loss could be very significant for some countries. Fourthly, because of higher marginal propensities to invest and consume, the final impact on GDP would be relatively high given the same initial decline in GDP. Fifthly, as these countries suffer from high current account deficits, foreign exchange constraints are expected to put further strain on investment and consumption.

To account for the direct and indirect factors, two scenarios were formulated in reference to the Trend. The first (Decline) is to assess the impact of the oil price decline, and the second (Norm), the impact of the lower net transfers that may follow. The simulations were run for Egypt and Syria as they are the major countries in this group.

The difference in the growth rates between Trend and Decline in Table 19.9 may be attributed to the direct impact of the oil price decline, while that between the Trend and the Norm may be attributed to the indirect impact due to the development in AMOEs. These results show the severe impact of an oil price decline on the development of these two countries, especially for the first forecast period, as it is expected to bring its adjusted GDP almost to a halt.

Table 19.9: Adjusted GDP Growth Rates for Egypt and Syria in Three Scenarios. Percentages.

	1985–90			1990–95		
	Norm	*Trend*	*Decline*	*Norm*	*Trend*	*Decline*
Egypt	2.9	1.8	0.0	3.2	1.8	2.6
Syria	3.3	2.2	1.1	4.2	3.3	3.1

They also show that the indirect impact is at least as significant as the direct impact. The simulations run provides a very depressing picture, especially if population growth rates are considered. As the average annual growth for the ten-year forecast period would be only 1.2 per cent for Egypt and 2.1 per cent for Syria, the adjusted GDP growth rate per capita in 1995 is expected to be less than that in 1985.

(c) *Arab Net Oil Importers.* The initial impact of the oil price decline on NOIs would be beneficial as we have seen before. For certain Arab oil-importing countries, the indirect impact is so significant that its negative impact could outweigh the initial positive impact. To investigate this aspect, two Arab countries that have close ties with the AMOEs (Jordan and Yemen AR) were selected.

Jordan is affected through the decline of its exports and re-exports to AMOEs as well as the net transfers and net factor incomes it receives. Its exports to MOEs, mostly to AMOEs, grew during the period 1973–81 at an annual rate of 44 per cent, while those to the rest of the world grew at only 24 per cent, to reach 58 per cent of its total exports at the end of the period. It would be affected also by the decline of the inflow of net transfers and net factor incomes. The combined ratio of these two variables to total exports declined from about 130 per cent in 1980 to about 120 per cent in 1985 (see Table 19.4) and is expected to decline much further in a scenario of price decline.

For Yemen AR, trade is not considered to be a major factor in the intermediate future even though in recent years its exports to MOEs have increased significantly. Net transfers and factor incomes would remain for some time the prime mover of the country's economy. Despite recent declines, they were estimated to represent more than 400 per cent of total exports in 1985.

The scenarios for these countries were run to measure the indirect impact. For Jordan, the main exogenous variables changed were re-exports, net transfers, and net factor incomes; for Yemen AR, they were net transfers and net factor incomes. Other exogenous variables were either left unchanged or adjusted slightly to avoid inconsistencies. The choice of the growth of these variables is no doubt subjective, but any reasonable assumption that considers historical developments is sufficient to show an order of magnitude for the impacts of these variables, keeping in mind that what is important for the purpose of this investigation is the difference in the assumed rate of growth between the two scenarios and not their level (see Appendix). The impacts of these variables are shown in Table 19.10.

These results show that changing the assumption about the possible flow leads to a sharp decline in the annual GDP growth of these countries in both forecasting periods. However, being net oil importers, these countries should benefit from the decline in oil prices as was initially explained before. The direct way to account for this benefit would be through an oil import function. It is not clear, however, whether this

Table 19.10: Indirect Impacts on Annual GDP for Two Net Oil-importing Arab Countries. Annual Real Growth Rates.

| | 1985–90 | | 1990–95 | |
	Norm	Decline	Norm	Decline
Jordan	3.6	1.6	3.6	1.8
Yemen AR	3.7	0.9	6.1	2.6

treatment would work in the present cases as the relevant domestic oil product prices were not linked to world oil prices, especially in the mid-1970s. Regardless, the models utilized for these two countries have no explicit oil import function.

An indirect approach to this problem is made by comparing the transfers of wealth in both directions: the positive transfer from the lower imported oil bill, and the negative one from lower net transfers and net factor incomes. The results are given in Table 19.11.

Table 19.11: Positive and Negative Transfers of Wealth for Jordan and Yemen AR. 1987–95. Hundred Million Current Dollars.

| | 1987 | | 1990 | | 1995 | |
	Positive	Negative	Positive	Negative	Positive	Negative
Jordan	322	158	375	652	731	1,758
Yemen AR	58	118	75	626	113	1,849

Given the assumption made about net transfers and net factor income it is clear that the negative transfer of wealth outweighs the positive transfer as the saving from the lower oil import bill is only a fraction of the loss from lower aid and net factor incomes. The relative values of the above figures provides a rough estimate of the final impact on GDP in the Decline scenario when combined with the results of Table 19.10. The growth rates of GDP in Decline would be higher and thus the spread between the two scenarios would be narrower. The compensating factor of a lower bill for imported oil is greater for Jordan. But for both countries the final impact of the decline in the oil price is expected to be negative.

Summary and Conclusion

Since late 1973 the oil price has taken an erratic path: two sharp increases and a crash with a slow movement, though coupled with unstable market conditions, in between. This development had and is expected to have a dramatic impact on the economies of the Arab countries. In the period between the two price increases the adjusted real GDP growth reached high annual rates for Arab oil exporters. For AMOEs these rates were in general higher than 10 per cent, and for some they were more than 15 per cent. Other oil exporters, as well as some net oil importers, fared well also with the annual real adjusted GDP growth rate averaging around or more than 9 per cent for the former group, and the real GDP growth varying for the latter but reaching respectable rates for some members such as Jordan with 10.5 per cent and Yemen AR with 7.5 per cent.

This high performance was, however, accompanied by various economic costs due to inefficiencies, inflation, high investment costs, uneven sectoral growth and increased dependence on one source of income.

During the period 1980–85 that followed, the Arab economies witnessed a reversal of the past trend with AMOEs being most affected as their adjusted real GDP declined very sharply. While the high economic growth rates during the 1973–80 period may be attributed to higher oil prices, the reversal of this trend during the period 1980–85 was mainly caused by lower oil demand.

The simulated scenario of price decline reveals that negative economic growth for AMOEs will continue during the period 1985–90 despite the expected increase in the quantity of their exported oil. For other oil exporters the initial shock would not be as severe but the added impact of lower transfers would bring their economic growth to a virtual halt during the same forecasting period. The simulation also shows that, for some Arab net oil importers with strong economic and political ties with AMOEs, the indirect negative impact from lower transfers could outweigh the positive impact of a lower import bill, with the final effect of the oil price decline being lower economic performance.

The results presented, combined with historical development, demonstrate the vulnerability of the Arab economies, especially those of MOEs, to fluctuations in the oil market. Other scenarios in the Interdependence System indicate that MOEs can achieve acceptable levels of growth rates and reduce their dependence on oil under conditions of a relatively stable real oil price, given a positive atmosphere for international and regional co-operation.

The paper also points to the importance of variables such as trade, requited and unrequited transfers, capital movements, interest rates, and energy development in determining the final impact of the oil price decline on NOIs. The behaviour of these variables could modify to a large extent the positive impact of the initial transfer of wealth. In such a situation it is not always the case that what one group of countries loses from the change in oil price the other gains. This calls for long-term price and production strategies that aim to minimize oil market fluctuations and realistically to reflect oil scarcity. It is preferable if these strategies are part of a broader co-operation strategy whose elements include in addition investment, trade and transfers.

APPENDIX

ASSUMPTIONS ABOUT THE EXOGENOUS VARIABLES FOR SOME ARAB COUNTRIES. PERCENTAGE ANNUAL GROWTH RATES

	Historical	*Norm*		*Decline*	
	1975–80	*1985–90*	*1990–95*	*1985–90*	*1990–95*
Egypt					
NT[1]	7.2	12.0	12.0	0.0	0.0
NIKL[1]	CD	15.0	15.0	9.4	11.5
F[2]	13.6	4.5	5.0	3.0	4.0
XNO[2]	−4.8	4.5	5.0	2.5	3.0
Syria					
NT[1]	20.0	12.0	12.0	0.0	0.0
NIKL[1]	CD	−15.0	−15.0	−2.0	−8.0
F[2]	6.8	4.5	5.0	3.5	4.0
XNO[2]	14.4	4.5	5.0	2.0	2.5
Jordan					
NT[1]	28.0	10.0	10.0	4.6	8.0
NIKL[1]	38.4	10.0	10.0	5.0	5.0
RX[2]	25.3	5.0	4.0	2.0	3.0
Yemen AR					
NT[1]	20.5	18.0	18.0	0.0	0.0
NIKL[1]	45.4	15.0	15.0	6.0	8.0
F[1]	44.6	13.1	13.0	11.4	12.3
XO[2]	−13.4	3.5	4.0	3.2	3.5

NT: Net Transfers;   NIKL: Net Factor Incomes;
F: Gross Capital Formation;   XNO: Non-oil Exports;
XO: Exports of Goods;   RX: Re-exports;

(1): Current Prices;
(2): 1980 Prices;
CD: Change in Direction

20 THE IMPACT OF THE OIL PRICE DECLINE ON THE ECONOMIC DEVELOPMENT OF ARAB COUNTRIES

Abdlatif Y. Al Hamad

For almost two decades now, the Arab development scene has been dominated by oil. Oil has been a determining factor in economic development for all Arab oil and non-oil countries, as well as a great many non-Arab developing countries. This resource has come to play a vital and decisive role in world politics and international economics, a role in which the question of its price and supply patterns is of absolute importance.

The dramatic increases in oil prices and revenues of 1973–4 and 1979–80 have had a generally positive influence on development in the Arab world. Yet this did not occur without a social and economic cost. It is generally agreed that the recent dramatic decline in prices and revenues will have a major impact on the international economy of a magnitude not less than that of the oil price increases in the 1970s. It is usually believed that lower oil prices are beneficial to the world economy, but very low prices will, in my opinion, pose serious problems.

Arab oil-exporting countries achieved high rates of economic growth over the past two decades, and some of them were in a position to effect major structural changes in their economies and in the fabric of their societies.

The increase in prices in 1973 and in 1979 provided the Arab countries with major financial resources which were used to make substantial investments, both at home and abroad, and for massive imports of goods and services. Great emphases were placed on transport, infrastructure, telecommunications, housing and the social services.

The immediate impact of this was to raise the level of per capita income in oil-exporting countries. For non-oil Arab economies, conditions were somewhat different, and there was

no immediate increase in income levels, yet oil revenues provided an indirect impetus to growth as new opportunities for
exports of goods and services emerged. In addition investment
and aid flows increased dramatically. GDP in the Arab countries as a whole rose from about $71 billion in 1973 to $152
billion in 1975 and then to nearly $403 billion by 1980,
reaching a peak of $432 billion in 1981.

The most salient feature of the accelerating economic
growth during the last decade was the increase in gross
domestic investment throughout the Arab world. Though the
investment boom took place in the oil-exporting countries,
other Arab countries registered very high rates of investment
as well. It is estimated that total investments in Arab OPEC
countries rose from $9.9 billion in 1973 to about $26.4 billion
in 1975, and then to $74.8 billion by 1980.

The overall effect of these dramatic economic changes was
the development of new institutions and fundamental trans-
formations in the economics and politics of the area as a
whole.

The development of commercial and banking infrastructure
and lending facilities also became necessary, and local and
regional banks were established. But in my humble opinion
the most significant development was the emergence of
development banks which were able to channel substantial
resources for development projects at the national and regional levels. The Arab countries became both agents and donors
of their own transformation.

Between 1973 and 1981 a number of developing countries,
both Arab and non-Arab, became dependent on the flows of
aid, trade, workers' remittances, commercial credits and
direct investment from Arab OPEC countries. For example,
remittances of Arab labour within the Arab countries
amounted to $7.2 billion in 1980. The overall figure for remit-
tances from oil countries to all neighbouring countries was
estimated to be around $12 billion in 1980.

Private transfers, mostly in the form of workers' remittances, represented an important source of foreign exchange
for Jordan, Tunisia, Egypt, Morocco, and North and South
Yemen. Their significance can be seen in the proportion of the
deficit in the balance of goods and services they helped to

cover. In these six countries, whose combined deficit represented 71 per cent of the total annual deficit for non-oil Arab countries during the period 1975–80, private transfers averaged 52 per cent of the annual deficit, rising from 33 per cent in 1975 to 69 per cent in 1980.

On the other hand, concessional aid disbursements by Arab donors increased from $2.1 billion in 1973 to a peak of $9.6 billion in 1980.

Several new Arab donor institutions were established in this period and other, older institutions, such as the Kuwait Fund for Arab Economic Development, the Arab Fund for Economic and Social Development and the Abu Dhabi Fund for Arab Economic Development, expanded both their volume and their geographical coverage. In addition, Arab countries took a leading role in funding organizations such as the OPEC Fund, the Islamic Development Bank and the International Fund for Agricultural Development, which represent innovative approaches to development finance and international cooperation.

Between 1973 and 1981 concessional financial flows from Arab oil countries amounted to about $55 billion. This represented over 14 per cent of their total surpluses during that period. In 1981 this ratio reached 17 per cent of the total.

The rapid growth permitted by oil revenues did not occur without cost. The most important manifestation of this cost was excess consumption and spending in both the public and private sectors in all Arab countries, not only the oil-exporting countries.

This resulted from the way oil revenues were being realized. Oil proceeds accrued to governments and filtered through government expenditures to the private sector. Income was not being generated through payments to factors of production but rather through the liquidation of a scarce resource. Governments, being the recipients of these revenues, had a major role to play in the distribution process. Mechanisms such as high wages, land appropriation and credit facilities at low or zero rates of interest served to pass oil revenues to the private sector.

Another important feature of the role of oil revenues on the development process in the oil-rich Arab countries was the role of capital in their development plans. In developing countries generally, planning is closely related to the rationalization of allocation of scarce capital resources. Thus, the social objectives of development become conditional on an economic growth process that is determined by capital allocation. This basic assumption did not apply to Arab oil countries before this decade since no capital shortages existed or seemed imminent, yet the effect of these facts on development planning proved unfavourable in many instances. The case of Kuwait provides a good illustration of this point.

Kuwait's traditional economic objectives of enhancing per capita income, ensuring more equitable distribution of national income, diversifying the economy, developing indigenous capabilities, and providing aid for regional economic integration have been consistently adhered to. Yet difficulties in implementation have consistently appeared. Although the country has been a model of development ever since 1946, pursuing a rational development course, nevertheless, well before 1973 the growth generated by oil revenues was seen to be slowing down, owing in part to a near saturation in the country's absorptive capacity and to the lack of an effective diversification programme.

Though economic diversification remained limited, large outlays for industrial growth accompanied the boom in surplus capital, and the quest for quick results led to abnormally high investment costs. In the process of implementing the huge development programmes society was compelled in many instances to bear an unduly heavy cost, largely owing to the availability of large financial resources. Investments, especially in infrastructure, were in most cases excessive, and the cost of capital goods and imported skills became extremely high; this in addition to exaggerated lavishness in the design and construction of projects.

At the regional level, the seemingly limitless wealth and opportunities encouraged labour migrations from other Arab countries, leading, as we have seen, to greater dependence by those countries on remittances from their nationals. But current private transfers tended to widen the gap between the well-to-do and the needy in these countries as the inflow of remittances contributed to inflation and to the emergence of new consumption patterns.

Another result of these developments was excessive migration to the urban centres denuding the countryside without a commensurate creation of new job opportunities and social amenities in the cities.

With the start of the 1980s, the oil situation underwent radical changes. There was a great fall in the demand for OPEC oil, from a peak of about 30 mb/d in 1979 to about 17 mb/d in 1986.

The past few months have witnessed the world's steepest fall in oil prices, slashing the income of the oil producers by almost 50 per cent. Spot oil prices, which averaged about $27 per barrel in 1985, had fallen to less than $10 by the middle of 1986. In real terms prices have dropped below the average levels prevailing in 1974–6. The suddenness of the price drop, like the rapidity of the price rises in 1973–4 and 1979–80, is having a dramatic impact on the economies of the Arab oil-exporting countries, in particular, and on the large number of developing countries in general. For the main oil exporters, or even lesser ones such as Egypt and Tunisia, the last six months have been disastrous.

While aggregate oil revenues for the Arab oil-exporting countries soared in 1980 to $205 billion, they declined to $97.5 billion by 1984 and are expected to decline further to $77 billion in 1985.

The estimates from American Express Bank provide a guide as to the extent of the revenue shortfalls facing major Arab oil producers in 1986. Assuming the price of oil remains at $10 per barrel for the rest of 1986 and output stays at 1985 production levels, revenues are expected to decline by 39 per cent (or $8.7 billion) while a price of $15 per barrel will reduce revenues by about 28 per cent (or $4.5 billion).

The countries that will least be able to weather the fall are the high absorbers: those with large populations and a high international debt (Algeria and Egypt). On the other hand, this fall will benefit oil importers already profiting from the decline in oil prices. With oil at a price of $15 per barrel, it is estimated that the world's industrialized countries will save around $100 billion in 1986. The greatest beneficiaries will be the heaviest consumers; for example, Western Europe will save about $45 billion on its oil bill, North America about $20 billion and the Far East about $25 billion. In the Middle East, Turkey, which has the largest non-oil economy in the region, will save nearly $2 billion if oil is priced at $15 per barrel.

To turn now to the implications and consequences of the fall in oil revenues on Arab economic and social development, one must recognize that these implications are varied and complex; because the socio-economic effects of fluctuations in revenue have both positive and negative effects.

Falling oil prices have a major impact on Arab oil-producing countries, where oil still accounts for 91 per cent of their export earnings, or about one-half of their GDP, and roughly 70 per cent of government revenues. The most immediate effect of declining oil prices is the loss of export oil revenues that is immediately reflected in the declining government expenditures, thus affecting overall growth.

In 1981 Arab oil countries had recorded a payment surplus estimated at $51 billion. By 1984 the surplus had been totally eroded and gave rise to a deficit of $4.3 billion. The 1985 deficit is estimated to be $6.0 billion.

As a result of the further and sharper decline in prices of oil and a drop in investment income due to the decline in the interest rate and the running down of foreign assets, the 1986 deficit is expected to rise sharply to $26 billion for the Arab Gulf countries alone. If other major oil exporters' deficits are added – such as Algeria's, Libya's and Iraq's – this figure will be several times higher.

The future outlook for the balance of payments will of course depend on oil prices and production levels, but with market conditions likely to remain difficult for the rest of the 1980s the continuation of revenues at the 1986 levels seems probable. But a stricter control of imports may improve the deficit: the average propensity to import for major oil producers had increased steadily during the 1970s and the early 1980s, and it is 37 per cent higher than before the 1973–4 oil price increases.

Imports continued to increase until 1982–3, despite the decline in exports. When the downturn in imports eventually came in 1983–4, it was fairly modest – amounting to a decline of only 3.7 per cent compared with a fall of 9.8 per cent in the value of exports. But although this trend of falling imports was slow to come, it is expected to be quite rapid in the coming years.

The decline in oil revenues implied austerity budgets for the majority of oil-exporting Arab countries, which has had a substantial impact on the financial structure of government spending. Allocations for all the main sectors have been cut sharply, with the largest reduction observed for infrastructure (including transport and communications) and municipal services. In 1980 oil revenues were in excess of government expenditures and net surpluses were being generated, but by 1984 these revenues were able to meet only 56 per cent of public expenditure.

The surpluses of 1980, of about $60 billion, became a deficit of $33 billion in 1983. The average deficit in most oil-exporting Arab countries was about 20 per cent of the total government budget. This ratio is not likely to decline much in spite of anticipations to the contrary. Kuwait's 1986/7 budget, for example, has been cut in line with projected revenues. Total expenditures are forecasted to drop by 11.3 per cent compared with those of the previous fiscal year, which was lower than the year before. For the first time since 1973 (or even before then), Kuwait is projecting a real deficit in the 1986/7 budget. However, Kuwait's national foreign holdings will enable it to make easier adjustments to this situation than many other oil exporters.

A fall in GDP of these countries was a natural result of these developments. The Arab oil countries' GDP declined from about $331.6 billion in 1981 to about $289.7 billion in 1984, and is estimated to have reached $289.1 billion for 1985. As a result, total GDP for the entire Arab world declined from $432 billion in 1981 to $405.5 billion in 1984, and is estimated to be around $411 billion in 1985 (in current dollars).

In the 1970s and early 1980s private entrepreneurs and contractors benefited greatly from the ambitious development schemes in the oil-exporting countries. However, as conditions changed and policies of greater austerity came into effect, competition for business became fierce, and 'survival of the fittest' is increasingly becoming the *mot de passe* for the present and foreseeable future.

The short-run cost of the process of adjustment now under way could be very high for the private sector, especially for the contracting and banking sectors. From a medium- and long-term perspective, however, a tight, dynamic and more efficient private sector will emerge which is a prerequisite for a more realistic and sustainable future growth of the Arab world's economy.

The decline in oil production and revenues in the Gulf countries will without doubt impose a new phase of development upon the Arab banks. This phase will not be characterized by easy expansion and high profits as in the past, but by a more competitive environment, with much more attention given to strategic planning and to the changing financial needs of the area.

In the case of Kuwait for instance, a number of abnormal factors have heightened the banking problem there. Not only have oil revenues declined, with oil production slowing down to less than 1.4 mb/d in 1984 and to 1.06 mb/d in 1985, but the economy is also suffering the impact of the Iran–Iraq war and, of course, the uncertainty and financial disarray caused by the Souk El Manakh collapse.

The implications of these factors for the banking business in Kuwait are, and will continue to be, profound, as the economy failed to grow between 1980 and 1983. The years 1985 and 1986 have witnessed a further decline in economic activities. The situation in other Gulf countries may be the same, although the causes may differ slightly.

Over the last decade Arab Gulf governments have built the foundation for industrial progress. The public sector has dominated their economies through the domination of physical and social infrastructure. In the future, however, the challenge rests with the private sector, especially with its most developed sector, namely the banking sector, which should take greater initiative in developing small business finance.

With world oil prices depressed and the Arab oil countries' development boom fading, many Arab and non-Arab developing countries are feeling the impact of these developments.

With the drop in oil revenues, however temporary, the stability of countries that either supplied labour or received substantial financial support, by way of repatriated earnings or as aid and direct investment, has been seriously affected.

It may be several years before the full effects of the current oil crisis and the associated economic cut-backs within the Arab world are fully felt, but when those effects show themselves they could leave not only economic but also social upheaval in their wake.

For millions of expatriates who have benefited from and enjoyed the challenge of working in the Gulf, winds of change have begun to blow. This change will affect their future role in the region and negatively affect their own countries.

Workers in the construction industry are the principal victims of these changes as national development programmes are scaled down and large numbers of expatriate workers are released. Similarly, those in secondary industries such as catering, transport or materials supply, which depend on construction, find themselves in the same situation.

Secondly, the slide in the oil market has affected budget forecasts and development plans alike. Pragmatic reappraisals brought about by diminished revenues have led to many projects being reduced in size or cancelled. These cuts, in a market already under pressure, lend weight to the Kuwait Planning Ministry's recent projections that more than 25 per cent of today's expatriate jobs in Kuwait will disappear by 1990.

However, despite the apparent recession, spending remains high in real terms. The industrial and infrastructural projects now starting up are the corner-stones of national development plans and will depend, at least in the short term, on skills and expertise not fully available in the Gulf. Communication networks, process engineering (particularly in chemical industries), air transport, ports, power station operations and maintenance are areas where the demand for expatriates is still growing.

This may be the explanation for the apparent paradox that, although thousands of expatriates are returning home, recruitment continues from East and West – albeit at an increasingly senior technical level.

Developing countries ranging from Egypt to the Philippines have enjoyed a rising flow of foreign exchange remittances from the large number of their workers in the Gulf. Now, however, these countries face the combination of declining foreign exchange flows and increasing flows of workers who will crowd their already difficult labour markets.

According to some calculations, Saudi Arabia, Kuwait and the UAE alone employ more than 650,000 Indians, 700,000 Pakistanis, 750,000 Egyptians and more than 100,000 Filipinos. Some think that these figures are rather conservative. Other estimates put the number of Egyptians working abroad at anywhere between 1.5 million and 3.5 million, mostly in the Gulf states.

Estimates of the amount of remittances from the Gulf to the immigrants' home countries also vary considerably. For some countries such as Egypt, Jordan and Pakistan this income has been a critical factor in sustaining their economies. Egypt is thought to have got around $3.3 billion from this source officially in 1983 compared with $2.0 billion the previous year. However, real remittances were almost certainly much higher as it is thought that some Egyptians were bypassing the official banking system and converting their earnings on the black market. Yet in 1985 remittances did not reach $1 million.

The future for immigrant labour and remittance flows will be determined to a large extent by what happens to the price of oil. A further fall would have far-reaching effects though to varying degrees for many countries in the South and East.

Even if the oil price shows some small recovery, it seems clear that the jobs boom that developed as a result of the extensive oil-financed development programmes in the past is now over. Long-term prospects in this context seem dim for most South Asian countries.

On the other hand, the set-back suffered by Arab oil-producing states as a result of decline in oil revenues will have a detrimental impact on the volume of development assistance these countries will provide in the future.

Arab development assistance in 1984 totalled $4.5 billion compared with the record level of $9.5 billion attained in 1980. Taking 1980 as the base year, Arab development assistance in 1984 was 46.8 per cent of what it was in the first year, while ratios for the years 1981 to 1983 stood at 86.7 per cent,

61 per cent and 54.8 per cent respectively, reflecting the prevailing trend in recent years.

A look at oil surpluses and Arab aid suggests that there is a strong correlation between aid and surpluses. Surpluses have been declining at a very rapid rate in the last few years and have disappeared altogether in 1985.

This point merits further consideration in view of the great changes undergone by donor countries' financial resources: the total current account balances of ten OPEC countries went from an unprecedented surplus in excess of $100 billion in 1980 to a deficit of more than $10 billion in 1982–3.

Yet the ratio of Arab development assistance to GDP, despite its anticipated decline, continued to be above that of the industrialized countries though these countries will achieve a saving of $80 billion in 1986 if oil prices remain at the level prevailing in the first quarter of the year. The saving in oil imports constitutes a transfer of the resources from the oil exports to the industrialized countries. This fact has had no impact on the overseas development aid flows of the industrialized countries to the developing world.

Projections of capital requirements of non-oil-exporting developing countries in the 1980s indicate that these requirements will grow rapidly during the remainder of the decade. The level of net capital inflows required to achieve a growth target ranging between 4 and 5 per cent is projected to be between $147 billion and $206 billion by 1990. These capital requirements are equivalent to 1.2 per cent of the projected GNP of the DAC countries and much less than the resource transfers they would enjoy from an increase in oil prices.

Notwithstanding the dramatic decline in oil revenues of oil exporters in 1986, it is almost inconceivable that the three big Arab donors, namely Saudi Arabia, Kuwait and the UAE, will stop giving aid altogether. It is almost certain, however, that they will continue to be active donors for as long as their oil revenues allow. But to keep their aid flowing, even at a lower rate than in the past, these governments will have to draw on their current income. On the other hand, it was the good fortune of the Arab Development Funds that their capital was increased in the second oil boom in 1980–81, and that their capitalization was fully paid up making them into permanent endowments. Moreover, the charters establishing most of these funds gives them the right to borrow in capital markets, thus increasing the resources available to them by almost two-and-a-half times their authorized capital.

Although declining oil prices have certainly had adverse effects on Arab economies, the overall picture is not quite so bleak. For example, some developing countries may see such a price decline as a welcome development as their energy costs are reduced, but on the other hand, it does not solve their longer-term problems of foreign debt and depressed commodity prices. On the other hand, Arab countries may see the current decline in oil revenues as a negative development that is thoroughly detrimental to their future prospects. None the less, adversity can lead to a more positive economic adjustment on the part of both oil and non-oil Arab governments.

It is clearly evident that the dramatic increases in oil prices after 1973 were not without high costs to the Arab oil-exporting countries despite the great financial surpluses they acquired.

However, it is only by looking back with the benefit of hindsight that these lessons become clear. Just as the adverse consequences of the great demand for oil and soaring prices during the 1970s did not become obvious until much later, the positive ramifications of the recent glut in the oil market and concomitant decline in revenues will not become obvious right away. Paradoxically, it may be that the 'cons' of rapid capital accumulation in the 1970s can be rectified by the 'pros' of rapid decline in the 1980s.

The illusion of progress came to an abrupt halt in the early 1980s with the decline in oil exports and prices, and sober re-examinations are now in order. Without doubt such re-examinations should be considered a positive potential development in that they may well motivate rationalization of public spending, manpower development, personal motivation, entrepreneurial initiative, capital allocation and economic diversification in the oil-exporting countries. It may also lead to policies of greater self-reliance on the part of both oil and non-oil Arab countries.

With lower inflation in the industrialized countries and strong competition in the construction business the oil producers are now getting better value from their development budgets than they were able to achieve in the 1970s. There is more and more realization that grand projects, built by 'guest' workers, give poor economic and social returns and that a less frantic pace of development could be more beneficial.

Moreover, high rates of extraction were rapidly reducing the life of oil reserves and most Arab oil-exporting countries were unable to absorb the revenues generated by the rising volumes of oil exports into productive investments within their national boundaries. The high extraction rates were depleting a real asset and replacing it by a foreign portfolio of paper assets subject to the vagaries of inflation, currency fluctuations, changes in rates of interest and the risks of default or expropriation.

As swing producers, and in the same way as they found themselves extracting too much oil in the years leading to 1973 and in the period 1973–9, today, Arab OPEC countries find themselves producing much below what they would have liked to produce. This is leading inevitably to conservation of their resources. Yet I would like to digress here for a moment and emphasize that I am by no means welcoming this sudden reduction in output. Conservation of resources should be a matter of explicit policy on the part of the producing countries, not the result of external forces over which they have no control.

Be that as it may, the reduction in revenues should be seen as an opportunity for improving the efficiency and management of their economies. The fall in oil revenues should induce governments to review their pricing policies, and subsidies for electricity, water, health services and food, to avoid the squandering of resources before it is too late. In fact, steps have already been taken in this direction.

The fall in oil revenues is a sobering experience which should stimulate both governments and people to concentrate on more productive and serious habits.

The world oil market has gone from shock to shock in the 1970s and 1980s. It has witnessed dramatic and quite long cycles. If the downswing phase proves to be as long as the upswing one, this might have many alarming consequences for both oil-producing and non-oil-producing Arab countries.

However, I am confident that oil will regain its supremacy in the near future. Yet I hope that this can be done without going through another price shock. For a commodity as crucial as oil, prices and production should be managed judiciously to avoid dramatic and sudden changes, which affect consumers and producers alike.

PART VII

THE FINANCIAL PROBLEMS OF
DEVELOPING COUNTRIES

21 THE BAKER PLAN: PROSPECTS AND PROBLEMS IN A CHANGING OIL MARKET

Said El Naggar

Background

The debt crisis erupted on 20 August 1982 when Mexico announced temporary suspension of payment on its external debt, estimated then at about $80 billion. The Mexican authorities asked for a ninety-day moratorium on $20 billion principal payments falling due in 1983 and 1984. This was the first request for debt rescheduling of such magnitude and sparked a series of similar requests from other debtors.

The Mexican crisis had the potential danger of bringing down the international credit system. More than 80 per cent of the external debt of Latin American countries is owed to commercial banks spread throughout the United States, Europe and Japan. In relation to their capital base, the major banks had a high degree of exposure. The nine largest banks in the United States, for example, had a combined exposure to developing country debt of more than 200 per cent of bank capital. Of this figure, the four major Latin American borrowers (Argentina, Brazil, Mexico and Venezuela) accounted for 128 per cent. Particular banks in the USA and the UK were even more heavily involved. Under these circumstances, default by a small number of debtor countries could have easily induced the insolvency of some major banks. The crisis would not have stopped there. There is a vast network of interlocking debtor–creditor relationships linking the major banks to thousands of medium-sized and small banks throughout the world. The collapse of a few major banks would have triggered a chain reaction engulfing a multitude of other banks and financial institutions. Since a good portion of external debt is trade related, widespread default would have disrupted the flow of international trade. This in turn would have brought to a halt the wheels of economic activity, thereby causing a depression of major proportions.

It is hardly surprising that the Mexican crisis brought forth a prompt and decisive response from the international financial community. Under the leadership of the IMF, a co-ordinated effort was made to ease the payments difficulties of Mexico. Help was also extended to three other major debtors facing a similar situation: Brazil, Argentina and Yugoslavia. Thus, four major 'rescue operations' were co-ordinated by the IMF in co-operation with the commercial banks, the Bank for International Settlements (BIS) and the US Government.

In all four operations the rescue package consisted of three basic elements:

(a) Provision of new credit by the IMF and the commercial banks. In addition, the BIS provided 'bridging finance', i.e. short-term credit pending the conclusion of negotiations between the IMF and the debtor country. The US Government also extended short-term credit and, in the case of Mexico, made advance payments for future imports of oil.
(b) Rescheduling a good portion of principal falling due during a period of two years.
(c) Agreement between the debtor country and the IMF on an adjustment programme covering macroeconomic variables such as foreign exchange, interest rates, budget deficits, credit ceilings and the like.

The IMF's role in the rescue operations was not limited simply to providing financial support from its own resources. The catalytic role of the Fund was much more important. The success of the operation depended on the assurance that other sources of finance, particularly the commercial banks which have the greatest stake, would provide fresh credit on a sufficient scale to avert default. That was brought about by insisting on reciprocity of commitments. The involvement of the IMF was made conditional not only on the debtor country undertaking an adjustment programme, which was customary, but also on the commercial banks undertaking to extend new credit, which was a novelty. That ushered in a new type of lending by the commercial banks in the context of rescue operations. It is referred to as 'involuntary' or 'concerted' lending. It is 'involuntary' since the commercial banks would not voluntarily have extended a new loan to a debtor on the brink of default. It is 'concerted' since the share of each bank in the 'involuntary' loan is proportional to the degree of its exposure in the debtor country.

The debt strategy underlying the IMF rescue operations was based on an appropriate blending of adjustment and finance. Effective adjustment was seen as essential to help restore the confidence of creditors and to lay the foundation for a return to sustainable growth in the future. It sought to strengthen export performance and curtail imports through monetary and fiscal action. At the same time, the provision of external financing was a basic element of the operation. It served to maintain the flow of essential imports and, more generally, to alleviate the unavoidable burden involved in the adjustment process.

The results of the debt strategy in 1983 and 1984 were fairly encouraging. The ten principal borrowers in Latin America, for example, collectively earned trade surpluses of over $100 billion during 1983–5 and greatly reduced their current account deficits. Commercial bank creditors gained a breathing space to build up their capital base, thereby lessening their exposure in the heavily indebted countries. In the three years ended June 1985, large US money-centre banks boosted their primary capital at a 13 per cent annual average rate, versus a 3 per cent annual growth rate in their claims on the ten major Latin American borrowers.

Despite these achievements, the debt strategy came to an impasse in 1985. During the two years that the strategy was in force, it became increasingly clear that the adjustment process was encountering serious problems. In the first place, the improvement on the current account was achieved through drastic cuts in imports rather than through expansion in exports. As compared with the average for the period 1981–2, the volume of exports in 1985 represented a cut-back of 43 per cent in Argentina, 26 per cent in Brazil, 34 per cent in Chile, 29 per cent in Mexico and 28 per cent in Venezuela. As was to be expected, such far-reaching cut-backs in the volume of imports were reflected in substantial reductions in investment programmes, real wages and the level of consumption. No less troubling is the fact that per capita incomes in most of the indebted countries remained below pre-crisis levels. At the same time, few of the debtor countries made such headway in stabilizing their internal economies. Progress on curbing budget imbalances and public sector dissaving has been patchy. Inflation remained a major worry and threatened to spiral further out of control.

Basic Features of the Baker Plan

It was against this background that US Secretary of the Treasury James A. Baker III announced at the Annual Meetings of the World Bank and the International Monetary Fund in Seoul, South Korea, in October 1985 a new initiative to deal with the debt problem. The Baker Plan is in a sense an extension of the IMF debt strategy. It builds upon the experience of the last three years while trying to avoid certain shortcomings. Thus it retains two essential features of the IMF approach:

(a) The solution of the debt crisis lies in a combination of adjustment by the debtor countries and financing by the international community. Both approaches hold the view that finance without adjustment is a waste of resources, while adjustment without finance is unsustainable.

(b) The solution of the debt problem rests on a case-by-case approach. Each country experiencing severe payments difficulties is a unique case which calls for a remedy specifically tailored to the situation.

However, the Baker Plan differs from the traditional IMF approach in three respects:

(*a*) *The Characterization of the Problem Facing the Debtor Countries.* According to the Baker Plan, the problem in these countries is not simply one of demand management. While this is certainly an important component of the problem, there are other structural imbalances that have to be addressed. These include savings ratios, investment incentives, allocation of resources, performance of public enterprises, efficient import substitution and export promotion. These structural imbalances can not be corrected through demand management measures. They are essentially supply side disequilibria which can only be corrected in the medium and long term. As such they fall outside the jurisdiction of the IMF and, therefore, outside the traditional focus of stabilization programmes. Stated differently, stabilization and prudent demand management at the macro level are certainly necessary, but they are not sufficient when the situation is one of structural disequilibrium.

(*b*) *Emphasis on Growth as an Essential Requirement of a Sustainable Adjustment Process.* The primary purpose of the adjustment process in the IMF approach is the restoration of external equilibrium, i.e. the reduction of current account deficits to sustainable levels. The instruments used to achieve that objective are as old as political economy, namely, devaluation and/or deflation. External finance could be, of course, a substitute for either or both. Under normal circumstances, however, external finance can not entirely obviate the need for a certain measure of devaluation and/or deflation. Within this framework, growth, at least in the short run, could become the victim of the need to achieve external balance. This explains why IMF stabilization programmes are accused of a deflationary bias. In many cases adjustment was associated with a rise in unemployment, a decline in real wages and a deceleration of growth. The Baker Plan purports to take deflation out of adjustment. Adjustment with growth is a key feature of the Plan.

(*c*) *The Role of the World Bank and Development Institutions.* As a corollary of emphasis on growth and structural imbalances, the World Bank and other multilateral development institutions, particularly the Inter-American Development Bank, are to play a key role in the solution of the debt problem. This does not mean that the IMF will cease to play a major role. In the words of James Baker:

> Emphasizing growth does not mean de-emphasizing the IMF. Through both its policy advice and balance of payments

financing, the Fund has played a critical role in encouraging needed policy changes and catalyzing capital flows. It must continue to do so ... The World Bank, and indeed all multi-lateral development banks, have considerable scope to build on current programs and resources, and to provide additional assistance to debtor nations which is disbursed more quickly and targeted more effectively to provide the needed stimulus to growth.

The increasing role of the World Bank in the international debt strategy has certain important implications. It means a greater degree of collaboration between the World Bank and the IMF than has hitherto been the case. Each institution will endeavour, of course, to maintain its distinctive character in keeping with its own articles of agreement. However, the line of demarcation between their respective areas of competence is becoming increasingly blurred. More than ever before the World Bank is involved in matters related to the macroeconomic policies of borrowing countries. Under the Baker Plan the Bank is expected to expand significantly the share of the so-called structural adjustment loans in total lending. These are non-project loans designed to address specifically structural imbalances. They cover practically all aspects of economic policies pursued by the borrowing countries including such matters as interest rates, trade regimes and budget deficits in addition to investment priorities, mobilization of domestic resources and efficiency of public enterprises. This type of loan has been aptly called 'policy-based' lending in contrast to the traditional 'project' lending. By its very nature policy-based lending is taking the World Bank into areas of macro-economic policies. On the other hand, adjustment programmes will be broadened to cover not only demand management measures, which constitute the core of IMF stabilization prog-rammes, but also structural adjustment measures. According-ly, the IMF will be increasingly drawn into areas that have traditionally fallen beyond its purview. These are important changes in the Bretton Woods institutions as we know them and as they were conceived by the framers of the articles of agreement. Whether or not these are changes in the right direction remains to be seen.

The Baker Plan spells out some specific financing targets for the next three years. According to the Plan, the commercial banks ought to commit themselves to increase their net out-standings to fifteen debtors by some $20 billion over three years, and the multilateral development banks should in-crease their disbursements to the same debtors by roughly 50 per cent from the current annual level of nearly $6 billion. The principal debtors referred to in the Plan are fifteen heavily indebted countries, ten of which are from the Latin American region: Argentina, Brazil, Chile, Mexico, Venezuela, Bolivia, Colombia, Ecuador, Peru and Uruguay. The five non-Latin American beneficiaries are: Nigeria, the Philippines, Ivory Coast, Morocco and Yugoslavia. It was pointed out, however, that the list is not necessarily limited to these fifteen countries. Others may qualify once they demonstrate their willingness to undertake appropriate adjustment programmes.

Prospects and Problems

When the Baker Plan was announced, it was welcomed by all parties concerned. It was hailed by the heavily indebted coun-tries as a step in the right direction. They saw in the Plan a significant change in the stance of the US Government to-wards the debt crisis. Heretofore, the US Government had taken the position that the crisis was largely a matter for the debtor countries and the commercial banks. This was no longer the case. In fact, Secretary Baker made it clear that his initiative represented a co-operative effort between the five actors in the debt drama: commercial banks, multilateral development banks, the IMF, governments of the debtor countries and governments of the creditor countries. Accord-ing to him:

> If creditor governments, in an age of budget austerity, are to be called upon to support increases in multilateral develop-ment bank lending to the debtor nations, and if the recipient nations are asked to adopt sound economic policies for growth to avoid wasting that financing, then there must be a commit-ment by the banking community – a commitment to help the global community make the necessary transition to stronger growth.

Similarly, the Plan received the strong endorsement of both the IMF and the World Bank. The centrality of the IMF's role in the adjustment process was preserved. The World Bank was given a well-defined role in a matter of crucial importance to the survival of the international financial system. No less important is the fact that the Plan signalled a significant change in the position of the US Government towards the World Bank. Henceforth, the US Government was on record as supportive of a general capital increase to enable the Bank to expand its lending levels. It was equally supportive of a shift in Bank lending from project financing to policy-based lending. Prior to the Baker initiative, the US Government, or rather the Reagan Administration, was strongly opposed both to a general capital increase and to non-project lending.

It is perhaps too early to pass judgement on the merits and demerits of the Baker Plan. At the time of writing the Plan is less than one year old. It is possible, however, to make some observations. There is no doubt the Plan has some positive elements. It is based on a correct characterization of the payment difficulties facing debtor countries as both structural and demand induced. The Plan recognizes that deflationary adjustment is unsustainable. It correctly opts for growth-orientated, sometimes called positive, adjustment. Last, but not least, the Plan recognizes that the debt crisis has implications which go beyond the financial relationship between the commercial banks and the debtors, and calls for the involvement of the governments of creditor countries alongside other parties.

At the same time, the Baker Plan leaves unanswered a number of questions. There is first the adequacy of the financial package. The Plan envisages net new lending by the commercial banks of some $20 billion plus $9 billion by multilateral development banks during the next three years. The facts of the case would seem to point to the gross inadequacy of these sums. During the period 1983–5 negative transfers from the ten heavily indebted countries in Latin America amounted to about $100 billion. These were offset by export surpluses which were realized only at extremely high cost in terms of investment and consumption. There is no reason to assume that the financial package envisaged by the Baker Plan will be enough to reverse negative transfers so as to spare the debtor countries the prohibitive cost of achieving export surplus through deflation. The Baker Plan is counting on the catalytic effect induced by positive adjustment, notably direct foreign investment, but it is doubtful, however, whether such flows, even on the most optimistic assumptions, would change the fundamentals of the situation.

The recent decline in the price of oil has greatly increased the financing needs of some major debtors, notably Mexico, Venezuela, Ecuador, Peru and Nigeria. Mexico is a particular case in point. It is the second most heavily indebted country (after Brazil) with an external debt estimated in 1985 at $98 billion. At the same time, it is heavily dependent on oil exports which accounted in 1985 for nearly $15 billion out of total exports of goods and services of less than $24 billion, i.e. about 63 per cent. As a result of the recent decline in oil prices, Mexico will suffer a loss in oil revenue estimated at about $8 billion. The adverse effect of this development can hardly be exaggerated. For the second time in four years the country was pushed to the brink of default. Once more the IMF came to the rescue. Under the most recent standby arrangement the Fund undertook to supply SDR1.4 billion in support of a comprehensive programme of adjustment and structural reform. For its part the World Bank will provide about $2 billion. Commercial banks are supposed to provide new credit of about $6 billion.

On the other hand, some of the major debtors are oil importers. For these the decline in oil prices was a boon. Brazil is the most obvious example. It is the most heavily indebted among developing countries with an external debt estimated at about $107 billion in 1985. As a result of the recent decline in the oil price, Brazil will be able to save about $3 billion on its oil import bill.

It should be noted, however, that in addition to these direct effects, the changing oil market will have some important indirect effects on the debtor countries. Inasmuch as it is responsible for a decline in interest rates, it will have a positive effect. However, for some countries, such as Egypt, workers' remittances constitute a major element in their foreign exchange earnings. As a net oil exporter, Egypt suffers a triple loss from the decline in the price of oil: oil export proceeds, workers' remittances and Suez Canal dues, all of which are oil related.

The Baker Plan assumes that the commercial banks will increase their exposure by some $20 billion in the next three years. It is vague as to the mechanism which would induce the commercial banks to do what they essentially regard as throwing good money after bad. This is all the more so since many American banks have of late significantly improved their position by strengthening their capital base and by increasing provisions for loan losses. Under the circumstances they are now in a position to withhold their support, which they were not able to in 1982 and 1983. Apparently, the commercial banks would like to see more than exhortation from the Secretary of the Treasury. Reportedly, they are seeking cast iron guarantees by the US Government and/or the World Bank for a resumption of normal voluntary lending.

Finally, the Baker Plan will have the effect of increasing the absolute level of indebtedness of the heavily indebted countries. It is not clear what the position of these countries will be at the end of the three-year period. From the viewpoint of the debt service burden, their position will presumably be made worse by the need to service the additional debts incurred in the 1986–9 period, plus the previously rescheduled debts. It is possible, of course, to visualize a high scenario which would greatly strengthen the debt-servicing capacity of these countries. The most important factor in this respect is the growth of the industrial countries. After the recent decline in oil prices, it was estimated that the debtor countries would be able to service their debts without resorting to deflationary policies if the industrial countries grew at about 4 per cent per annum. Such a rate of growth would boost the export earnings of the debtor countries and reverse the declining trend in the price of non-oil export commodities.

Being heavy importers of oil, most of the industrial countries benefited from the decline in oil prices. Table 21.1 shows that the United States, Japan, West Germany, Italy and France would save about $87 billion on their oil import bill assuming a decline in the price of oil from nearly $30 to $14

Table 21.1: Net Oil Import Savings. 1986. Billion Dollars.

Country	Savings
United States	28
Japan	25
West Germany	13
Italy	11.2
France	9.6
Total	86.8

per barrel. On the other hand, the United Kingdom would lose about $6 billion and Canada about $1.7 billion in their foreign exchange earnings as both are net oil exporters. On balance the major industrial counties would experience a net saving of about $80 billion. Such a beneficial effect would, other things being equal, boost the economic growth of the industrial countries taken as a group by nearly 1 per cent. Unfortunately, other things are never equal. The positive effect of the decline in oil prices has been swamped by more dominant factors. In the case of the United States the major operative force has been a considerable and persistent trade deficit matched by an equally considerable budget deficit. In the cases of Japan and West Germany the oil effect was more than offset by a cautious non-expansionary policy.

On balance the prospects for growth in the industrial countries are far from encouraging. According to current projections, the rate of growth is likely to be about 3 per cent per annum for the next three years. This is well below what is required to accelerate the foreign exchange earnings of the debtor countries. The problem is further compounded by the resurgence of protectionism. For this reason, some of the critics of the Baker Plan believe that it does no more than postpone the day of reckoning. In their view the Plan is based on the mistaken assumption that the present crisis is one of illiquidity. In other words, it assumes that the difficulties currently experienced by the heavily indebted countries are due to a convergence of exceptionally unfavourable circumstances. Once these circumstances recede, the debt service burden would be well within the payment capacity of the troubled country.

The critics take issue with this assumption. According to them, the crisis is one of insolvency, not illiquidity. The debtors are simply insolvent in the sense that even under the most optimistic assumptions they are not in a position to service their external debt except at a cost which is unsustainable both economically and politically. If the insolvency hypothesis is accepted, it follows that the solution of the debt problem lies in some measure of debt relief in the form of 'write-downs' and 'write-offs' of a certain proportion of present debts. Senator Bradley has recently declared himself in favour of debt relief by proposing to cut interest rates and forgive some of the debt outstanding owed by the debtor countries in Latin America. According to his proposal, interest rates should be cut by three percentage points, and outstanding debt by 9 per cent in a three-year period. These write-offs would release the fifteen countries covered by the Baker Plan from some $57 billion of debt. That would represent a permanent reduction in their external liability as compared with an increase of $20 billion they would get in commercial bank loans under the Baker Plan. However, the idea of debt forgiveness has not yet taken hold as a serious policy option. This is not likely to happen until the Baker Plan is put to test and proven to be a failure.